SR 150

Please return/renew this item by the last date shown

North Somerset
COUNCIL

Previous page. Mainstay of the West were the LSW T9 4-4-0s which lasted right through Southern Railways days on services in the far west of the Southern system, but could be found on all types of duty over lines of all three of the Southern's principal constituents. No 116 is seen here in enemy territory at Exeter St David's with a train for Plymouth.

Main line locomotives from the LBSCR did not last as long as their compatriots from the other Southern constituents since they were soon displaced by main line electrification. Here Marsh 4-4-0 Class B2 4-4-0 No B321, as rebuilt by Billinton, passes Purley with an express for the coast in the mid 1920s. The wires are up for the short three-year life of ac electrics to Coulsdon which was converted to dc third rail in 1928.

A century and a half of
SR 150
THE SOUTHERN RAILWAY

David St John Thomas & Patrick Whitehouse

David & Charles

A DAVID & CHARLES BOOK

Hardback edition first published 1988
Reprinted 1989
Paperback edition published 2002

Distributed in North America
by F&W Publications, Inc.

A catalogue record for this book is available from
the British Library.

ISBN 0 7153 1376 2

Printed in China by
Hong Kong Graphics & Printing Ltd
for David & Charles
Brunel House   Newton Abbot   Devon

Previous page
South West holiday train. The
Atlantic Coast Express *with its
many through portions serving
Devon and Cornish destinations was
the Southern's equivalent of the
GWR's* Cornish Riviera Express.
*With so many sections, all needing
first, third and luggage
accommodation, the train included a
large number of brake composites,
five of which are seen behind the
locomotive, King Arthur class 4-6-0
No 789* Sir Guy *in the Malachite
Green livery of the Bulleid era,
working the Exeter–Salisbury leg of
the up journey.*

New Pacific. The post war Golden
Arrow *about to leave Victoria in
1946 headed by West Country class
4-6-2 No 21C119 (named* Bideford
*on 29 August 1946, and never
rebuilt). This was the regular engine
for a few weeks after preliminary
trials with Merchant Navy No
21C1. The locomotive was
temporarily converted to oil burning
between July 1947 and 1948.*

CONTENTS

FOREWORD

History is an art - the combination of Time and Events, without which we should still be primitives. So it is right that the one hundred and fiftieth anniversary of the London & Southampton Railway, the progenitor of the Southern, should be commemorated.

Few people today will realise that the Southern Railway Company had only a quarter century of separate existence, from January 1921 to December 1946*, the product of two Acts of Parliament, one which created it, the other which destroyed it.

Though the Southern laid no claim to a glorious tradition such as those of the Great Western and the London & North Western, it was always very much a part of the counties, cities, and towns which it served – a hard-worked affair, moderately profitable, with differing characteristics within itself, reflecting the quiet West Country, the ever-growing South, to the dour, hectic scramble of suburbia with which the capital had surrounded itself.

It boasted few 'famous trains', but by common consent the railwaymen and women from Kent to Cornwall had few equals in the movement of masses of people to and from their work and to the countryside and the sea for happiness; not for nothing was it called 'the Gateway to Sunshine'. The statistics, year after year, showed the Southern carrying more passengers in the summer than the other three railways together. They were carried safely and cheaply though, as on other traffic-jammed systems, not always strictly to time. Certainly, the provision, in May 1940, at the shortest of notice, of hundreds of special trains for the evacuated and exhausted British soldiers from Dunkirk via Dover and Folkestone – a non-stop operation for three days and nights – to destinations all over Britain, will remain a monument to efficiency and dedication.

The story of the Southern Railway is largely the story of Sir Herbert Walker. Elsewhere† I have paid tribute to him and his devoted team who devised and completed, over fifteen to twenty years, the world's largest suburban electrification, at the then vast expenditure of £25,000,000, with interest at 2½ per cent!

Walker was a natural leader and a tireless worker. His day was long, his patience and his stamina inexhaustible, his judgement sound, being based on natural ability plus a massive practical experience, and his two chief goals for the railway were always clearly before him – electrification on the widest (and most economical) scale, and the expansion of the docks at Southampton. He had the clearest of minds, and a remarkable gift for accounts and statistics which, applied continuously to the commercial problems of the undertaking (and they were many), ensured that every officer with any responsibility was made perpetually aware of the fact that the successful raising of new capital for the new schemes was dependent on earning enough money to pay 5 per cent on the Preferred Ordinaries and something (usually 1¼ per cent) on the Deferred. Yet it was as an operating general manager above all that Walker stamped his image on the line. The 'even-time' services, suburban and main-line, for which the Southern became renowned, the early application of colour-light signalling, the wholesale rebuilding of out-of-date stations and depots, and the relentless pursuit of safe operation and good time-keeping, all stemmed from him and set the pattern for the whole system.

In the long period covered by this book, the names of the earlier pioneers – who they were, what they did and how and when they did it – are all set down, along with colleagues on the Southern itself. It is a privilege for me, with a lively record of service for a quarter of a century at Waterloo, to offer this Foreword, with gratitude to those who have so loyally and successfully undertaken and completed their arduous and important task.

Sir John Elliot
The Southern Railway's last General Manager

†*The Early Days of the Southern Railway, The Journal of Transport History*, November 1960.

*The railway, as opposed to the company, was in being from 1 January 1923, the date that 'Grouping' was implemented, until 31 December 1947.

1
INTRODUCTION

Until you consider it in detail, the statement may sound bland, but it is full of great meaning: the Southern Railway was one of the most sensible large transport organisations the world has ever seen. It had a touch of magic, and among those who really knew it, its achievements were wondered at, its demise on nationalisation bitterly regretted.

Among the Big Four of the 1923–47 Grouping era, it was of course not the largest (it was in fact by far the smallest) nor the grandest, and despite the fact that Southern Electric became a household name neither it nor its services were best known, at home or among the many thousands living elsewhere in the world who then took a keen interest in Britain and her railways and played a major part in determining 'popularity'. Railway modellers, for example, were naturally more attracted to anything but the Southern, for the other three all had more glamorous trains and locomotives passing through more dramatic scenery. Very few of the best-known stations, those large cathedrals of steam, were on the Southern, and the same went for Britain's famous industries.

Yet the Southern went about the business of steadily improving the scope and quality of what it did with masterly determination. Its policy, based on common sense rather than dogma, was pursued consistently and therefore economically; but it was not too proud to admit mistakes and to change when need be. Its management atmosphere was that of a large, reasonably happy family. Above all, it controlled its finances wisely. Save in one locomotive matter right at the end of its life, it virtually made no investment that it regretted. And as later pages will tell, it certainly never threw anything away – locomotive, train or piece of equipment – that could continue to be used usefully or incorporated into something else.

Before the air age, the Southern was of course Britain's front door, at least three quarters of all visiting royalty and political and other famous people first glimpsing our countryside through its windows. In the days that Gatwick airport was a grass field and London's airport was at Croydon all the world of politics and fashion was to be seen at Victoria before the departure of the *Golden Arrow*. One of its main successes was in the development of Southampton, often described as the jewel in its crown, and to attract the final generation of larger Cunard liners there. It had unrivalled experience in carrying great crowds, going to the seaside on day trips and later on for longer holidays, visiting the numerous racecourses on its territory, and so on. This of course proved invaluable in the various wartime evacuations of London and especially in the brilliantly-executed operation of dispersing the nearly a third of a million soldiers brought back from the beaches of Dunkirk.

Southern uniform. Double breasted brass buttoned guard's uniform with brass letters SR on the lapels, all emphasising the requirements of smartness and cleanliness important to the man in charge of the train and custodian of passengers' safety.

7

Pioneer Ventures

Though the first trunk line in its region, as the London & Birmingham was in the Midlands and the Great Western toward the west, the London & Southampton was by no means the first railway.

The L&S's Act in fact received Royal Assent later in the month that down in Cornwall the Bodmin & Wadebridge Railway opened its 22-mile steam-hauled and partly passenger-carrying system, July 1834. The story has often been told how the South Western illegally acquired the B&W in 1847, when its own main line was still 200 miles away, but how the purchase gave driving force to conquer – however belatedly – a substantial slice of West Country territory. It took the South Western half a century to reach Wadebridge, but the triumph was in keeping the GW off the Atlantic coast all the way from Minehead to Newquay.

Even earlier, however, was the Surrey Iron Railway, from the Thames at Wandsworth to Croydon. The world's first public railway, it opened, double-track but of course horse-operated, on 26 July 1803, a branch to Carshalton following eleven months later. A route through to Portsmouth was planned, but thanks to Nelson winning the Battle of Trafalgar and reducing the need to convey goods to the naval port, the only extension was the Croydon, Merstham & Godstone, which ended in a lime works at Merstham.

The year of the opening of the Liverpool & Manchester, 1830, saw the region's first steam-powered passenger and freight line, the Canterbury & Whitstable, built like many short routes of its day in place of a navigation improvement scheme. It involved heavy gradients up to a gable summit and a 1,012yd tunnel. It was worked almost entirely by stationary engines until the South Eastern took it over in 1844, the sole locomotive,

continued on page 10

Yet it was essentially an everyday railway, carrying workers and crops. It had no special sophistication, but a great aptitude for getting the detail right. Not merely did it develop the world's largest electrified suburban system, but it made it work with much precision. Indeed, throughout the system there was a smartness of operation that was the envy of other railways. Fifteen seconds was all that trains were normally allocated for station stops, a few more at junctions. Different portions of trains were joined and separated in two or three minutes, at dozens of locations and at many of them hour by hour. Electric train motormen would often be seen running the whole length of their train to ensure a punctual departure were the arrival at the terminal late.

While the arrival of an Anglo-Scottish train was always an occasion at Leicester or Preston, and the Great Western always announced its departures with a preliminary whistle as if to enhance the moment, most Southern electric and steam services arrived and went with as little fuss as those of tramcars or buses. The joy was rarely in the individual occasion. The collective music was the almost non-stop sound of wheels on the crossings outside the major traffic centres, especially the London termini. Visual memories are of parallel trains snaking round curves, of the passage of more services going in the opposite direction on relatively short suburban journeys than over hundreds of miles of trunk routes north of the Thames, of crowds alighting without hustle, everyone going about a familiar process and – for example – bringing everyday life *into* the railway station (the Southern was far ahead of others in developing shopping and other letting incomes) as opposed to keeping it something special.

The everyday, the routine, were indeed the great objectives. Special events were judged not by the splendour of the occasion but by how well the traffic was handled, how little disruption regular customers had been subjected to. Thus even the carrying of great crowds was done in a matter-of-fact kind of way, and indeed so many were the occasions on which many tens of thousands had to be carried in addition to ordinary traffic that collectively they *were* routine. The very mood of the railway changed less than on other lines. All and everything was in the day's work. Thus even down the Kent Coast line, though the pressure on summer Saturdays was little less acute than on the Great Western in South Devon, there was not the feeling of enacting special performances for the history book. Which is not surprising when you consider the frequency of trains on electrified sections ('Got to stay an hour or so but shouldn't be more than five or six trains late') and the affect that had on operation thinking on almost all routes out of London.

Which is not to say that the Southern lacked contrasts. Hopefully these are well presented in the following chapters with their 'fillers' shorter features in between and 'snippets' in the outside columns. In some ways the Southern had more contrasts than any other railway. Most were of geography, though history played a major role. There was absolutely nothing in common between the pulsating London termini and busy suburban electrified routes and the quiet, rural branches in Devon and Cornwall. Waterloo certainly seemed less relevant to Southern men at Bodmin than Paddington did to the Great Western ones at the other one-platform terminus. Nor was it only the South West that

The Brighton at Clapham Junction. An unusual photograph taken on 25 July 1926 with a Gladstone class 0-4-2 as Southern Railway No B190 at the head of a heterogeneous collection of stock including an ex Great Northern Railway six-wheel brake third and wagons containing wheel sets. Note the overhead gantries for the LB&SCR electrified suburban lines. The signals to the far right are those giving access to the West London line.

South Western scene. Fareham viaduct with an ex LSWR H15 class 4-6-0 crossing at the head of a fast freight. These were mixed traffic engines, Urie's first design which appeared in 1913. They could be found at work over most of the South Western section right up until the end of steam.

continued

Invicta, being confined to the Whitstable end. The Southern closed it to passengers in 1931; the Southern Region to freight in 1952.

The London & Greenwich was the first to become a busy part of latter-day railways. Opened in sections from 8 February 1836, it was perhaps seen as the start of a trunk route to Dover, but that ultimately involved numerous separate schemes. Built largely on viaducts (stores under them later provided valuable rent), its own traffic was disappointing, but tolls soared when other companies began using it. The South Eastern eventually leased it, though the company retained nominal independence until Grouping.

First over part of the Greenwich were the trains of the London & Croydon, opened formally on 1 June 1839, when two trains took guests to see Croydon station, 'excellently arranged and containing every comfort that can be desired'. With its own terminus at London Bridge, a train almost hourly, and expectations of trains of other companies developing longer routes using its tracks, it showed that the Railway Age was on the way, the scene set for the first trunk line, the London & Southampton.

Top right. Maunsell's largest passenger engine. The up Golden Arrow *express leaving Dover behind 4-6-0 No 850* Lord Nelson *in 1934.*

Right. Modernisation. The all-electric signalbox at Woking showing the distinctive form of architecture developed by the Southern in the 1930s, brickwork and concrete used in tandem to give a modern image. The lettering would have been green on a cream background.

had branch lines where time stood still and the railway had been absorbed into the countryside it served. Some of the most rural and rudimentary of all railways were surprisingly close to London. For example, trains from Appledore on the Ashford-Hastings line served the one-time separate branches to New Romney and Dungeness, splitting at Lydd. Sometimes passengers were supposed to wait at Lydd until the train had served one branch before returning to set out down the other. In practice they were almost bound to be invited to take the extra ride free.

And though changes in traffic volumes on main lines were handled in a very matter-of-fact manner (incidentally often with the most extraordinary contrasts of modern and Victorian equipment), seasonal changes inevitably made themselves felt in the countryside, the hop pickers' specials being but one special Southern feature. But if there were contrasts enough on the mainland, the Southern alone of the Big Four had the pleasures (management visitations!) and perils (indigenous individualism?) of running an island system, and moreover made up of as many constituents as the vast majority of the mainland system. Even the Drain, the Waterloo & City, was part of the Southern, even less part of the main railway than the Isle of Wight's system or the narrow-gauge Lynton & Barnstaple.

The examples help make an interesting point. The Southern eschewed change for its own sake, as again the antiquated nature of many of its trains emphasised; yet during its quarter of a century, it changed a great deal. Thus the Dungeness and Lydd branches were combined into one, the Isle of Wight systems integrated into possibly the best-run small island system the world has ever seen, the Waterloo & City was totally rejuvenated with considerable ingenuity and expense, and the Lynton & Barnstaple was the most famous of the portfolio of unremunerative backwaters the Southern chopped (one by one, individually, not as a programme), though new country lines were added to an almost identical extent so that the total mileage changed little.

And now to the main threads. The Southern, it has been said, was an everyday railway. Unlike the others, it was a truly main-line affair, and it is indeed the 150th anniversary of the opening of a major part of its trunk, the London & Southampton, that this book celebrates. In passing, while the uniform *LMS 150* came just half a century after the LMS celebrated its centenary with gusto, the war prevented the Southern marking the completion of the London & Southampton; but a 150th celebration of the opening of the first major portion, paving the way for long-distance traffic and the railway revolution in much of Southern England, was held at Woking in 1988. The London & Southampton was one of the world's truly great trunk routes, better built than anything else from the capital to the South Coast, and like the London & Birmingham and the original Great Western has served its successors extremely well. Though stations and junctions have been substantially replaced, some several times over, a surprising part of the infrastructure dates from the excellent start. Following this chapter is one of the best accounts published of what in its day was of course a work of tremendous scale.

The original name of London & Southampton was changed to LSWR

when the company broadened its scope, firstly by taking in Portsmouth, but it was very much the same company throughout its independent history, and the traditions of Waterloo established last century set the tone for much of the Southern after 1923. Managed by men who had come up the hard way, it lacked the flamboyancy of the GW, which was its great enemy on much of the northern as well as the very broad western front. Eventually, of course, more traffic passed down the West of England line from Worting Junction (the subject of the jacket illustration) than along the original London & Southampton, though that is not to underestimate the Southern's achievement in the development of Southampton as Channel and Transatlantic port. Only on matters concerning the Great Western was the South Western aggressive or generally even original. But it was broadly liked by its passengers, a large middle-class affair. 'Homely, practical and even humdrum,' is one description.

In great contrast, next door the London, Brighton & South Coast – always just The Brighton – was so small that the whole could easily be seen in a single day, but a vigorous, colourful concern with real style though spending its money exceedingly carefully. Though small, it was a line of contrasts of the kind the Southern was to develop. For example, it already had a luxury Pullman train to its star resort, Brighton, and

11

King George's Funeral

The number of people who flocked to London on Tuesday 28 January, to pay their homage to our beloved Monarch, was simply amazing. At Victoria Station over 10,600 alighted before 7.0am, followed during the next hour by another 26,500 (the normal number for that hour being under 6,000) while between 8am and 9am. 17,600 more arrived, a total for Victoria alone of nearly 55,000.

In addition to the full normal week-day business service special facilities were provided. The 5.58am special from Brighton was full and standing from Redhill, the 6.25am Brighton up had an extra four-car unit attached and was stopped at Merstham and Coulsdon to pick up passengers. The 7.8am from Brighton was sent through to Victoria intact instead of detaching four London Bridge cars at East Croydon as originally arranged and the 7.36am Coulsdon to London Bridge was diverted to Victoria. Traffic was heavy in the Sutton-W Croydon-Wallington area and the 7.20am W Croydon to Victoria was so full that 400 people were left behind at Streatham Hill, a special being run from there at 8.45am, the first possible path. From East Croydon alone 3,000 booked to Victoria and Charing Cross from Norwood 1,500 and from Purley 1,000, all before 8am.

In the early afternoon four specials were arranged from Victoria, three to Selhurst and the fourth to Wallington.

In view of the absence of any information as to the proportion of our usual early morning travellers, or of the number of additional passengers for Victoria &c., that might be expected in the early hours, all possible arrangements were made beforehand. Controllers were posted at East Croydon, Sutton, Balham, Three Bridges, Redhill, Brighton, Worthing, Haywards Heath, Polegate and Streatham Hill in the

continued opposite

SOUTHERN ELECTRIC

NEW CHEAP ZONE TICKETS DAILY

February 1st and until further notice.

| WEEK-DAYS | .. .. .. | By all Trains from 9.30 a.m. |
| SUNDAYS and BANK HOLIDAYS | .. | By all Trains. |

ZONE 1.

FROM **PECKHAM RYE** TO
LOWER SYDENHAM
BELLINGHAM
BECKENHAM HILL
RAVENSBOURNE
SHORTLANDS
NEW BECKENHAM
BECKENHAM JUNCTION
3rd Class Return s. d. -/9

ZONE 5.

FROM **COULSDON NORTH** (Week-days only) **SMITHAM** (Daily) TO
THORNTON HEATH
NORBURY
ANERLEY
PENGE WEST
CRYSTAL PALACE
3rd Class Return s. d. 1/-

ZONE 2.

FROM **SUTTON CARSHALTON BEECHES WALLINGTON** TO
NORBURY
STREATHAM COMMON
BALHAM
STREATHAM HILL
3rd Class Return s. d. 1/-

ZONE 6.

FROM **RAYNES PARK WIMBLEDON WIMBLEDON CHASE MERTON PARK** TO
TULSE HILL
STREATHAM HILL
BALHAM
WANDSWORTH COMMON
CLAPHAM JUNCTION
3rd Class Return s. d. -/10

ZONE 3.

FROM **ORPINGTON PETTS WOOD** TO
STREATHAM HILL
BALHAM
STREATHAM COMMON
NORBURY
THORNTON HEATH
SELHURST
CROYDON WEST
ADDISCOMBE
3rd Class Return s. d. 1/6

ZONE 7.

FROM **BROMLEY SOUTH BICKLEY** TO
STREATHAM HILL
BALHAM
STREATHAM COMMON
NORBURY
THORNTON HEATH
SELHURST
CROYDON WEST
ADDISCOMBE
3rd Class Return s. d. 1/3

ZONE 4.

FROM **GRAVESEND CENTRAL** TO
SLADES GREEN
ERITH
BARNEHURST
CRAYFORD
3rd Class Return s. d. 1/6

ZONE 8.

FROM **GRAVESEND CENTRAL** TO
BELVEDERE
ABBEY WOOD
BEXLEYHEATH
BEXLEY
3rd Class Return s. d. 1/9

Tickets are available for travel to or return from any Station within the specified zones on the day of issue.

FREQUENT ELECTRIC TRAINS.

CHILDREN UNDER 14 YEARS OF AGE, HALF-FARE.

Tickets obtainable in advance at Stations and Agencies.

NOTICE AS TO CONDITIONS.—These tickets are issued at less than the ordinary fares, and are subject to the Notices and Conditions shown in the current Time Tables.

Passengers holding Cheap Day Tickets may take with them, free of charge, at Owner's Risk, goods for their own use (not for sale) not exceeding in the aggregate 60 lbs.

Waterloo Station, S.E. 1.

H. A. WALKER, General Manager.

C.X. 78/ 15/25182 January

Printed by McCorquodale & Co, Ltd., London.

served a string of other resorts well, and with its French partner ran a Newhaven–Dieppe sea route in keen competition with the short ones from Dover and Folkestone. But most of its passengers used the dense suburban services from London Bridge and Victoria. Apart from the lack of train heating (provided only on the Pullman and boat trains), they were well run, and electrification was started using an overhead system that to this day many people believe would have been better for south of the Thames as its modern counterpart has been adopted north of it. The South Western had started the third-rail system; electrification is of course one of many detailed aspects studied more closely in later chapters.

Predictably electrification was still a pipe dream on the third constituent, again quite different in kind, a law unto itself and indeed made up of two formerly bitter enemies competing often senselessly against each other. The South Eastern & Chatham was a managing committee, operating the South Eastern and the half-bankrupt rival London, Chatham & Dover. Though by 1923 the management committee had been in place as long as the Southern Railway itself was to last, the old rivalries had not yet been eradicated; and though some unification and economies had been made, the heritage of an over-abundance of lines and stations continued to drain resources. Much of it, especially on the Chatham side, was poorly built. Especially its commuter services (out of five London termini: London Bridge, Cannon Street, Holborn, Charing Cross, Victoria – or six if you include Blackfriars with its terminal bays) were a well-known musical hall joke.

Premier electric train. The Brighton Belle, *once the most famous electric multiple-unit in the world, seen here on the Quarry Line which avoids the flat junctions at Redhill, south of Quarry Tunnel before 1939.*

continued

early hours of Tuesday, which, together with stand-by trains provided at Brighton, Epsom Downs, Coulsdon North and Selhurst, enabled the specials, diversions, &c., to be directed to the best advantage. – Southern Railway Magazine, March 1936.

Local to Reading. Three-cylinder Mogul (Maunsell 1931) No 1895 at Guildford in 1948 at the head of a Redhill–Reading train. Classed as U1 these three-cylinder 2-6-0s were a development of the prototype, itself a rebuild of the one three-cylinder River class 2-6-4 tank No 890.

Right. Typical Southern Electric. Most of the stock for the Southern's suburban electrification of the 1920s and 1930s was obtained by rebuilding older coach bodies on new underframes and adding driving cabs and the electrical gear. Here an eight coach train formed of two 3SUB motor units (the leading one made up of ex SECR stock), with a two-coach trailer unit sandwiched between, emerges from the Chislehurst loop on to the former SER route at Petts Wood, heading for Orpington on 18 April 1931.

However hard it tried, it could do little good in the public's eye. Perhaps only railwaymen appreciated the quality of its management – and unlike the others it was a gentleman's line, mainly run by public school men with a liking for culture – which kept it together, stretching scant resources to form almost daily miracles in carrying armies of workers into London, day trippers to the Kent coast. Though it had more freight than the Brighton, its only money spinners were the Continental boat services.

Welding these three into a viable whole to cope with the increasing commuter and pleasure traffics of the brave new post-war world, while maintenance – leave alone improvements such as electrification – had been seriously delayed by hostilities, was task enough. Yet from the start it was clearly a challenge that might be won, a much more possible task than that facing the LMS, for example, which in addition to its great size across all four countries of the United Kingdom and the need to weld numerous arch-rivals together was still left facing keen competition over a large proportion of its services. Even before 1923, substantial parts of the South Western and the Brighton were without practical competition, and now it was only the South Western's old rivalry on the western flank that was possibly to deflect the Southern from pursuing its own sensible policies.

The new railway had a logical territory and also benefitted from a relatively small board, for much of its history no more than eighteen members, though including many distinguished figures especially from

14

the business world. It worked so much as a team that unanimous decisions were the rule. Generally the Southern was more orthodox than most railways, setting out to run itself on traditional lines as any other large business. The board thus always represented the shareholder's interests, and its meetings were no formalities. Tension mounted as the monthly cycle of reports, consultations and formal meeting came round, senior staff waiting for the news from Waterloo with keen interest (especially no doubt when their salaries were up for review).

Again sensibly, the territory of the three main constituents now became the Sections under which considerable continuity would be preserved and even public timetables presented: Western, Central and Eastern. But a serious mistake was made in not sorting out the overall management soon enough; to begin with the three general managers continued in parallel, salaries of £7,500 each, every decision requiring all three signatures. Only when Sir Percy Tempest (SE&C) became ill and, though he had at first insisted on the superiority of the Brighton way of doing things, Sir William Forbes recognised that Herbert Walker was the best man for the job, and so retired, was serious progress begun with turning the three railways into one. The appointment of Walker, the man that was to transform the Southern, was ratified by the board in

January 1924. He had earlier, incidentally, been informally asked to head the LMS, but believed the Southern could be a real achiever. He also believed in continuity, and the South Western's chairman, Drummond, who had earlier been instrumental in bringing him from the LNWR, was first chairman of the Southern. It was most likely the wish to prevent the merger looking like a South Western take over that prevented crisper action earlier. And though many key posts did inevitably go to South Western men, there was never any dogma of the kind that characterised the Midlandisation of the North Western. Even so, many Brighton men were disappointed that its line's unique character and practices were inevitably eroded.

From many points of view Walker was the Southern. There was no comparable appointment elsewhere on Britain's railways after 1923. Like the good managing director, he knew what was his to command and prevented operating interference from board members, yet thoroughly respected the board's role. He could only authorise capital expenditure of £250 without its authority. But his personal stature and command not merely prevented time-wasting in-fighting but brought great drive and enthusiasm to the railway like a large family business determined to serve its customers better and protect its revenue and profit. He was the arch operating enthusiast, always out on the line testing its quality, absorbing reports on performance (no railway paid greater attention to guard's journals) and at the regular traffic meetings – novel in their day – encouraging, quietly demanding, better. And his eye was constantly on the finances. Thousands of times he explained that the railway must make sufficient profit to continue paying some kind of dividend to make it possible to finance further electrification. Only through electrification and its 'even time services' (trains departing at the same times past each hour so that passengers would not have to consult a timetable, or be kept waiting too long) would the Southern prevent the disappearance of much of its passenger business.

If that sounds slightly dramatic, it needs to be remembered that all railways were struggling in the 1920s, and trams and buses were eating deeply into non-electrified suburban traffic. Then came the depression coupled with more general bus competition, resulting in most stations in rural areas such as North Devon losing up to half their passengers within a few years, the railway indeed ceasing to be the general carrier and beginning to rely on specialist traffics, of which the growing long-distance holiday one was of course the chief saviour in North Devon's case. No question of electrifying down there, but a great determination to replace infrequent, slow and above all expensive steam trains with three times as many short electric ones over as wide an area as possible. Success may be gauged from the fact that by 1938 the number of passengers carried overall was up by half.

It did not take long to decide on the adoption of the South Western's third rail system already serving important suburbs and proving reliable. That meant converting Brighton's 'Elevated Electric Railway', but extensions to this were opened as late as the mid-1920s and the last train at 6,700V 25Hz did not run until 1929. The SE&C dreamed electrification but lacked the funds to make a start.

Never was electrification better planned or executed more economically. There was none of the start-stop-start, assemble teams and disband them, of BR days. One scheme was immediately followed by another. And neither did electrification give the signalling and rolling stock people an opportunity for a 'clean sweep'. Everything was pragmatic. That meant some new signalling, of course, but there seemed nothing peculiar in electric trains being controlled by Victorian semaphores, or in the bodies of two four-wheelers being placed on a new chassis to provide a 'new' vehicle for the electric fleet. The more you study the Southern, the more you regret that its type of management was not more readily adopted on Britain's railways – and realise it was only possible because it ran itself almost free of politics and, like a typical business of the day, was conventional but thorough.

There was no mistaking its product: train miles. The weekday average in 1923 was 130,000. By 1938 it was 170,000, achieved with a reduction of 12 per cent in the number of passenger vehicles and an overall staff reduction of 3,350 (mainly steam locomotive firemen). Punctuality had also improved. The railway's catalogue was the timetable. Though it relied on reprints from *Bradshaw*, and because so many of its routes were alternative through ones or run in close association with London-bound trains, it lacked many individual branch tables and was less interesting (or harder to understand, even in the case of the Isle of Wight system) than those of most. But its *content* improved dramatically. Ever more and faster trains were introduced, though once an improved service had been established it would normally remain unchanged for many years. The effort lay in preventing the exceptional. Staff were constantly exhorted to

A decade into Nationalisation. Orpington in August 1959 showing grimy Schools class 4-4-0 No 30925 Cheltenham *with a Ramsgate–Dover–London train passing stabled electric multiple-unit stock which retained Southern green livery until the late 1960s.*

The Reason Why

Regular passengers using the Southern Railway between Surbiton and Waterloo, both local and main, will have noticed, during the past few months, the considerable amount of work in progress along the line; the numerous gangs of permanent way and engineering staff; the constructional work in course of erection at Wimbledon on the London side, the new signal box at Waterloo, and so on. At the same time, as the Company is aware, these passengers are suffering considerable inconvenience due to late running of their trains.

There is a definite connection between these two phases, and the Company feels that if their regular patrons are given a frank statement of the position and the why's and wherefore's, they will be as patient as can be expected, and perhaps recognize that the benefits to be obtained are directly in their own interests.

As already announced, the Company is spending £500,000 on improving the running lines between Waterloo and Surbiton; and about one thousand men are at present employed on this work. This area of the line is one of the most congested and difficult to operate on the system; and the scheme has raised profound engineering problems.

The difficulties have been accumulating for a long time. Electrification, with its increase and acceleration of train services, has been the main cause. But the Company knows that electrified services will continue to expand: new areas will have to be served; new houses will be built; new stations; new lines on which more trains will run; the difficulty of track accommodation on London's threshold will grow. Unless something drastic is done these problems will become insurmountable.

One instance: in 1925, 1,046 trains came into and out of Waterloo Station during a normal

continued opposite

ensure the timetable delivered what it promised, no detail being too small to miss management attention. Above all, utilisation was developed into a fine craft. The entire railway's staff could see productivity rise, which led to increased pride in the job, not in the GW tradition of greatness but in a matter-of-fact let-us-get-on-with-the-job attitude which helped eradicate sloppiness and delay. By 1938 there were 670 miles of electrified route, including of course to Brighton (the announcement of that scheme was one of the great Southern moments) and Portsmouth. Yet the board, unable to reach unanimous decision, had to turn down electrification from Sevenoaks to Hastings, some members fearing inadequate traffic. That was Walker's one major rebuff, something he never forgot.

Walker's other great success was the development of Southampton. His shortcoming was not realising soon enough the potential of the shorter-crossing sea traffic via Dover and Folkestone, but when this became clear he tried to make up lost time and among other things introduced the train ferries enabling through trains to run from London to Paris. He was always open to persuasion. He was not a great communicator and neither was he much interested in the aesthetic side of the railway. But very early on he was worried by the company's poor Press. Especially when the first stages of major electrification reduced reliability and increased overcrowding, every journalist seemed to have a go at the Southern. Why, Walker asked Lord Ashfield, its founder, did London Transport get much kinder treatment. The answer proved to be one of those vital turning points in the story of any successful venture: LT took care to inform the Press, the Southern ignored it. Indeed Walker liked to keep new developments secret until they were ready, so that passengers did not know why timetables were disrupted. The result was the appointment of John Elliot, a rising journalist, as Britain's first 'public relations' man. He reported directly to Walker and rapidly had his ear on a wide range of things, down to the style of cloth in the new electric trains then being not well chosen by the officers' wives. The Southern went into attack, telling the world what it was planning and doing. Steadily a Southern style evolved, great posters were produced, slogans taken into the everyday language of life south of the Thames, stations given contemporary display boards extolling the virtues of the frequent electric trains . . . and confidence so increased until most people served by it believed in and even loved the railway.

Continuity was important in all this. Walker had transformed the business by the time of his retirement in 1937. The board's style had remained constant, though during this period there were no fewer than four chairmen, Drummond, the first, dying in 1924. Relations between Walker and all four seemed to have been good, a remarkable record compared with what happened on most railways. Two of his key officers also went with Walker: Edwin Cox, who had been largely responsible for the vital traffic side, and the chief mechanical engineer R.E.L. Maunsell, who had had only a limited budget to improve steam traction (electrification not only required priority but made numerous older locomotives available for service elsewhere) but did so with splendour, his Schools and King Arthurs still being fondly remembered.

Changes after 1937 were more frequent for a variety of reasons, including the war, but the die had been firmly cast, and the railway's overall style and management and aims continued as little altered as they might be in the violently changing world until after nationalisation. Only the doings and products of one man were totally at odds with tradition. Replacing Maunsell, Oliver Bulleid was a contrast, producing some of the finest but most controversial and finally the most useless steam locomotive ever built, spending money in a most non-South Western or Southern way. John Elliot the journalist was drawn into the main fabric of the company and served as last general manager and indeed on into BR days, when the Southern – though left to its own devices more than any other – fought for the continuity of its independent policies and lost, electrification now depending on other people's (including the politicians') whims. The shining war service has already been mentioned but is studied in greater detail later: it is a remarkable story.

There are surprisingly few 'if onlys'. The Southern was a railway sensibly created and especially sensibly run. It never totally overcame economic problems, and though better than that of the LMS and LNER its dividend record in the end was at best mediocre and ultimately electrification was provided more by cheap government finance than from the market backed by the company's own performance. It should have started train ferries at least a decade sooner, and had the wherewithal to do so after World War I (three train ferries were actually sold to the Harwich route), and undoubtedly Bulleid should have been better controlled. But these are minor, nit-picking matters. If not great, because by its very nature it did not seek grandeur or status, it was utterly sound.

It enabled enormous numbers of people to live further from their work in more pleasant suburbs. It of course played a major part in promoting residential development, making various commercial arrangements with developers and publishing a popular *Residential Guide: The Country at London's Door*. Would-be borrowers are also reminded that the various Building Societies now make advances almost to the same extent as do the Local Authorities. As more middle-class families settled in the suburbs or deeper in the countryside, the emphasis among commuters steadily changed from blue to white-collar workers. It enabled ever larger numbers to take first days and then whole weeks and fortnights by the sea and greatly increased the prosperity of the numerous resorts it served, but especially Brighton and the Isle of Wight whose ferries were also reached by fast electric trains. From Whitstable to Padstow, the resorts were well contented. It made Continental visits practical for the first time for tens of thousands of middle-class families, and brought the first mass foreign tourists into London. Though carrying little heavy freight and always having a higher cost of freight conveyance because of the short distances and light flows (which unfortunately cancelled out part of the benefit of its economical passenger working), it did play a major role in providing fresh meat, fruit and vegetables, from its own territory on which much of Britain's horticulture was concentrated and increasingly from overseas. Quite apart from electrification, it substantially improved large slices of its infrastructure, bringing the South Eastern line up to really main-line standard following the 1927 Sevenoaks accident (generally the Southern was a safe railway, but it

continued

twenty-four hours. To-day the number is 1,242 trains. *Two hundred more have to be moved, over the same layout of lines as existed ten years ago.*

At present, all electric trains going up to London, stopping at stations on the way, have to cross the paths of all the up and down steam and fast electric trains just outside Waterloo. Southern men are intent upon obviating this difficulty. To-day they can only use ten platforms for main line trains that come into or leave Waterloo. They need sixteen such platforms for the smooth conveyance of the public. *The work in hand will give them that number.* Boat trains and expresses have become so long that they can only be berthed at certain platforms: wherefore, on leaving Waterloo, they must cross all the up main lines between there and Vauxhall, to the detriment of rightful possessors.

What is the big job? It is the construction of what is called 'A Fly Over', just north of Wimbledon Station: a stretch of line over which nine hundred trains pass during twenty-four hours of a normal day. None of these trains has been stopped: all are allowed to proceed while work is going on; BUT THEY MUST GO SLOW.

Along seven hundred yards of train-occupied (and electrified) track, railwaymen are building, by day and by night, an up and a down gradient, which will take electric trains up a gradual slope and down the other side, while other trains will cross beneath it all the time. This will enable the Company to arrange its layout of lines between Waterloo and Surbiton so that the present difficulties will be relieved, and punctuality improved generally.

Constructional work of this nature and magnitude, while in progress, impairs, temporarily, the strength of the permanent way: *and trains which normally pass here at a speed of sixty miles an hour*

continued overleaf

continued
must, for safety, be restricted to a speed of fifteen.

The reaction to this is two-fold. The driver, being so near Waterloo, is unable to make up time before arrival. So he comes in late – and all his passengers wonder why. But his train is timed to go out again from Waterloo on another journey, probably in five minutes. It cannot: therefore it starts late; arrives late at one of its junctions; to find the track ahead occupied by a train that has been through no trouble, and so is in its right place. Thus the sinister snowball begins to accumulate in size as the day advances.

They tried hard to 'improvise'; by swopping trains over at Waterloo; using one instead of another not so busy – juggling in fact. But you can't go on doing this indefinitely, because you ultimately come to the condition of having no train 'left up your sleeve'. *Official SR explanation of 1930's delays.*

suffered a succession of serious accidents around nationalisation), making circular working to Dover out by Chatham and back via Ashford possible (which helped enormously in the Dunkirk evacuation), and updating numerous stations (far more than on any other line in the Grouping era) including the building of several Odeonesque stations right down to Exeter Central which gave the impression the railway was commercially solid and was going to remain vital in the second part of the present century.

Comfort it generally was not known for. The *Brighton Belle* and other Pullmans, yes. 'Pink lampshades and deep armchairs . . . this is luxury living,' thought Alan Melville taking his first trip for one and sixpence. But even on the Pullmans the limited menu often disappointed. On ordinary restaurant cars meals were seldom up to the standard enjoyed elsewhere, the seating ungracious. Much catering, including many refreshment rooms and of course the Pullmans, was put out to contract along with a variety of ancillary services, including local cartage in many smaller places and most hotels. Walker, the businessman, saw such matters distracting attention from the main function of running – and *electrifying* – the railway, fearing also that railwaymen would lose money on things they did not understand. But the Charing Cross Hotel was different, the one plaything all the directors and top managers had a finger in influencing, the place where all top consultations and publicity events were staged and the board held its working dinner the night before the formal meetings. Housing for its workers it did maintain and extend during its quarter century.

But the trains . . . the enormous numbers of them, smartly, unfussily stopping and starting. Clean, busy, precise, it was the ultimate model railway.

The London & Southampton

The South Western's trunk line originated in a proposal for a ship canal from Spithead to London, for which Francis Giles was retained to make the survey. When the impossibility of the scheme became obvious, thoughts turned to railways. The first practical step was not, however, taken until 1831 (the year after the Liverpool & Manchester's opening). On 26 February a meeting was held at the house of A. R. Dottin, M.P. for Southampton and later a director of the London & Greenwich. Sufficient money was promised to allow the appointment of Giles as engineer.

On 6 April there was a public meeting at Southampton at which the Southampton, London & Branch Railway & Dock Company was formed. The title is revealing: the initiative was coming from Southampton and the railway and the docks were regarded as complementary, as they were until nationalization. The branch referred to a Basingstoke–Bristol scheme.

Evidence of traffic potential, even in the under-developed and sparsely peopled Hampshire of the day, was considerable. But the common sense of the promoters deserted them in calculating expenses. To earn a total income of £181,241, working expenses were not going to exceed £61,241, no more than £1 per week per locomotive being allowed for motive power. The chairman made the extraordinary statement that 'two locomotive engines making two trips a day each would suffice for passengers . . . and three engines would be adequate for the transport of goods'.

In all this the promotors were undoubtedly led astray, not only by the natural optimism of company floating, but by the general ignorance of railway operation. Giles was also to blame. He was a good engineer, but lacked a business sense. His prestige had also been lowered by a wild miscalculation which resulted in his attacking Stephenson upon the grounds of the impossibility of crossing Chat Moss, on the Liverpool & Manchester.

The promoters held back to await the fate of the London & Birmingham Bill, which was eventually passed in 1833. Meanwhile the docks side had been dropped completely and the Bristol scheme held in abeyance. The Bill therefore went forward at the next session as the London & Southampton Railway. Support had been widely canvassed and evidence in favour was given before the Committee by the Lords of the

Admiralty, the Quartermaster-General of the Army and by fishing and agricultural interests. The Act received the Royal Assent on 25 July 1834. Its passage had cost only £31,000, a very modest sum compared with the £150,000 of the Brighton Act.

At the first meeting of the Company, held on 24 October 1834, Giles reported that work had begun. Next February it was decided to present a Bill for the Bristol line, the GWR Bill not having yet been passed. But after a 46-day enquiry, the latter gained the victory, to the mortification of the Southampton Company, which thenceforward reserved its special enmity for the GWR. For its part Paddington rubbed salt in the wound by obtaining powers for a Thingley–Melksham and Trowbridge line across the only possible line of advance towards Bath. A statement that the loss of revenue to the London & Southampton 'would not amount to one or two per cent' was pure face-saving.

Though construction had begun, all was not well. Progress was slow and costs were rising, iron rails jumping from £7 18s. 6d. a ton to £14. It became quite obvious that Giles's estimates were wildly optimistic and powers for capital increases had to be obtained. Furthermore in 1836 the Southampton Docks Company was incorporated. It also retained Giles, who thenceforward gave less time to the railway than he should.

Public confidence was undermined and it became difficult to obtain calls on shares. Stephenson, no doubt to pay Giles off for the Chat Moss incident, announced that 'the whole wealth and strength of the Company would be for ever buried in the cutting through St. George's Hill, Weybridge' a prediction fortunately as far wide of the mark as Giles's had been over Chat Moss. The coaching interests, too, were active in stirring up opposition. From this time dates the famous remark that the London & Southampton 'would be used only for the conveyance of parsons and prawns, the one from Winchester, the other from Southampton'. In short, in the words of a shareholder 'to be connected with the Southampton Railway is to make the choice of being considered a fool or a rogue'.

Fortunately the situation was restored by the recruitment of two great personalities in the early history of railways, Joseph Locke and W. J. Chaplin. Locke was appointed engineer upon the resignation of Giles in 1837. His first act was to clear out numerous small and inefficient contractors. One, however, was considered 'very able and responsible' and was given all the unfinished work as far as the Wey Navigation, Byfleet. He was Thomas Brassey, of whom more will be heard anon. From now on work went ahead rapidly.

Chaplin, the other recruit, was a large road carrier, owning 64 coaches and 1,500 horses. In 1834 he had been called upon by the Southampton promoters to supply them with figures of possible traffics. As a result he became convinced of the great future awaiting the new form of transport – to such an extent that he sold his road interests and put the money into the London & Southampton. Always active, he became chairman of the LSWR in 1843 and piloted it through the difficult years following the Mania. With Locke as engineer and with

the faith and integrity of Chaplin among the directors, the tide was turned. The London terminus of the railway was at Nine Elms (near Waterloo).

On 19 May 1838 an official party travelled to Woking Common (23 miles from London), where a cold collation awaited them. Speed was retarded on the return journey by a headwind and the situation was not improved by the number of gentlemen riding on the carriage roofs, no doubt mellowed by the junketing. Public traffic began on 21 May. A service of 5 trains a day each way (4 on Sundays) was provided, and there were connecting buses from all over the City and West End. At the stations passengers were booked over open counters, a practice which lasted until the conventional *guichets* were introduced in 1847. The tickets were slips of paper with the destination printed on them. Intending passengers were given a handbill setting out the Company's regulations. These included one that passengers were not to alight without the assistance of a servant of the Company, and another that on approaching a habitation or crossing the guard would blow his whistle (surely a reflection on the sparsely inhabited route). The whole procedure was a curious blend of former coaching practice and subsequent air travel.

For the Derby, which took place a few days after opening, an excursion to Kingston (Surbiton) was announced. The response caught the Company completely unawares, for early in the morning a vast crowd, estimated at about 5,000, was found milling about in front of the gates of Nine Elms. Several trains were got away, but the crowd increased and eventually invaded the station. The police had to be summoned to restore order. Perhaps because Sir John Easthope, a well-known figure in racing circles, was chairman, the Company was by no means discouraged and a few weeks later advertised excursions in connection with Ascot, an even further walk from Kingston. Thus, from the very start, the tradition of handling large race-going crowds grew up, a tradition which has persisted to this day. Waterloo lost the Epsom traffic but served Sandown Park and Kempton Park as well as Ascot.

On 24 September 1838, the railway was extended to Shapley Heath (Winchfield), 38½ miles from Nine Elms. It was now long enough for people travelling from all over Southern England to transfer to it, and one can picture the lively scene at Shapley Heath as coaches brought passengers and luggage for the new means of transport. As in the West Country, the coaching business flourished during the short-lived partnership with the railway; but soon, of course, the coaches were left with merely the unremunerative territory. As for the railway, by February 1839 receipts totalled £42,158 2s. 9d. and operating expenses £24,788 9s. 7d. and nearly 8,000 passengers a week carried. This was a most satisfactory position and gloomy prognostications had already been refuted.

On 10 June 1839 came the formal opening of the Shapley Heath–Basingstoke and Southampton–Winchester sections, 8 miles and 12½ miles respectively. Another year passed before the works on the most difficult intervening section were ready, excitement rising the while. The long-awaited day was 11 May 1840.

The directors and 'bands of music' left Nine Elms at 8.0am and arrived at Southampton, amid a twenty-one gun salute, at 11.0. On their return, Brassey had a cold collation laid on for them at his camp at Warren Farm near Andover Road Station (Micheldever). The festal air of the train crews aroused some apprehension among passengers, but the only casualty was a dog decapitated by a train, while Northam crossing gates were run through in an excess of *joie de vivre*.

The Southampton line is a fitting monument to its builders – a high-speed route from end to end which carries traffic infinitely greater than that envisaged by the most sanguine of the promoters. In spite of the need to climb to 430 feet at Litchfield, in order to cross the chalk plateau, gradients were kept to a minimum. There are long steady climbs, but never at over 1 in 250. There are no severe curves and but six short tunnels.

The line has been quadrupled all the way to Battledown (50 miles from Waterloo), the actual point of divergence of the West of England line, though the junction is at Worting. The widening has been on a most spacious scale and there are but three flat junctions. Unfortunately one of these, with the Portsmouth Direct line at Woking, is the busiest of all.

The original intermediate stations were 13, while a further 15 have been added over the years. Only two, Wandsworth (later Clapham Common), and Bramshot Halt (serving a golf club), have been closed. It is noteworthy that Micheldever is still the only intermediate station in the 18¼ miles between Basingstoke and Winchester. Modernization has swept away most of the early stations, which were severely plain, almost featureless two-storey brick buildings. Characteristically, Micheldever remains unaltered.

But generally low architectural standards did not prevent the London & Southampton retaining Sir William Tite, designer of the Royal Exchange, for the termini. These he planned with great effect, adopting a simple classical style which reminds us that the Age of Elegance did in fact survive into the Railway Age. The *façade* of Southampton Terminus survives intact and is one of the glories of British station architecture. The sadly battered *façade* of Nine Elms survived, buried in the goods depot (closed 29 July 1968), until the latter gave way to the new Covent Garden.

In 1846 the Company had reputedly the fastest trains in the world with its 110-minute schedule to Southampton, 42.9mph. On one occasion the Gooch 2-2-2 'Elk' did the up journey in 93 minutes, 50.3mph. The coaching stock was reasonable for the standards of the time. The firsts had 3 compartments each seating 6, while the seconds had wooden seats and open sides. Luggage was carried on the roofs of the first and in boots in the second. Guards and brakesmen were seated at the roof ends.

The thirds were apparently removable bodies mounted on the chassis of goods wagons, which gave rise to the epigram 'in some of the trucks was the swinish multitude, in others a multitude of swine'. At first they were attached to goods trains, but the public, and who can blame them, tended to fight shy of this form of conveyance, especially after a bad accident on the GWR at Sonning. The chairman, making a virtue of necessity, said in 1842:

> The Goods Trains were not so secure from danger as the passenger trains and therefore we have adopted a third class conveyance by an early morning train, which gives the industrious poor not only a greater sense of security, but also encouragement for early rising.

In 1841 a train was hired by an enterprising person who was organizing an excursion, and the Company began running its own excursions to satisfy a growing demand for cheap rail travel. But not everyone was yet converted. The Duke of Wellington lived at Stratfield Saye, 7 miles from Basingstoke, and in 1842 the chairman said 'Although a special train was always in readiness for His Grace, this has not been taken advantage of by him'. The next year however the Queen patronized the Company for the first time, and she was attended by the Duke. With justifiable pride the chairman reported they were both 'highly pleased with our mode of conveyance'. The accolade of social respectability had been bestowed.

Initially goods wagons were attached to the last passenger trains in the day, but freight trains were run when the extension to Basingstoke was opened. Traffic, however, did not develop satisfactorily, as the railway would not accept goods from ordinary consignors, but only from certain carriers. Sir Sam Fay, from whose work *A Royal Road* so many details of early operation have been culled, paints a vivid picture of these trains. At first they were conducted by three 'juvenile delinquents' but these were later replaced by a guard. There were no brake van and no brakes, the guard riding in a wagon known as the 'Noah's Ark', which conveyed small packages for roadside stations. The wagons, 12 feet long, had dead buffers and springless drawgear. To start a train the guard scotched the last wagon and the engine backed up to slacken the couplings. Two of these equipages were run each way, mercifully under cover of night.

Trouble was experienced in recruiting staff in those early days when there was a general lack of experience. Easthope was alleged to have recruited all the staff from Leicester, of which he was M.P. and in 1852 he was forced to resign. Meanwhile a fiery Irishman, one Davies, was recruited from 'A Northern Line'. He brought with him a number of porters to help train the ignorant Southerners. After a violent quarrel however he was relegated to station agent, Weybridge. Men of all classes were taken on at first, a station-master might be a gentleman, a former stage coach proprietor, shopkeeper or farmer.

2
PERSONALITIES AND CHARACTERS

'The Southern Family' as Holland-Martin was wont to call it, was fortunate in having a number of outstanding railwaymen among its officers, managers and engineers. Biographical notes and character sketches of a few appear below.

Not the least of its worthies were the five chairmen; Sir Hugh Drummond, who came from the LSWR and who had brought Walker from the LNWR; the Hon Evelyn Baring; Lord Wakehurst; Robert Holland-Martin (see below), and Eric Gore-Brown. It was their support for the general managers that underlaid the modernisation of the Southern which took that railway ahead of the rest of the 'Big Four'. While their obituaries over-emphasised the part played by the chairmen, Klapper's excellent study of Walker plays down their part. A balance between the relative importance of direction and management must be maintained in the history of the Southern.

The ranks of management included F. Bushrod, a fanatical LSWR man who could see nothing good coming from the SE&C, but who came to accept working under Cox. The Southern managed to keep inter-company rivalry within bounds, unlike the LMS. H.E.O (Toby) Wheeler was another of Cox's able assistants. Captain Payne, Commodore-Master of the Dover–Folkestone fleet attained fame on D-day, while A. Newbold, general agent for France was a significant figure in Anglo-French commercial circles. While engineering was dominated by Maunsell, Bulleid and Raworth, the chief civil engineers, Szlumper and Ellson must not be forgotten, their tasks including upgrading the poor permanent way of the Eastern Section. Maunsell's team was also outstanding, including the technical assistant, H. Holcroft, and the Ashford works manager, G. H. Pearson, who became assistant CME.

But tribute must also be paid to the rank and file railwaymen. Station masters and signalmen were given wide-ranging devolved responsibilities and used them to full advantage to keep traffic moving in the service of the public. Driver Stainer of Bricklayer's Arms, who has left us such an evocative account of his horrific experience when Cannon Street was bombed in 1941, and Fireman Fairey, hero of an attack on a Guildford–Horsham train the following year, may be taken as typical of the skill, initiative and loyalty among thousands of steam and electric train crews.

Berth allocations

Until Bulleid (secretly?) built one, the Southern was a railway without a sleeping car, and normally an LNER car (or two) was included in the inspection train taking officials to the further-flung part of empire in Devon and Cornwall. Between 19 and 21 May 1943, a special toured the West, noting the new war-time connections with the GW and the need for extra sidings for freight traffic from Templecombe to Lydford.

Berth Allocation
Toilet

10	Mr W. J. England
9	Mr R. G. Davidson
8	Mr R. M. T. Richards
7	Mr G. Ellson
6	Col E. Gore-Browne
5	R. Holland-Martin
4	E. J. Missenden
3	Sir Alan Mount
2	O. V. Bulleid
1	J. L. Harrington

Shower
Attendant Taylor, King's Cross, LNER

By the next time Mr Bulleid was in an LNER sleeper heading west, shortly before victory in Europe, the major item on the agenda was the arrival on the scene of his West Country Pacifics, taking heavier trains over the hills and cutting down double-heading though necessitating the lengthening of crossing loops.

SIR HERBERT ASHCOMBE WALKER, KCB

Reading this book soon reveals the all-pervading influence of Sir Herbert Walker. More than any other one man he established an international

Sir Herbert Walker.

reputation for the company and he was undoubtedly one of the great names in railway history. Born in 1868, he joined the London & North Western Railway at the age of 17. He eventually became outdoor goods manager, Southern area, but this position rather obscured his contribution to the company – which included reform of the North London Railway in 1909.

The LNWR *Athletic Gazette* summed him up as 'a strict disciplinarian, very just and ready to stand by his staff'.

In 1911, aged 43, he became the LSWR's general manager. He soon demonstrated his powers of leadership and evolved a much-needed development strategy. In 1914 he became deputy and then substantive chairman of the Railway Executive Committee, which controlled the railways during the World War I.

At Grouping he was placed in an impossible position as joint GM with the former Brighton and SE&C GMs. Threatened resignation and the support of his chairman got him the substantive post which he held with such distinction and with profit to the Southern until he retired in 1937, being subsequently elected a director. Tall, impressive physically, at the end with distinguished grey hair, he died in 1949.

Austerity of manner obscured a deep interest in his railwaymen, aided by a phenomenal memory, refreshed from files before visits, made himself popular by calling them by name and displaying knowledge of their life and work.

His insistence on constant visiting – with a deliberate walk – resulted in unique knowledge. During the 1926 general strike he demonstrated his ability to work Waterloo 'A' Box. He was in the control room at Three Bridges when current was switched on to Seaford in 1935. An anguished phone call came from Seaford Box 'Me levers are alive!'. Walker, the story goes, drily remarked that something must be done and left the box. When an engineer arrived at Seaford he was already there and said 'just run a copper wire from the buffer stops into the sea.'

Walker was able to unify the diverse constituents of the Southern without the bitterness experienced by the LMS. He was able to spot talent among his juniors, and inspired self-reliance and individuality of thought in all grades. His financial flair, ability to state his case and tactful handling usually enabled him to swing the board behind him. His only major failure was their refusal to sanction electrification to Hastings via Tunbridge Wells. His vision too sometimes did not extend beyond the railway. Bromley North Station was rebuilt without thought of bus interchange.

The plaque at the entrance to the Waterloo offices bears these words: 'This station, the development of . . . Southampton, and electrification of . . . the Southern Railway to which he gave his genius and leadership are his memorial.'

Giant of the Past

'Perhaps I am too much of an over-simplifier, but it seems to me that a little more study of the personality, attitudes and methods of H.A.W. are worth far more than the reports of all those management consultants to whom it has been the fashion to submit us. The problems faced by those giants of the past were no less difficult than those of today, but our apparatus of analysis is now so much more exhaustive which induces a feeling of immense complication.' – *David McKenna, retired BR Southern Region general manager, in a letter to Sir John Elliot, the last general manager of the Southern Railway. H.A.W. of course refers to Sir Herbert Walker.*

OLIVER BULLEID

It has been truly said that an engineer can achieve for £10 what any fool can do for £12. If this were the only criterion, Bulleid's professional status would have been open to serious doubts.

He was fortunate in being chosen, aged 29, to serve the great Nigel

24

Gresley as personal assistant. In this position, which he held for 25 years (less 4½ years' army service during World War I) he might fairly be described as a mixture of organiser, trouble shooter and ideas man. Inevitably he was closely involved with new developments – welded underframes, boosters, *Cock o' the North*. But it was Gresley who decided the strategy, and Bulleid had to sell his own ideas if they were to be translated into metal. We may guess that some were not fully digested.

Bulleid would try anything – well, almost anything – once. Picture him on the footplate of a long, loose-coupled GNR freight in the fenlands south of Peterborough and instructing – nay, ordering – the driver out of the blue to make a full emergency brake application so that he could see the effect. The train comes to a violent stop, divided, and the unfortunate guard is hurled the length of his van in the close company of his hot stove. By the greatest good fortune he does not need an ambulance and the train is not derailed and foul of the adjacent line. It was a classic instance of how *not* to conduct an experiment, and Gresley reprimanded him for it.

Maybe his subservience to Gresley lasted too long and began to corrode the soul. Certainly the old Maunsell order at Waterloo departed for ever with Bulleid's arrival in 1937 as chief mechanical engineer at the age of 55. Revolution! Routine administration was loaded on to a general assistant and he took design and development to his own bosom. Technical assistants were reduced to little more than consultative figureheads. Ideas, some good, some highly dubious, poured into the drawing office in a steady stream, supplemented by the offerings of enthusiastic salesmen (who regarded Bulleid as a fairly soft touch) and his own patents (which surprisingly the Southern allowed him to take out as his own property). What was needed was a tough chief draughtsman *à la* Tom Coleman at Derby, someone who would argue from experience, prevaricate, skirt round the wilder flights of fancy with more practicable alternatives, and generally act as a buffer between his chief and the men on the board. Instead, the word from above was 'Even if he wants the chimney on the tender, give it to him'. So came the nonsenses of chain-driven valve gears, ashpans wthout dampers, and steam locomotives which actually *caught fire* and had to be extinguished by the fire brigade.

Bulleid's Pacifics were expensive to build, showed appalling availability and were a shed fitter's nightmare, yet there was little effective follow-up of their serious deficiencies. Bulleid's mercurial mind, behind the gentle smile that said 'These things happen . . .' was busy with new ploys, and was reluctant to be diverted by unhappy experience. He could legitimately point to their excellent performances when in traffic, doing everything asked of them and earning the appreciation, even adulation, of the men who drove and fired them.

Bulleid's extrovert character could never be satisfied. He would produce what no-one had done before, a new concept of the steam locomotive, a flexible, all-adhesion general purpose tank engine which would mop up every job left over by the Pacifics and Q1s. He took proved, conventional design and wrung its neck, often changing for change's sake. *Everything* had to be different. Even the class name would

James Stirling

Stirling . . . was a designer who saw no need for the steam dome in locomotive design and consequently all the engines that came out of Ashford in his time were without this traditional feature. He was, likewise, a man who saw no necessity for the outer world to be notified of what was going forward within the confines of his works, and paid his small son pocket-money to scan through all the technical journals for news items naming Ashford, in order that he might call down fire and slaughter on the heads of the offending editors. He painted his engines (up to 1895) black, with red lines, equipping them all with his own labour-saving steam reversing device, which might not have become an adjunct of locomotive design for some years had not his mother once expressed to him the compassion she felt towards certain perspiring enginemen she had seen hauling over the heavy reversing gear of their locomotive by muscular strength alone.

proclaim its unique virtues. After much prodding, and dragging a reluctant traffic manager with him, the Southern in 1946 authorised an initial build of five (without really knowing the machine they were to get), and immediately before nationalisation a further 31 – though this latter was largely by way of staking a claim. Riddles at the Railway Executive, faced with this expensive proposal, earned Bulleid's utter contempt by agreeing to the five guinea-pigs only, and the rest in LMS 2-6-4 tanks. It was too much. Bulleid shook the BR dust from his feet in disgust and left for Inchicore. The *Leader* proved one of the most monumental failures in British steam locomotive history.

But the old spirit survived; the blame for the demise of his masterpiece was seen as lack of vision at Marylebone Road. One great problem overshadowed the CIE scene, Ireland's dependence on imported coal and oil while it lay smothered under a potential fuel, turf. It was exactly the challenge that Bulleid's active mind would unhesitatingly rise to. The *Leader* design was resurrected for adaptation as the new master-piece; some simplification of the bogies was swamped by the complexity of the boiler and its fuel supply and draughting arrangements. With plenty of development work and modification, and a cadre of skilled firemen, it *might* have been made to work, a high cost answer to the problem. But the Irish railway climate was never going to provide this, and 2,000 miles of test running saw it consigned to the scrap yard. The Irish christened him 'The Bull', and it was apt.

EDWIN CHARLES COX

Walker was fortunate (though he also had the ability to select good assistants) in Cox as his chief-of-staff. The son of a SER railwayman, he joined that railway in 1883 and by 1911 had risen to become superintendent of the line of the SE&C. The post was exacting, especially during the 1914–18 war, and he displayed great competence, among other things introducing 'parallel working' in the London Bridge area to ease awful congestion at the flat junctions. He became chief operating superintendent of the new Southern and when in 1930 the operating and commercial sides were merged he became traffic manager. Although Cox was due to retire earlier, Walker insisted on his staying until he himself retired in 1937.

A timetable and operating genius, it was he who demanded trains of 500 tons at 55 mph overall speeds for the Eastern Section, a demand met by Maunsell with his 'Lord Nelsons'. But Cox was inclined to be hasty and in an excess of rationalising fervour in 1923 alienated customer opinion by concentrating all the fast services to Portsmouth on the Haslemere line at the expense of the Mid-Sussex. In this case Walker officially took the blame and the status quo was restored.

He chaired the electrification steering committee and Walker re-marked 'without Raworth (chief electrical engineer) and Cox it (electri-fication) could not have been done'. Like Walker he was tall and impressive. A hard and sustained worker with ceaseless creative energy, he was also a hard taskmaster, respected but not popular. More extrovert than Walker, he was fond of making long public speeches. Elliot tells of him haranguing the Dorchester station master and the serried ranks of his three staff: see separate 'snippet'.

SIR JOHN ELLIOT

It takes all sorts to make a railwayman. Sir John Elliot is not only a great railwayman, but is the very antithesis of his predecessor Missenden (see separate entry). The son of R. D. Blumenfeld, the famous editor of the *Daily Express*, he was educated at Marlborough and Sandhurst and served with the Hussars in the 1914–18 war. He afterwards went into Fleet Street, changing his name to his second Christian name on Beaverbrook's advice, who foresaw a second German war and resultant disadvantage of a German name.

In 1925, he was called in by Walker to reform the bad public relations of the Southern. He insisted that he report direct to Walker and became 'Public Relations Assistant', the first outside the US. His work has been summarised elsewhere. After a year's trial he had learned to love the railway and was glad to be given a permanent appointment. On his advice, Maunsell's first 4-6-0s were named from the Arthurian legends. There was trouble over *Joyous Gard*; the ASLEF representative complained 'What about the drivers?'

He was much under Walker's influence and learned a great deal from him, especially on the financial side. He was selected for further advancement. In 1933 Walker told him 'It's time we put you out on the line, you have a lot to learn. Spend as much time outside as you can'. A typical remark by Walker, typically taken to heart by Elliot. He was created assistant traffic manager. He eventually became assistant general manager under Szlumper and later became Missenden's deputy. Both men relied on him heavily.

On Missenden's departure for the Railway Executive, Elliot assumed the title of Acting General Manager. The government refused to allow the company to give him substantive rank in case he qualified for an enhanced pension, but he was still the last of the Southern's outstanding general managers: he got away with posters signing him such. With nationalisation he was effectively demoted to chief regional officer, an agent of the Executive, no longer a manager. In 1950 he was transferred to the London Midland Region with the remit of restoring morale. But a year later he took the chair at the Railway Executive, chosen by the Minister of Transport and recommended by Missenden as the best man to bridge the gap with the Commission. Yet at their first meeting Hurcomb told him: 'I want you to know you were not my choice.' He did his best in an unworkable situation. With the abolition of the Executive under the 1953 Act, he became chairman of London Transport, until he retired in 1959. One of his major contributions was to get the Victoria line 'off the ground'. He was knighted in 1953.

Not only one of the foremost railway managers of this age, he emerges from his writings as a most engaging personality, with a great depth of humanity and much more outgoing then his predecessors just considered. It is no coincidence he was in constant demand for public speeches and it was right that it was he who gave the Southern's funeral oration on 31 December 1947. And on 31 December 1987, just short of his ninetieth birthday, he enthusiastically gave further help in the preparation of this book, to which he writes the *Foreword*.

Memories of Guildford

Much of the charm of observation in this area lay in the cross-country lines; at Peasmarsh Junction the Horsham line (single) joined, the passenger trains on this branch comprising Marsh 'balloon' coaches hauled/propelled by motor fitted Stroudley class D1 0-4-2Ts. This ensemble, the diminutive locomotive overshadowed by the coaches, was known locally, but not without affection, as the 'Sprat and Winkle'. There was a mixed train early in the morning, producing a class E5 0-6-2T, and in the afternoon a leisurely pick-up goods in the care of a class C3 0-6-0. The only non LBSC type to venture down this typical LBSC branch were Guildford based class M7 0-4-4Ts, which took commuters from Waterloo on from Guildford as far as Cranleigh, and no further. For example, the 6.34pm from Guildford, returning immediately from Cranleigh as light engine or empty coaching stock.

The next signalbox towards Guildford was Shalford Junction, a truly busy place at peak times, especially after electrification when the Portsmouth services were expected to run with clockwork precision but at the same time the more unpredictable steam services not only from the Horsham line but also from the ex SE&C Redhill line had to be fitted in. The Redhill–Reading passenger services were largely in the hands of the aged SEC class F1 4-4-0s, technically quite unsuitable with their 7ft driving wheels for a line which included Gomshall bank at 1 in 96, and the 1 in 116 up from Deepdene to Betchworth. But loads were light, and the class U 2-6-0s took the heavier trains including the through Birkenhead–Hastings from the Great Western. The signalmen at Shalford Junction exercised considerable expertise and uncanny judgement in accomodating these literally conflicting interests— R.A. Savill.

R. E. L. Maunsell.

ROBERT HOLLAND-MARTIN

The Southern's third chairman – he succeeded Lord Wakehurst after the latter's sudden death in 1934 – was Robert Holland-Martin. He held the post until his own death in 1944. He was an ideal chairman, always a leader and never a driver, he was well aware it was the function of the board to formulate policy and not to dabble in management.

With perhaps one exception, his relationship with Walker and the other GMs was excellent, and his support of Walker had much to do with the building up of the Southern's reputation from the abysmal depths of its early years.

Holland-Martin came from a private banking family, but though serving continuously on the LSWR and Southern boards, for him the fascination of railways was not financial – he left that side to Walker and Docker – but the human side, 'the Southern Family'. He was interested in making the trains as cheerful and attractive as possible. He supported the advanced decor of the Bognor buffet cars and the malachite green livery.

He was much liked for his friendly manner. He had a habit of losing his agenda papers, and leaving meetings in other people's hands, but was always capable of shrewd assessment of the advice given him.

RICHARD MAUNSELL

Maunsell (the 'u' was superfluous for purposes of pronunciation) was the archetypal example of the chief mechanical engineer whose interests lay in running a tight ship to the satisfaction of general manager and board, rather than in major innovation. He enjoyed his department. He picked his subordinates with great care, delegated, communicated and listened. He was a man who put together a team, told them what he wanted, laid down the parameters and judged their performance accordingly; when they had earned his confidence, he supported them loyally. Not for him the burning of midnight oil; he firmly believed in running the department between nine and five, leaving a clear desk behind him.

His training under H. A. Ivatt at Inchicore, Dublin, and subsequent experience elsewhere, had taught him how to extract value for money in an environment that was very far from wealthy. He returned to Inchicore to take over as works manager (a staff of 1,500) at a youthful 28, and remained in the post for fifteen years. As Joynt, the chief draughtsman wrote: 'He was splendidly energetic . . . full of ideas, enterprising, enthusiastic, hardworking and expecting hard work from others.' He undoubtedly left his trademark on the place. But his subsequent two years as locomotive, carriage and wagon superintendent of the GS&W did not immerse him very deeply in the design field and this lack of experience of the overall design concept was vividly shown on his arrival on the SE&C at Ashford in 1913. The design of the new L class 4-4-0 was virtually complete, but Maunsell had not yet had the opportunity to appraise his design staff and build up confidence in them. So the principal drawings were sent off to Inchicore for vetting, and the changes which they recommended proved retrograde. But never again would he put himself in that position; he was his own man. Without going through the mechanics of what passes for consultation today, he nevertheless listened to the opinions of his designers, users and maintainers, evaluated them and then made his own mind up on the evidence. His aim was to ensure that what he built was right.

Having weighed up his key staff and found no satisfactory 'in-house' succession, he promptly went outside for his new appointees. From Swindon came Pearson, his Assistant CME, Holcroft to modernise Ashford Works, and Lynes to lead on carriage and wagon design. From Derby he brought Clayton as leading locomotive draughtsman, later personal assistant, and from Inchicore, Hicks as assistant works manager. He picked well, and the team was to hold together, little changed, until Maunsell retired 23 years later – a remarkable record.

Inevitably he was often frustrated; there was never enough money left over after putting down more third rail. While the LMS was using cheap Government money to build new locomotives and carriages in their hundreds, Maunsell had to be satisfied with penny numbers and keeping the veterans running. He accepted it philosophically.

Listener and communicator? One thinks of his regular visits to his works: no mere walkabouts, but purposeful probing by a practical man. Searching questions on design, manufacturing techniques and repair procedures flew at his managers. One of them likened it to fielding in the slips when Don Bradman was batting. Again, he was in his element at major staff functions; he attended annually the 'Pupils & Premiums Association' dinners in London and gatherings of works supervisors, not as a chore but as a chance to renew old friendships and set up a dialogue.

In the latter years of his office he was dogged by ill-health, and his steadfast senior team began to fray at the edges with sickness and old age. The zest had gone, and – albeit at the age of 69 – he retired. His staff felt a real sense of loss wrote one: 'After he had gone we felt it was the end.' Maunsell died just over six years later.

SIR EUSTACE MISSENDEN

The Southern's wartime general manager was an out and out railwayman who had come to the top the hard way. The son of a stationmaster, on leaving board school he became a booking clerk. It was a tribute to his competence, perseverance and capacity for hard work that he rose through the ranks of the SE&C, a railway whose management tended to be recruited from university graduates. But it left him with a lifelong antipathy for public-school men, 'intellectuals' and civil servants.

On the formation of the Southern he became divisional operating superintendent (London East), and later came across from London Bridge to Waterloo as assistant superintendent of operation under E. C. Cox, Walker's right hand man. Cox and Walker retired together in 1937 and the former's place as traffic manager was taken by Missenden under the new general manager, Gilbert Szlumper. It was during this period he launched the 'Southern Sales League' aimed at making stations and depots more revenue conscious.

In 1939, on the outbreak of war, the War Office requested Szlumper's release for war service. Holland-Martin the chairman perhaps foolishly acceded, expecting Missenden to accept an acting appointment. This he refused, threatening resignation unless he was made substantive general manager. So when Szlumper was released from war service, he was forced to accept a golden handshake.

> **Maunsell's 'Annual Dinner'**
> A social occasion that might almost be described as a living memorial to R. E. L. Maunsell – greatly loved and deeply respected at the works – is the annual dinner of the Ashford & District Foremen's Association. From the first assembly held in the winter of 1919 at the George Hotel, in Ashford, Maunsell took the opportunity afforded by the dinners to reveal to his staff particulars of the programme of work laid down for the months ahead, and these speeches were fraught with such significance for the men (not infrequently haunted by the spectre of 'short time') that the Kent newspapers came to give them the utmost prominence in their columns.

Sir Eustace Missenden.

Missenden was a lifelong operating man, and knew the Southern inside out. He lacked Walker's financial flair, but undoubtedly was the right man to lead the wartime Southern with its vastly increased traffic to be handled by reduced stock and staff, interrupted by years of bombing, but when there were no worries about making profits or planning investment. His work was recognised by a knighthood in 1944.

Missenden left the Southern in the months before the date of nationalisation to become the first chairman of the Railway Executive, knowing he was not the first choice for the job. The hopeless constitutional muddle of the relationship between British Transport Commission and the Executive, described by Elliot as 'The Corridors of Confusion', were made worse confounded by the personal animosity between Hurcomb, chairman of the BTC and arch-civil servant, and Missenden, the arch-practical railwayman.

Missenden's was not a warm personality and he did not get on well with many of his peers, including Raworth, the chief electrical engineer. But 'though he trusted few people, he was entranced by Bulleid' (Elliot) and defended his eccentricities, including the *Leader* locomotive, though he ordered windows to be fitted in the 'Tavern' buffet cars.

He refused to work long hours and delegated well. Usually a shrewd judge of character and ability, he kept the loyalty of his assistants, and was never afraid to see that loyalty got its reward. His sponsorship of Elliot speaks volumes for both men.

GILBERT SAVIL SZLUMPER

Szlumper (the z is silent) was the son of A. W. Szlumper, a civil engineer on the LSWR and Southern, becoming chief civil engineer on the latter. Gilbert himself trained as an engineer, as pupil under Jacomb Hood, the LSWR chief civil engineer. He turned to the management side, and in 1914 Walker appointed him as his assistant. He also took up the duties of secretary to the REC under Walker. In 1919 he became deputy docks and marine manager and on the formation of the Southern became substantive head. In 1925 he also became assistant general manager, relinquishing the docks and marine post in 1929. But he had laid the foundations of the expansion of that jewel in the Southern crown, Southampton Docks, including the planning of the new Western Docks.

On Walker's retirement he became general manager, but had little time to impose his stamp on the already well run railway before the outbreak of war. He had been a territorial officer since 1908, and his release was requested by the war office.

He said of himself 'I had to overcome the handicap of being the son of the chief civil engineer and to mind my step when I was young'. His was a tireless capacity for hard work and early rising. He was a clear and forward thinker. Unlike Walker, he saw the rise of road transport could free railways of the need to maintain uneconomic and closely spaced goods depots and rural stations. Popular, his was a breezy style, and his affability and good humour extended to all except those he classified as 'bloody fools'. The other two categories into which he placed the Southern's top-brass were 'good chaps' and 'fools'. His fondness for risqué stories did not apparently get him into trouble with Walker who could not be expected to appreciate them.

Tree of Growth

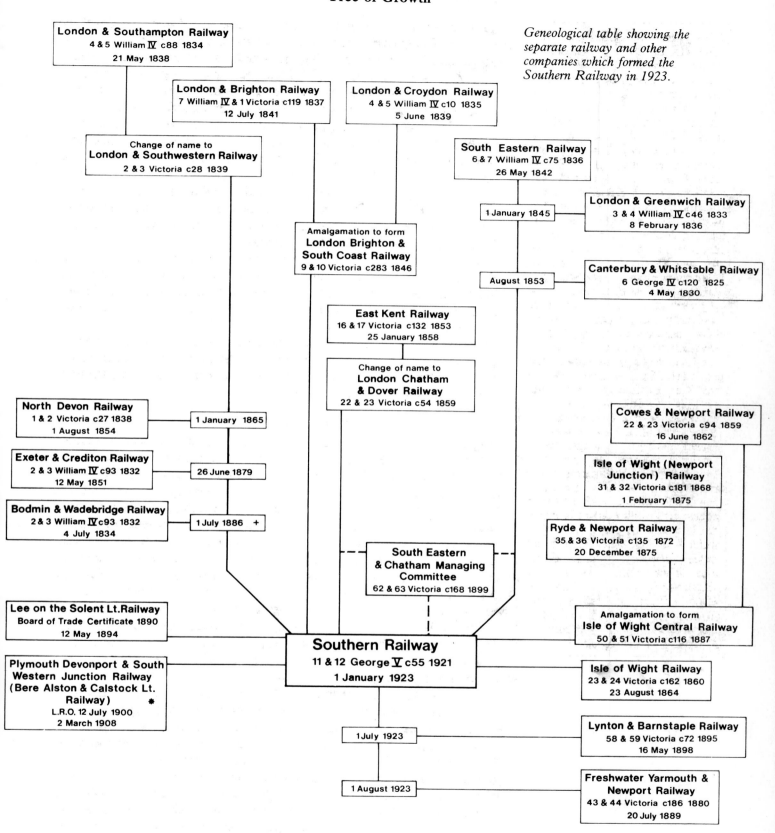

Geneological table showing the separate railway and other companies which formed the Southern Railway in 1923.

London & Southampton Railway
4 & 5 William IV c88 1834
21 May 1838

London & Brighton Railway
7 William IV & 1 Victoria c119 1837
12 July 1841

London & Croydon Railway
4 & 5 William IV c10 1835
5 June 1839

South Eastern Railway
6 & 7 William IV c75 1836
26 May 1842

Change of name to
London & Southwestern Railway
2 & 3 Victoria c28 1839

1 January 1845

London & Greenwich Railway
3 & 4 William IV c46 1833
8 February 1836

Amalgamation to form
London Brighton & South Coast Railway
9 & 10 Victoria c283 1846

August 1853

Canterbury & Whitstable Railway
6 George IV c120 1825
4 May 1830

East Kent Railway
16 & 17 Victoria c132 1853
25 January 1858

Change of name to
London Chatham & Dover Railway
22 & 23 Victoria c54 1859

North Devon Railway
1 & 2 Victoria c27 1838
1 August 1854

1 January 1865

Exeter & Crediton Railway
2 & 3 William IV c93 1832
12 May 1851

26 June 1879

Cowes & Newport Railway
22 & 23 Victoria c94 1859
16 June 1862

Isle of Wight (Newport Junction) Railway
31 & 32 Victoria c181 1868
1 February 1875

Bodmin & Wadebridge Railway
2 & 3 William IV c93 1832
4 July 1834

1 July 1886 +

Ryde & Newport Railway
35 & 36 Victoria c135 1872
20 December 1875

South Eastern & Chatham Managing Committee
62 & 63 Victoria c168 1899

Lee on the Solent Lt. Railway
Board of Trade Certificate 1890
12 May 1894

Amalgamation to form
Isle of Wight Central Railway
50 & 51 Victoria c116 1887

**Plymouth Devonport & South Western Junction Railway
(Bere Alston & Calstock Lt. Railway)** *
L.R.O. 12 July 1900
2 March 1908

Southern Railway
11 & 12 George V c55 1921
1 January 1923

Isle of Wight Railway
23 & 24 Victoria c162 1860
23 August 1864

1 July 1923

Lynton & Barnstaple Railway
58 & 59 Victoria c72 1895
16 May 1898

1 August 1923

Freshwater Yarmouth & Newport Railway
43 & 44 Victoria c186 1880
20 July 1889

+ Bodmin and Wadebridge Railway purchased by LSWR without Parliament's authority in 1846.

* Also incorporated the East Cornwall Mineral Railway (Calstock to Callington) originally 3ft 6in gauge, converted to 4ft 8½in gauge c1907/8.

3
ELECTRIFICATION

Last Workmen's

The first workmen's trains, special trains on which cheap fares were charged, were operated by the London, Chatham & Dover. Clause 134 of the Act of 25 July 1864 required the company 'to run a train every morning of the week from their Loughborough Park and Peckham Junction stations to their Ludgate station' and back in the evening at 'one penny per journey'. The trains started in 1865, leaving both Victoria and Ludgate Hill for the other terminus via Herne Hill at 04.55, returning at 18.15 (14.30 on Saturdays).

Anxious to exploit any source of passenger traffic, the Southern's constituent companies extended the scope of workmen's services. By the 1930s, the Southern would quote workmen's fares between any two stations and available by any train reaching the destination before 08.00. Workmen's traffic from 'Southern Electric' stations in London East Division had reached enormous proportions.

In 1938 the workmen's fares from Charlton to London Bridge were 6½d (2.7p), Cannon Street 7d and Waterloo and Charing Cross 7½d. These were overwhelmingly the main destinations, largely because the tram services paralleling the North Kent line were cheap and frequent. The booking clerks divided their customers into the baddies who presented a half-crown for a 7d ticket and the goodies who gave a penny along with the silver 6d.

The total cost of workmen's tickets at six per week was little less than the monthly season, *continued opposite*

'It's a wonderful thing, an electric tram' enthused the author of an Edwardian children's poem. Two lines later he was down to technical details: 'There's a little wheel and a wire and lo! a handle is turned and off we go.' But there was much more to it than interesting technicalities. The spread of the tramway networks brought new opportunities and convenience of travel, more nearly door-to-door than the suburban railway. And its coming put the fear of death into railways the length and breadth of the country. The LBSC's South London line from London Bridge to Victoria via Peckham Rye, saw its bookings fall from 8 million in 1903 to 3 million five years later. Catastrophe indeed.

The adage 'If you can't beat 'em, join 'em' was never more appropriate than in South London. Only electrification could stem the tide. It would reduce train crews from three to two, give greater crew productivity in terms of train miles, and save fuel through greater thermal efficiency.

The LBSC was early off the mark. It obtained powers to electrify the South London line in 1904, and after consulting an eminent electrical engineer, Sir Philip Dawson, accepted his recommendation that single phase alternating current at 6600v 25Hz, with overhead contact wire, would best suit their requirements. It was a brave decision, for the single phase series traction motor was still at the development stage. The South London line, on which electric trains came into service in December 1909, became what LBSC publicity described as the 'Elevated Electric Railway' (because of the overhead wire, not because much of it ran on viaducts). The resulting traffic growth due to a faster, more frequent and cleaner service quickly demanded longer trains. By 1912 the overhead had reached Crystal Palace and Selhurst, but the war interrupted further work. After hostilities ended, traffic flows dictated more extensions and the ac system reached Coulsdon North, and Sutton via West Croydon, in the spring of 1925, by then under the Southern Railway.

London United Tramways had spread equally into LSWR territory. By 1903 the trams were in Hampton Court and expansion was continuing. If they were not particularly attractive to City commuters from the leafy suburbs, they were certainly mopping up the local journeys. So the LSWR was also forced down the electrification road. The decision was made in 1913, the first service opening from Waterloo to Wimbledon via East Putney in October 1915. By November 1916 electric trains had reached out to Shepperton (both via Wimbledon and via Richmond), the Hounslow loop and Claygate, all current supplied from a new railway power station at Durnsford Road, Wimbledon. The war then stopped further extensions and no further services began until July 1925, at which date Dorking North and Guildford were brought into the fold.

By contrast, the impecunious SE&C, every bit as strongly assailed by the tram, could only watch as the others did what it could not afford to do itself.

The man on the Clapham Junction platform must have been puzzled by what he saw. Since 1911 he had been conditioned to the Brighton line with its overhead structures festooned with contact wire and cables, through which the pantographs on the motor coaches picked their way with a gentle swish. Now, on the LSWR's Windsor line platforms, they did not need any of this complexity; they just came along with a load of insulating pots, screwed them to the sleeper ends, dropped a steel conductor rail on to them, coupled it to the 600v direct current supply – and they were in business. Why did they have to have two different systems to do the same job? Nobody in authority considered it necessary, or even desirable, to tell the Clapham observer that the Brighton company selected their system with the ultimate objective of carrying it to the South Coast. It was a system for a forthcoming main line electrification with express trains to Brighton and elsewhere. The South Western, on the other hand, saw the third rail as confined to a suburban network; they ran long-distance expresses to Bournemouth and the West of England, and clearly *they* would *never* be worked electrically.

Even before the birth of the Southern Railway in 1923, the dice were loaded against the Brighton's ac system. The Kennedy committee on electrification policy acknowledged the high cost of conversion to dc but recommended it be seriously considered in the new unified company to facilitate through running and interchangeability of rolling stock. With the LSWR's Herbert Walker as general manager the outcome was all but inevitable. Thus in 1926 the Southern decided that the third rail would become universal, and three years later the overhead was finally laid to rest. The late S. B. Warder, architect of BR's ac system, suggested in 1966: 'this system was conceived . . . as eventually extending to Brighton, but the railway managements of the day had insufficient foresight to contemplate electrification for anything except suburban operation in competition with tramways . . . It was never given a fair

Waterloo & City Railway. Single car No 16, with driving cabs at both ends for use on off peak services. There were five single cars built by Dick, Kerr & Co in 1899 and 1900 which ran until 1940 when they were replaced, along with the remaining W&C stock, by the trains still running on the line. The photograph was probably taken when the cars were new and shows the original centre third rail arrangement.

continued

about the same as the quarterly rate. But the £3-15-0 (£3.75) quarterly special from Sidcup for example, represented a large cash outlay against a weekly wage of about £2. From many suburban stations in London East, horny-handed sons of toil were distinctly in the minority. Most passengers travelling on workmen's tickets were junior office workers, clerks and typists. Since workmen's tickets were available only on trains arriving before 08.00 and offices usually began at 09.00, the rush was on for the last 'workmen's'. City coffee shops benefitted from the early arrivals.

Pressure on the last workmen's train became especially serious as suburbs grew up round stations such as Albany Park almost overnight. In 1938 the last available

continued overleaf

The LBSCR suburban electrics. The Brighton company adopted high voltage ac electrification with overhead conductor wires strung from lattice supports for its initial conversions before World War I, which some say in the light of hindsight might have been a better bet than the LSW's dc third rail system. This view depicts a train working the second route to be converted, in 1911, between Victoria and Crystal Palace, leaving Clapham Junction heading for Victoria. The trains were three-coach formations with a motor coach and two driving trailers.

continued
train for Charing Cross was the 07.38 and for Cannon Street the 07.46, both of which by a fortunate coincidence were booked to arrive at the termini at 08.00. Of the 300 or so workmen's tickets sold at Charlton daily, about three-quarters were for travel on these two trains. The organised minority bought their tickets on the way home the previous night; tickets were of course Edmondson cards, and a second dating press was provided, kept with the next day's date. The late turn booking clerk would date up a few tickets short of the usual sale, as there would be no time in the morning. If more were sold they went out dateless; if less, the unsold dated ones had to be cancelled.

Booking clerks tended to judge the relative work done at various stations by the number of workmen's tickets issued. To the new recruit on his own for the first time, Charlton seemed busy enough, but the legendary station was Grove Park, where, due to its proximity to the vast LCC estate, 3,000 workmen's tickets were issued daily from five booking windows. At Charlton a second window was opened only when Charlton Athletic Football Club, then in the First Division, were playing at home, but that is another story.

trial.' Walker himself later admitted that even when the Southern electrified to Brighton it was regarded as an extension of the suburban network – not main-line electrification.

The decision made, it was applied energetically both to infill schemes within the surburban area and to the gradual advance of its boundaries. Orpington and Dartford in 1926, Epsom in 1929, Windsor and Gravesend in 1930, the rolling programme rolled inexorably on. There was a brief slowing down with the onset of the Depression, but the resolve was still there. Walker announced to his officers in 1929, 'Gentlemen, I have decided to electrify to Brighton!' At last the suburban shackles were to be thrown off. The process was aided by the development of mercury arc rectifiers to produce the dc current; they could be installed in unmanned substations, remotely controlled. It was the beginning of the end for rotary converters in manned substations. In the leap from Coulsdon North to Brighton and Worthing in 1932 and 1933, power came from 18 rectifier substations overseen from a windowless central control room at Three Bridges. But did anyone consider at the time that with the Brighton's ac system they would probably have needed only five substations?

Commercial results from this project were such that there was no hesitation in pushing further. July 1935 saw Eastbourne, Hastings and Seaford 'on the juice' and two years later the third rail was pushed through Woking and Haslemere to Portsmouth. The first of the old LSWR's main lines had fallen! Still the march to the South Coast continued, reaching Bognor and Littlehampton in July 1938. Some of the last outposts of the suburban area were invaded in the last year of peace – Reading came on stream in January, Maidstone, Gillingham and Rochester in July. There remained two yawning gaps. The Chatham main line to Margate and Dover was electrified in 1959 as Phase I of the Kent Coast electrification. Phase II in 1961 at last took the third rail down the South Eastern main line beyond Sevenoaks – over thirteen years after the Southern Railway became Southern Region.

Last of the major schemes involved the Bournemouth line, worked electrically from July 1967. For this service special provision was necessary to preserve through coach working to Weymouth, which at that stage was not to be electrified. After extensive 100mph testing to

34

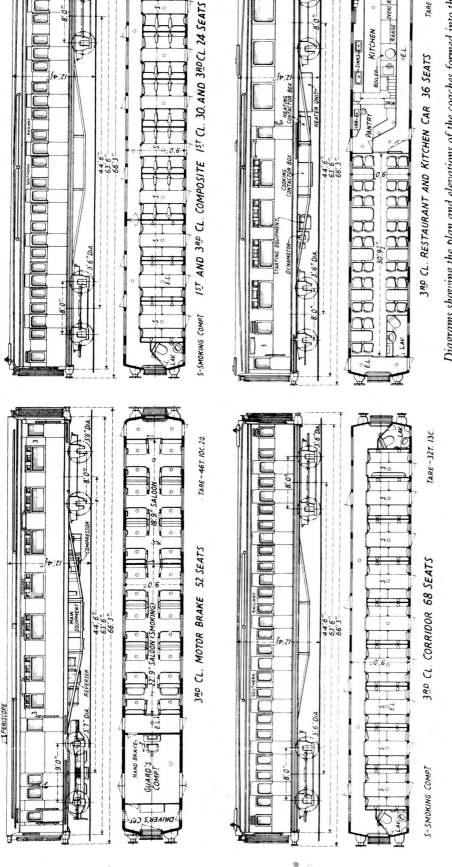

1ST AND 3RD CL. COMPOSITE 1ST CL. 30. AND 3RD CL. 24 SEATS   TARE—32 T. 12C.

S—SMOKING COMPT

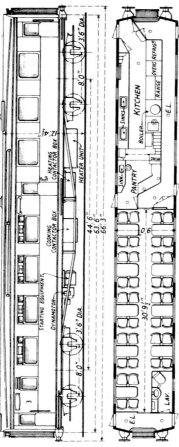

3RD CL. RESTAURANT AND KITCHEN CAR 36 SEATS   TARE=35 T.

3RD CL. MOTOR BRAKE 52 SEATS   TARE—46 T. 10C. 20.

3RD CL. CORRIDOR 68 SEATS   TARE=32 T. 13C.

S—SMOKING COMPT

RESTAURANT AND COMPARTMENT FIRST. 42 SEATS   TARE—33 T.

S—SMOKING COMPT

Diagrams showing the plan and elevations of the coaches formed into the 4COR and 4RES units for the Portsmouth electrification of 1937.

Top left :   Third class motor-coach used at each end of four-car set. Each of these cars has two traction motors

Middle left :   Third class corridor coach used in non-restaurant four-car sets

Top right :   Composite first and third class coach used in non-restaurant formations

Bottom right :   Third class restaurant and kitchen car

Bottom left :   First class restaurant and compartment coach

To the Man who Lives in London

It may safely be said that no great city in the world has such an intensive suburban train service as London. And, of the districts north, south, east and west of the Metropolis, the south has more electric trains to the suburbs and beyond than all the rest put together.

The recent developments of the "Southern Electric," pushing out into the very heart of Kent and Surrey, and opening up virgin country for the busy city worker are altering the conditions of living in a degree not dreamed of hitherto.

The electrification of the Southern Railway's suburban lines has *continued opposite*

Two generations. Comparison between SR electric stock of the 1920s on the left, formed from ex LBSCR stock, only 8ft wide, and the post World War II all-steel 9ft wide bodied Bulleid stock on the right. Note the letter headcode of the old stock, 'H' indicating a Hampton Court – Waterloo service.

prove the suitability of push-pull working, the ingenious solution was adopted of forming 12-car trains of two 4-car driving trailer sets, with a high-power 4-car 'pusher' set at the London end. At Bournemouth the driving trailer sets were hauled to Weymouth by diesel-electric locomotive, the 'pusher' set being left behind to haul the next return service. The driving trailer sets were propelled back from Weymouth by the diesel locomotive and attached behind another powered 4-car set. With the recent electrification through to Weymouth, these unique arrangements are no longer required.

Southern electric multiple unit trains, after a long period of relative technical stagnation between the wars, and even after, have come a long way in recent years. The electro-pneumatic brake was standardised in the late 1940s, but it took a long time for the Southern Region to accept that slam doors brought as many problems as they solved and that sliding powered doors should be adopted. Air suspension bogies and the Westcode type of brake were taken aboard rather more readily, but the Southern jibbed at incorporating air and electrical connections in the Tightlock automatic coupler. Only very recently has the ultra-reliable camshaft-operated power controller been supplanted by thyristors.

What of the people whose lives have been changed by Southern electrification? Railwaymen from other companies might describe the Southern Railway disparagingly as a glorified tramway, but to those who entrusted their behinds to its carriage seats that view cut no ice at all. They were more impressed by those green enamel signs at station entrances that proclaimed 'Frequent Service of Electric Trains to . . .' The housewife at Cooden Beach, going shopping at Bobbies store in Eastbourne before the days of two cars in every drive, soon learned that she had a train at 1 and 31 minutes past each hour for her convenience.

Everyone enjoyed quicker and cleaner journeys, electrification unleashing suburban development on an unprecedented scale. The Southern encouraged developers, made special offers to new commuters (they would not then have recognised the word), and for ever kept in touch with publications, posters and other practical advice. Just how dramatically journey times came down is illustrated by the Teddington service. From Waterloo by steam it had taken 35 minutes to Kingston, 47 to Teddington. Now it was 28 and 34 minutes respectively – though on most routes it was the increase in frequency and regularity that passengers felt benefitted them more.

To the staff in the thirties it was something different again. For the motorman at a suburban depot it could be a lonely and soul-destroying job; he exchanged banter with his guard as they crossed on the platform while changing ends, and perhaps with colleagues during his meal break. Otherwise it was a life of 'Rightaway – power on – watch for the coasting board – shut off – brake – 15 second station stop – Rightaway', and repeated a hundred times or more round the chimney pots, and roll on enough seniority to get something better. For the guard, before the days of the 'Ding, ding and away' syndrome, it was a case of keeping close to his van door when he waved his green flag or risk being left on the platform gazing ruefully at the receding tail lamp. The man on the track, long before the days of high-visibility vests, needed to keep an extra sharp lookout for the quietly approaching train, and perhaps felt the tingle as his long wet macintosh brushed the unguarded conductor rail. The substation attendant, ear unconsciously tuned to the hum of his rotary converters, knew that it was his future that was on the line as technology marched on to unmanned substations.

And for the badger on his nocturnal rambles in search of succulent pickings, it was sudden death in the pungent reek of singeing fur.

ELECTRIFICATION DATES

Victoria–London Bridge (via South London line)[1] . . .	1 Dec 1909
Battersea Park–Crystal Palace (Low Level) (via Clapham Junction and Streatham Hill)[1]	12 May 1911
Crystal Palace–Norwood Junction–Selhurst[1]	1 Jun 1912
Peckham Rye–West Norwood (official; trains began on 3 Mar 1912)[1]	1 Jun 1912
Waterloo–East Putney	25 Oct 1915
Point Pleasant Junction–Clapham Junction via Kingston including Shepperton branch	30 Jan 1916
Clapham Junction–Wimbledon–Strawberry Hill . .	30 Jan 1916
Hounslow Loop	12 Mar 1916
Malden–Hampton Court	18 Jun 1916
Hampton Court Junction–Claygate	20 Nov 1916
Balham–Coulsdon North[1]	1 Apr 1925
Sutton (via West Croydon)[1]	1 Apr 1925
Victoria–Orpington (via Penge East) . . .	12 Jul 1925
Raynes Park–Dorking North	12 Jul 1925
Nunhead–Crystal Palace (High Level) . . .	12 Jul 1925
Leatherhead–Effingham Junction	12 Jul 1925
Holborn Viaduct–Orpington (via Nunhead) . . .	12 Jul 1925
Claygate–Guildford (via Cobham)	12 Jul 1925
Hayes–Elmers End	21 Sep 1925

[1]The LBSC's overhead system

continued
brought within easy daily reach of London many places actually in and surrounded by the real, beautiful country to be found everywhere south of the Metropolis. Thus, London's daily workers can spend their leisure, and sleep, in pure air and in a beautiful country which before was more or less inaccessible because of the time taken, the infrequency of trains, and the greater comparative cost. It is the special aim of the present book to make known the attractiveness of these places.

In this book, comprehensive practical information is given concerning the cost of, and possible situations for, new houses, and – it is believed for the first time – the financial assistance available in the different areas. Speaking generally, houses cannot be rented nowadays. They must be bought. The practical questions for persons of moderate means are, then: Where can I get a house within my means? What cash must I be prepared to put down at the outset? What financial help can I get from the Local Authority under the provisions of Housing Acts, or otherwise? So much information as to the price and class of house available in each district is here presented, that the reader should get some real idea as to whether he is likely to obtain what will suit him at a particular place, and whether he can count upon such assistance as he needs.

Readers who desire financial assistance to enable them to build or purchase, should, in addition to noting the particulars on the point set out in the separate sections, consult the special article on page vii.

Introduction to an SR booklet listing facilities of new suburban electric areas, 1926.

Fast to Reading

For some years the fastest thing through Clapham Junction was not the *Atlantic Coast Express* (40mph) nor the *Brighton Belle* (60mph) but any one of the faster trains to Reading (no limit, line straight) which happened to have an F1 on it. These were Stirling's first express designs for the SER and, even after re-boilering and re-cabbing by Wainwright, looked gloriously ancient and ramshackle with their large 7ft drivers and tenders with outside springs.

Built for the Continental expresses in 1883 (the B class, very similar but with slightly larger boiler, followed in 1898), they were remarkably fast. Long since displaced on the Eastern side from anything except stopping trains, some of them proved ideal for the tightly-timed Reading semi-fasts, non stop to Staines. The steam reversing gear was quite terrifying, with lots of little handles and wheels suddenly spinning round and they rode as if they wished they were going right or left – anywhere except straight on – and the cab seemed even narrower than the earliest batch of T9s. But with a clear road from Waterloo, once under way past Doulton, their drivers could catch up and pass *anything* else that moved – even a Portsmouth electric (new then) and they frequently did.

It was good to sample one of these archaic machines at speed; 71mph was clocked through Clapham with four on.

Charing Cross/Cannon Street–Orpington	28 Feb 1926
Charing Cross/Cannon Street–Bromley North	28 Feb 1926
Charing Cross/Cannon Street–Addiscombe and Hayes	28 Feb 1926
Charing Cross and Cannon Street–Dartford (via Greenwich, Blackheath, Bexleyheath and Sidcup; some trains began 6 June 1926)	19 Jul 1926
London Bridge–Crystal Palace (Low Level)	25 Mar 1928
Charing Cross–Caterham and Tadworth (extended to Tattenham Corner)	25 Mar 1928
London Bridge–Victoria (via South London Line; overhead system replaced)	17 Jun 1928
Streatham Hill–London Bridge (via Tulse Hill)	17 Jun 1928
London Bridge–Coulsdon North (via Streatham and Streatham Common also via Norwood Junction)	17 Jun 1928
London Bridge–London Bridge (via Norwood Junction and Selhurst)	17 Jun 1928
London Bridge–Epsom Downs (via Streatham and via Norwood Junction)	17 Jun 1928
London Bridge–Crystal Palace (Low Level)	17 Jun 1928
London Bridge–Dorking North and Effingham Junction (via Tulse Hill and Mitcham Junction)	3 Mar 1929
Victoria–Epsom (via Mitcham Junction)	3 Mar 1929
Victoria–Beckenham Junction (via Crystal Palace; overhead system replaced between Victoria and Crystal Palace, Low Level)	3 Mar 1929
Victoria–Holborn Viaduct–Wimbledon (via Tulse Hill and Haydons Road)	3 Mar 1929
Wimbledon–South Merton (new line)	7 Jul 1929
Victoria–Coulsdon North and Sutton (overhead system replaced)	22 Sep 1929
South Merton–Sutton (via St. Helier) (New line)	5 Jan 1930
Whitton Junction and Hounslow Junction–Windsor	6 Jul 1930
Dartford–Gravesend Central	6 Jul 1930
Wimbledon–West Croydon (via Mitcham)	6 Jul 1930
Purley–Three Bridges and Reigate (via Redhill)	17 Jul 1932
Three Bridges–Brighton, Hove and Worthing	1 Jan 1933
Lewisham–Hither Green	16 Jul 1933
Bickley–St. Mary Cray	1 May 1934
Orpington–Sevenoaks (Tubs Hill)	6 Jan 1935
Bickley and Chislehurst–Sevenoaks (Tubs Hill) (via Swanley and Otford)	6 Jan 1935
Brighton and Haywards Heath–Eastbourne	7 Jul 1935
Brighton etc.–Hastings and Ore	7 Jul 1935
Haywards Heath–Horsted Keynes	7 Jul 1935
Brighton–Seaford	7 Jul 1935

The famous Hovis advertisement using the Southern Electric headcodes H (Hampton Court) Ō (Hounslow) V (Teddington and Kingston) I (Claygate) S (Shepperton) which appeared in compartment advertising panels for many years.

Nunhead–Lewisham	. . . .	30 Sep 1935
Woodside–Sanderstead	. . . .	30 Sep 1935
Hampton Court Junction–Chertsey and Staines	. .	3 Jan 1937
Hampton Court Junction–Guildford (part services)	. .	3 Jan 1937
Waterloo–Portsmouth (via Woking and Haslemere)	. .	4 Jul 1937
Woking–Farnham (part services)	. . . . .	3 Jan 1937
Woking–Alton	. . . .	4 Jul 1937
West Worthing–Bognor Regis	. . . . .	22 May 1938
Motspur Park–Tolworth	. . . . . .	29 Mar 1938
Dorking North–Havant (via Horsham and Arundel)	. .	3 Jul 1938
Three Bridges–Horsham	. . . . . .	3 Jul 1938
Littlehampton branch	. . . . . .	3 Jul 1938
Virginia Water–Ash Vale (via Ascot)	. . . .	1 Jan 1939
Ascot–Reading South	. . . . . .	1 Jan 1939
Tolworth–Chessington South (New line)	. . .	28 May 1939
Frimley Junction–Sturt Lane Junction	. . . .	1 Jan 1939
Aldershot–Guildford	. . . . . .	1 Jan 1939
Otford–Maidstone East	. . . . . .	2 Jul 1939
Swanley–Gillingham (Kent)	. . . . . .	2 Jul 1939
Gravesend–Maidstone West and Rochester (via Strood)	.	2 Jul 1939
Gillingham–Margate and Ramsgate (via Herne Bay)	. .	15 Jun 1959
Sittingbourne–Sheerness	. . . . .	15 Jun 1959
Faversham–Dover Marine (via Canterbury)	. .	15 Jun 1959
Buckland Junction–Ramsgate (including the Minster "triangle")	. . . .	2 Jan 1961
Sevenoaks–Dover Priory	. . . . .	12 Jun 1961
Paddock Wood–Maidstone West	. . . .	12 Jun 1961
Maidstone East–Ashford	. . . . .	9 Oct 1961
Ashford–Minster (via Canterbury West)	. . .	9 Oct 1961
Brookwood–Basingstoke (part service)	. . .	2 Jan 1967
Ryde Pier Head–Shanklin (Isle of Wight)	. . .	20 Mar 1967
Basingstoke–Bournemouth (part service)	. . .	3 Apr 1967
Brockenhurst–Lymington Pier	. . . .	2 Jun 1967
Brookwood–Branksome (full service)	. . .	10 Jul 1967
Tonbridge–Hastings	. . . . . .	12 May 1986
East Grinstead–South Croydon	. . . .	5 Oct 1987
Branksome–Weymouth	. . . . .	May 1988

Summer Saturday express. Although from the 1930s the Southern's electric stock was classed as suburban, semi-fast, and express, all types of stock could be found on peak Saturday holiday services. This ten-coach train on a Waterloo–Portsmouth express working passing Surbiton in the late 1950s is formed of a 2HAL and two 2BIL semi-fast units, with a 4SUB suburban unit bringing up the rear.

Invalids Welcomed

NOTICE TO INVALIDS. A First Class Railway Carriage, constructed expressly for Invalids, is in attendance at the principal Termini, fitted up with full length Sofa Couch capable of being elevated from the level to any degree of incline, with ante-room for attendants, supply of water, and every accommodation required for an Invalid. . . . Also, for the convenience of Invalids requiring to be conveyed from house to house without being disturbed, an Invalid Road Carriage has been built, to travel on the road with horses, and on the railway upon a carriage truck, in the same manner as a *private carriage*. – London Brighton & South Coast Railway timetable, October 1855.

The Navy link. The genuine Portsmouth express stock was affectionately known as the 'Nelsons', partly because of its link with Pompey and the Royal Navy, and partly because with the headcode panel on one side of the gangway and the driver's window on the other they had a rather one-eyed look. A twelve-coach formation of 4COR/4RES/4COR is seen passing New Malden bound for Waterloo in the 1950s.

Opposite. An operating problem for the signalman at Worting Junction as Cunard Ocean Liner special hauled by Lord Nelson class 4-6-0 No 860 Lord Hawke *coasts over Battledown flyover bound for Waterloo at the same time as the up Atlantic Coast Express rounds the curve of the West of England main line hauled by Merchant Navy class 4-6-2 No 21C 9* Shaw Savill. *Both trains would be scheduled to take the through line track from Worting Junction to London although one could have been sent up the local line but would risk being delayed by stopping trains. The period is 1947 in the last year of the Southern Railway, and such operating decisions like this were commonplace for SR junction signalmen handling intensive services, normally with a high standard of punctuality.*

Hampshire branch. Even though the Southern electrified several of its main lines in the 1930s, related branches were not always converted and remained steam worked where they did not fit in with a complete electrification package. Here at Petersfield, the Midhurst branch remained a steam worked connection off the Waterloo–Portsmouth line until closure in the 1950s. The push-pull train is headed by ex LSWR Class M7 0-4-4T No 30060.

Pre-Grouping and Southern colours. Reproductions of coloured postcards showing Southern Railway constituent company stations and trains in their old liveries and SR trains. These are typical examples of cards issued in their tens of thousands during the Edwardian and 1920/30 period showing trains of the day by such well known firms as the Locomotive Publishing Co, Raphael Tuck, Valentine and Salmon; others by smaller companies exampled by Knight or Pouteau. Today these are collectors' items but they provide a very real and fascinating insight into the more colourful days of Britain's railways.

The illustrations show, Top, Richard Tilling card series No TC1 with a caption 'Southern Belle' leaving Victoria in 1921, depicting Marsh Atlantic No 422 heading the Pullman train with a D3 class 0-4-4 tank No 380 to the right and a small tank engine, probably a D1 0-4-2T, in the platform to its left. The livery is dark umber brown and all the engines are spotless. The headcodes are not correct for 1921 as by then the boards with a cross had been discontinued. The Atlantic carries the 1910 Brighton via through (Quarry) line, while the D3 tank carries the Brighton via Redhill code.

Centre. Another Richard Tilling card, this time No TC7 with the caption 'SE&CR Charing Cross station London 1907'. A Wainwright D class 4-4-0 waits in the platform with a Dover via Sevenoaks train with two trains in adjacent platforms, one almost certainly headed by an H or Q class 0-4-4 tank the other by an LCD 4-4-0.

Bottom. A Raphael Tuck & Sons 'Oilette' card in the London Stations series showing the old Waterloo before rebuilding. The caption reads – 'Waterloo Station is situated in the Waterloo Road and at the southern end of the bridge of the same name. It is the terminus of the London and South Western Railway and thence run frequent trains to various up-river resorts and South Western suburbs and also Expresses to Southampton and the south west coast.'

WATERLOO STATION. L&SWR.

Top. Another Tuck 'Oilette' card, this time based on a photograph. It is from Series II of Famous Expresses (postcard No 9040) with a caption reading 'Bournemouth Express. The distance from London to Bournemouth 108 miles is covered by the London and South Western Railway express in 2½ hours.' The 12 coach train is double headed by a pair of Drummond T9 class 4-4-0s. The third vehicle is a Pullman car.

Centre. The famous all-electric Pullman, the 'Brighton Belle', on its run from Victoria to Brighton, which succeeded the 'Southern Belle' after electrification. The unit is depicted with its original number 2051 which within a year had become 3051.

Bottom. A further Tuck 'Oilette' card from a later Famous Expresses series (Postcard No 5304). The scene is from an oil painting on a photograph with a caption reading – 'Atlantic Coast Express. The "ACE" or "Atlantic Coast Express" runs daily between Waterloo and Padstow, a distance of 260 miles. The normal seating accommodation is for 396 passengers but during the summer it is amplified.' The engine is Class S15 4-6-0 No 827 and is probably working a Summer Saturday extra portion. The head discs have disappeared in the painting.

BOURNEMOUTH EXPRESS L&SWR

THE "BRIGHTON BELLE"
Southern Railway.

SOUTHERN RLY.
"ATLANTIC COAST EXPRESS"

Every Hour, on the Hour

'There's a good train at 3.20 for Hastings.' 'An express for Bournemouth at 10.15.' 'A fast train from Charing Cross at 3.18 for Dover.' Look at any month's railway timetable before World War I: there were many express, fast, good, bad, or indifferent trains (the latter three categories not put in so many words in the train timing columns) to most places in Southern England. Yet whatever the type of train, whether calling at all stations, a handful of selected stations on the way, or non-stop to principal towns whether it be Ashford, Brighton, Lewes, or Salisbury, there was little consistency in departure times. Sure there was a train from Victoria to Hastings at 3.20 and another at 5.20, both carrying slip portions for Hastings detached at Polegate off Eastbourne services. A two-hourly interval service? Hardly for other Hastings services left Victoria at 9.45 (with Pullman car), 12.00 (without Pullman car) and 1.25. In all this the Southern's predecessors were no different from other railways, and indeed parts of Britain are served the same way today.

But Herbert Walker, the dynamic general manager of the London & South Western Railway, had other ideas. He demanded train times that could be easily remembered – and regular interval sequences repeated right through the day. Clearly there would be variations at peak times, whether for commuters heading for town in the morning or returning home in the late afternoon, or for the hordes of holidaymakers on summer Saturdays, but as far as possible the commercial need was for a continuing all-day pattern. Almost as soon as Walker had joined the LSWR he was involved in suburban electrification.

What better time to put his timetable ideas into practice! Thus as the South Western electrics were introduced during 1915 and 1916 the new trains were working on intervals of four to the hour (curiously spaced at 10 and 20min intervals to work in with other services) or three an hour at 20min intervals or half hourly, according to traffic needs. In contrast the neighbouring LB&SC electric services on the South London line between London Bridge and Victoria, and from Victoria to Crystal Palace, were running on anything but an even interval service. There might have been four services an hour on the South London line but all were to odd minute permutations.

But it was not just on the new electric services that Walker pressed home the advantages of interval timetables. By 1922 they could be seen to a large extent on the principal main line services to the West of England and to Bournemouth and Weymouth. At that time long-distance travel had not reached mass market proportions so there was not the call for trains at every hour day long, and with varying intermediate traffic potential, identical

Top left. The Southern at Oxford. Through trains from the Great Western system running on to Southern stations beyond Reading, for example Birkenhead to Bournemouth, could change engines at Oxford. N15 King Arthur class 4-6-0 No 742 prepares to move south in April 1939.

Left. Devon Belle. Bulleid Pacific 21C11 General Steam Navigation at Clapham Junction with the down 'Devon Belle' in August 1947. This was a full Pullman train with its importance widely evident by its title carried not only on the buffer beam of the engine but also on the smoke deflector sides.

Above. Interval service. The Brighton main line was the epitome of interval services with express, semi-fast and stopping trains interwoven in a regular pattern of connections. Here one of the hourly London Bridge–Brighton stopping services which formed a half hourly pattern with a similar service from Victoria to Brighton, arrives at Three Bridges.

stopping patterns could not be maintained all the way. But with the Waterloo starting times at the same minutes past each hour, those trains making the same calls on the way at least had the same intermediate timings, and even with differing stops there was some uniformity and structure. By summer 1922 there were trains for Exeter or beyond from Waterloo at 9.00, 10.00, 11.00, 12.00 (for Sidmouth), 1.00, 3.00, 5.00 and 6.00. On the Bournemouth line the 30min past the hour sequence had been adopted but in this case, at least in high summer, the service was hourly from 9.30 in the morning right through until 7.30pm. Of course Sir Herbert Walker himself was not the timetable clerk but certainly his policy was imposed, even if those concerned did not always share his passion. Even senior operating officers had to be convinced of the advantages of interval services. Walker scored by his able and detail grasp of train operation, seen not from behind his desk but from many journeys as an ordinary passenger travelling incognito – much to the chagrin of stationmasters and other ground level operating staff. Many found themselves at Waterloo for interview with the general manager to explain why a connection had not been held, or to sort out an operating problem that regularly arose by a timetable inconsistency which nobody had bothered to rectify. Of course as electrification spread, it was taken for granted that increased, regular-interval services were part of the package. To the ordinary traveller they were indeed the essence of electrification.

The greatest scope of all for time-interval services was offered with electrification through to Brighton in 1933. Here it was not just principal trains (as on the Exeter and Bournemouth routes) or as a series of broadly self-contained routes to branches fanning out from the central core (as on the South Western suburban services from Waterloo) but a plethora of principal expresses – by 1935 serving Brighton, Worthing, Eastbourne and Hastings – semi-fast trains providing linking services with selected intermediate stations, all-stations main-line trains connecting with the extremities of the London suburban area, and finally branch workings to Reigate, Horsted Keynes and Seaford. Regular-interval working embraced connections, overtakings, and more connections, spreading out down the line like ripples in a pond and then bouncing back as the interval pattern returned to London. Moreover, services started from two London termini, Victoria and London Bridge, with the emphasis on the former during the day and the latter during the business peak, which all added to the complexities.

The new timetable was lavish. Principal services were the Brighton non-stops – every hour, on the hour, in the hour – which provided the Southern's publicity men with one of the best slogans ever, although it perhaps held back the operators from going faster as more power became available in later years. The almost every hour, at mostly five minutes past each hour, in fifty-one minutes with one stop, of today's fastest interval services might just have the commercial edge but certainly does not roll off the tongue quite so readily. There were expresses with intermediate calls leaving Victoria at 25min past each hour for West Worthing and at 45min for East-

bourne and Hastings, a semi-fast for Brighton at 28min, and a Clapham Junction, East Croydon, Purley, and all stations to Brighton at 48min past the hour. From London Bridge there was a semi-fast to Brighton on the hour (which followed the Victoria non-stop from East Croydon) and at 18min a stopping service which gave a half-hourly interval with the 48min past from Victoria between East Croydon and Brighton. The stopping services, running on the local line via Redhill to Balcombe Tunnel Junction were overtaken by one or other of the faster services, while the hourly Horsted Keynes to Seaford stopping service connected at Haywards Heath out of and into a Brighton stopping service and out of the Eastbourne and Hastings fast service which the Seaford train then followed.

It was much the same on the Portsmouth line from 1937 where the hourly fast service leaving Waterloo at 50min past each hour called at Guildford and Haslemere to Portsmouth, and connected at Guildford into and out of one of the half-hourly stopping trains at 27 and 57min from Waterloo to Portsmouth.

The stopping Portsmouth trains included an operating feature of many Southern electric services which survive in one form or another, the multi-portion train dividing or attaching en route. They were invariably combined with an Alton portion as far as Woking (the army in the front portion, wanting Brookwood or Aldershot, the navy in the rear portion for Pompey!), while on the Brighton line the Brighton stopping trains usually carried a portion for Reigate detached at Redhill. Some of the express services combined two destinations, Seaford and Worthing for example. Indeed many SR junction stations divided and coupled portions with a slickness not seen anywhere else in Britain – Staines for Weybridge and Windsor, Ascot for Guildford and Reading, Purley for Tattenham Corner and Caterham, Swanley for Maidstone East and Gillingham and Strood for Maidstone West and Gillingham. Often no more than two minutes were needed to disconnect the brake and electrical connections and take off the screw coupling. Many dividing points survive today, though others have disappeared as multi-portion trains have been replaced by a single through service and branch connection.

But interval timetables were not confined to SR electric routes, for many linking or interworked steam services were also later turned over to interval timetables – and sometimes with multi-portion trains, as for example the permutations that at one time, until the Beeching closures in BR days, were available on Oxted line routes to Brighton, Eastbourne, and Tunbridge Wells West.

Certainly Sir Herbert Walker's theories set up the Southern Railway's operating discipline to a standard not seen on the other three groups, and which has extended in BR years to the development of interval timetables all round the country although not as completely as some would like. Perhaps it needs a present-day Walker to instill the will in BR to make an all-embracing country-wide interval timetable work in Britain just as it now does in Switzerland. It could indeed be said that Walker's spirit lives on in the Alps rather than the Downs!

LONDON AND THE SOUTH COAST

Week Days—Continued

	1	2	3	4	5	6	7	8	9	10	11	12	13	14	15	16	17	18	19	20	21	22	23	24	25	26	27	28	29
VICTORIA ....dep.																													
Clapham Junction ...."																													
LONDON BRIDGE ...dep.																													
New Cross Gate ..."																													
Norwood Junction **B** ..."																													
East Croydon ....dep.																													
Purley																													
Coulsdon South																													
Merstham																													
Redhill 274																													
Earlswood																													
Salfords																													
Horley																													
Gatwick Airport																													
Three Bridges (below) 234																													
Balcombe																													
Horsted Keynes.......dep.																													
Ardingly																													
Haywards Heath **C** 239																													
Wivelsfield (below)																													
Burgess Hill																													
Hassocks **D**																													
Preston Park																													
Brighton (below) ....arr.																													
Haywards Heath ...dep.																													
Wivelsfield (above)																													
Plumpton																													
Cooksbridge																													
Lewes 239 ....arr.																													
Brighton ....dep.																													
London Road (Brighton)...																													
Falmer																													
Lewes ....arr.																													
Lewes ....dep.																													
Southease and Rodmell																													
Newhaven Town ...(Halt																													
" Harbour....																													
Bishopstone Beach Halt																													
Bishopstone																													
Seaford...........arr.																													
Lewes ....dep.																													
Glynde																													
Berwick																													
Polegate 239																													
Hampden Park **F**																													
Eastbourne ....{arr. dep.																													
Hampden Park **F**......																													
Pevensey and Westham...																													
Pevensey Bay Halt......																													
Norman's Bay Halt......																													
Cooden Beach.........																													
Collington Halt........																													
Bexhill (Central) **G**....																													
St. Leonards (W.M.)....																													
" (W.S.)....																													
Hastings 56, 59.......																													
Ore................arr.																													

	1	2	3	4	5	6	7	8	9	10	11	12	13	14	15	16	17	18	19	20	21	22	23	24	25	26	27	28	29
Three Bridges (above)..dep.																													
Crawley																													
Ifield																													
Fay Gate																													
Littlehaven Halt																													
Horsham, 244, 245..arr.																													
Sutton ....dep.																													
Dorking North **H**																													
Horsham 244, 245...{arr. dep.																													
Christ's Hospital, West																													
Billingshurst....{Horsham																													
Pulborough **J** 246....																													
Amberley																													
Arundel																													
Brighton ....dep.																													
Holland Road Halt......																													
Hove																													
Aldrington Halt........																													
Portslade and West Hove...																													
Fishersgate Halt.......																													
Southwick																													
Shoreham-by-Sea **K**....																													
Shoreham Airport **L**....																													
Lancing																													
Ham Bridge Halt **N**....																													
Worthing Central......																													
West Worthing **U**......																													
Durrington-on-Sea......																													
Goring-by-Sea.........																													
Angmering **V**																													
Ford (Sussex).......dep.																													
Littlehampton {arr. dep.																													
Ford (Sussex)																													
Barnham ....arr.																													
Bognor Regis {arr. dep.																													
Barnham ....dep.																													
Chichester **Y**																													
Fishbourne Halt.......																													
Bosham																													
Nutbourne Halt........																													
Southbourne Halt......																													
Emsworth																													
Warblington Halt.......																													
Havant 244, 366 ...arr.																													
244 Hayling Island ...arr.																													
Bedhampton Halt......																													
Fratton 380																													
Portsmouth & Southsea.arr.																													
Portsmouth Harbour....																													
525 RYDE PIER (Boat)..arr.																													
359 SANDOWN ...."																													
359 SHANKLIN ...."																													
359 VENTNOR ...."																													
359 NEWPORT ...."																													
359 COWES ...."																													
359 YARMOUTH ...."																													

d Departure time.   F Sats. only. Not after 9th Sept.   g Arr 3 mins *earlier* on Sats.   H Sats. excepted until 8th Sept. daily commencing 11th Sept.
L 6 mins later on Sats.   P Pullman Car facilities available.   U Stops to take up only.   y Arr. 2 mins. *earlier*.   Z 4 mins. later on Saturdays.   * Change at East Croydon.   † Change at Sutton.
SX Saturdays excepted.   R Restaurant Car facilities available between London & Bognor Regis.   SU Saturdays only.

For Other Notes, see page 195; for Continuation of Trains, pages 166 to 195; for Return Journey, pages 196 to 233.

The Brighton line timetable for weekdays, Summer 1939, showing an hour or so of the interval services linking the main line and the coast.

47

4
THE ULTIMATE IN STEAM

Baltic Symphony

Fareham, LSWR, a quintuple junction between Portsmouth and Southampton, early on a rather cold morning:

The warning bell indicating that something was coming round the very sharp curve from the Portsmouth direction had been ringing for ages, so it must be going to be something very slow. The bell went on ringing. And on. And then a desperate light puffing with many wild slips and re-starting. Something very heavy was coming. Then the noise was interspersed with slow, very laborious long hissing noises. The bell went on ringing.

And then round the corner, almost at walking pace, came a Brighton 0-6-0 Terrier tank haul-ing an engine never seen before – for the best of reasons; it would not have gone under the bridges – a VAST Baltic tank from the old LBSC, its cab removed as well as its dome cover, and loaded into a wagon behind it, but with its motion still connected, hence the hissing from the open cocks. Men all over it, fussing. So passed Baltic No B331, after waiting at the end of the platform for ages, taking the single tunnel line towards Knowle Junction and Eastleigh, where it was to undergo general overhaul, Brighton works being then closed.

Folkestone Junction. Waiting in the engine sidings to take over a Continental boat train for Victoria, a nicely cleaned Bulleid 'West Country' Pacific simmers gently, a lazy plume of smoke drifting at the front of her air-smoothed casing. The crew listen with professional appreciation to the sound of their train fighting its way up the mile of unrelenting 1 in 30 from the Harbour, the increasing roar of random exhaust from several sure-footed engines working nearly flat out disturbing the otherwise peaceful scene. A cloud of black smoke rises to the heavens above the adjacent houses marking its progress. Finally the train itself takes shape as it comes round the curve making perhaps 15 miles an hour. And in contrast to the sleek machine which will whisk it the 72 miles to Victoria, on the front are three game little ex-South Eastern Railway Class R1 0-6-0 tanks of Victorian vintage waddling under the effort, their firemen grinning from canopied cabs. The bark from their tall chimneys quietens as the weight of the train comes off the grade and into the level dead-end roads, but the slow clickety-click of coach wheels on points is overlaid by the exhaust of another little R1 assisting in the rear and still shoving. Her driver shuts off steam as he approaches the Pacific, and the clank of rods and squeal of flanges replaces the stack music. Within a couple of minutes the banker is away clear and the West Country is backing down on to her train.

It is an everyday picture that highlights the perpetual contradiction of the locomotive scene (and the Southern scene in particular); new engines come, but the old live on in useful endeavour.

At birth, the Southern was an overwhelmingly steam railway, with an elderly locomotive stock of 2,285. Though in 1923 there were still only 77½ miles of electrified route, the commitment to extensive electrifi-cation (eventually for South Coast express work as well as suburban services) severely constrained the steam scope of its chief mechanical engineers. Yet, greatly to its credit, throughout its life it was among the leaders in locomotive technical design.

Of the three constituent companies the largest contributor, with 915 locomotives, was naturally the London & South Western. The great Dugald Drummond, a martinet if ever there was one, had been dead for barely a decade, and had left what was essentially a 4-4-0 and 0-6-0 railway. His attempts at anything bigger, just as with many other engineers, had been very much less than triumphant. But the far-seeing Robert Urie, who had succeeded him from the works managership at Eastleigh, had very different ideas, focussed on 4-6-0 tender engines, simple, rugged, accessible, built for hard work yet on top of the job. But for World War I it is probable that more Urie engines than the 51 actually in service would have been available. The weaknesses of the

King Arthur 4-6-0 No E795 Sir Dinadan *was one of the last batch of 14 'Arthurs' built at Eastleigh in 1926. It has the later pattern cab to conform to the composite loading gauge and six-wheel tender for working on the Central Section.*

Lord Nelson 4-6-0. Official view of the first of the class No E850 Lord Nelson *in works photographic grey when new at Eastleigh in 1926. The flattened sides of the valve chests disappeared when new cylinders with larger piston valves were fitted from 1939 onwards.*

Schools class 4-4-0 No E907 Dulwich *new from Eastleigh in 1930. The rather open front of the original tenders, with no coal bulkhead is apparent. The engine has dry sanding for the leading coupled wheels only: this was later replaced by steam sanding to all four coupled wheels to minimise slipping.*

original 16 Drummond four-cylinder 4-6-0s were well understood, and Urie had already rebuilt one drastically as a two-cylinder engine. In addition a programme of superheating the smaller Drummond engines was well in hand.

The South Eastern & Chatham brought a dowry of over 700 engines. It was a difficult railway to operate, compounded by restricted axleloads due to the number of weak underbridges (notably on the Chatham side), the rebuilding of which would not be completed for some years. The result was the use of medium-sized 4-4-0s on heavy Continental boat trains and expresses. The chief mechanical engineer, R. E. L. Maunsell, had recently rebuilt numbers of these 4-4-0s with superheaters, new cylinders and long-travel valve gear to produce, in the D1s and E1s, first-class locomotives with axleloads not exceeding 17½ tons and weighing only 52½ tons in working order. Their performance could only be described as brilliant; they handled 300 ton boat trains with complete confidence. But looking to the future, six-coupled wheels were going to be essential, and Maunsell had been persuaded that only two designs were needed to meet foreseen traffic requirements, a 2-6-4 tank for express passenger trains – the longest haul was no more than 80 miles – and a 2-6-0 tender engine for freight. Prototypes had been built in 1917, and follow-up orders were in hand at the grouping. They were thoroughly modern machines, with much commonality of components, reflecting the best aspects of Swindon practice through the influence of Pearson and Holcroft together with high superheat.

New Traffic
'Locomotive Excursion. As Advertised.' A typical Edmonson ticket, but on 23 April 1939 a British enthusiasts' first, for footplate rides on the Bisley branch. Two Drummond 0-4-4 tanks, coupled back to back, carried over a hundred passengers over several trips, the fare (including ordinary train from Waterloo to Brookwood) being 7s 6d.

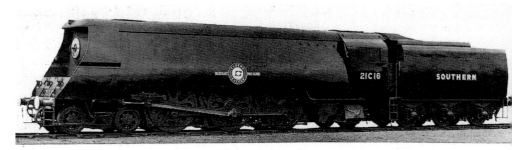

Merchant Navy. By the time No 21C16 Elders Fyffes *was built in 1945, the front end cowling had been modified and cab and tender altered to improve crew comfort and lookout. It is depicted in wartime black livery.*

Rebuilt West Country. The rebuilding of the Bulleid Pacifics in the 1950s and 1960s took away most of their quirks and made fine, reliable locomotives of them. No 34016 Bodmin *typified the rebuilds. The outside Walshaerts valve gear was arranged to suit the original cylinders with outside admission valves.*

Lucky Class

The 'Lord Nelson' class was to become rather lucky in that potentially dangerous accidents involving the engines would result in no more than slight damage and little hurt to life or limb. The first of these occurred on 23 January 1930 when No E853 became partly derailed while approaching Kent House station on the outskirts of London and then re-railed itself, the train crew being completely oblivious to the whole affair until arrival on time at Victoria!

The train concerned was the 12-vehicle 'Golden Arrow', leaving Dover Marine at 4.57pm, which was running slightly late with driver Chapman of Battersea trying to make up arrears. At 6.23pm, when passing through the up facing junction at Kent House, the leading and middle driving wheels became derailed; the middle wheels appear to have been re-railed at the crossing a few feet further on but 880yd were covered before the leading wheels re-railed themselves at the trailing junction, leaving in their wake 117 broken fishbolts, 11 damaged chairs, one smashed sleeper, one damaged crossing, three broken insulators and about

continued opposite

The London, Brighton & South Coast brought in the smallest locomotive fleet, a little over 600, of which three-quarters were tank engines. They were a mixed bag. Only three attempts had been made to produce modern six-coupled locomotives, the best being the two J class 4-6-2 tanks and the 17 K class 2-6-0s, though the latter lacked the versatility of the comparable Maunsell engines. Billinton's big 4-6-4 tanks left a great deal to be desired. There was nothing in the Brighton stable which could compete with the Eastleigh and Ashford products.

With a strong SE&C influence in the initial appointments, Maunsell was the natural choice for the new railway's CME; he had shown himself a fine administrator, picked his assistants with care and wisdom, and delegated to them within clear bounds. He was 54 and in his prime, while Urie was 68 and ready for retirement and the Brighton's Billinton, though only 39, was easily persuaded – with financial inducement – to step down. Maunsell had been backed by a first-class team at Ashford, and this he transplanted to Waterloo during 1924. G. H. Pearson remained assistant CME with J. Clayton as personal assistant and H. Holcroft in charge of the 'primary' (ie development) drawing office. Eastleigh's status was reduced to that of principal locomotive and carriage and wagon drawing offices working to Waterloo's directions, which caused some chagrin.

It was to Maunsell's everlasting credit that he made no attempt to apply his own SE&C products slavishly to the system as a whole. The short-haul Eastern Section with its heavily-graded crossings of the Downs, and the slightly easier Central Section, represented one set of conditions; the 172 mile route to Exeter (though engines were invariably changed at Salisbury) and the Bournemouth road, with generally heavier loads and combining lengthy but moderate gradients with a fast roller-coaster profile in the West Country, was something else entirely. 21-ton axleloads were acceptable on the Western Section main lines but not immediately on the Eastern Section. And engines built to the generous Western loading gauge were severely restricted elsewhere.

Overshadowing the inheritance, the aftermath of World War I lingered on. The locomotive fleet as a whole was in a run-down state and failures and resultant train delays were unacceptably frequent. It took some years for the works to get fully on top of the backlog of classified repairs and for the campaign to overcome mechanical failures to bear fruit. In the meantime, a strategy for new construction quickly emerged. There was an immense range of duties on which the modern Ashford six-coupled designs could progressively take over from elderly 4-4-0s and 0-6-0s on mainly secondary routes throughout the system; they already conformed to the new SR composite gauge. It was entirely natural, therefore, for a family of engines designed round the Ashford concepts to be built for service from Cornwall to Kent. But for the Western Section main routes the groundwork done by Urie with his 4-6-0s for the longer heavy hauls could be built on, while applying Ashford practice to the less satisfactory features of the design. The two new important locomotive builds by Maunsell which fell outside this framework still represented a direct blend of these two philosophies.

Right from the start came a traffic demand for a new locomotive able to haul 500 ton passenger trains at an average speed of 55mph. To design and build a new machine was going to take time, and so a holding operation was put in hand by building more Urie 4-6-0s. There was an

continued
850 dislodged or damaged keys. Damage to rolling stock was minimal and to staff, passengers and by-standers nil.

A speed of between 50 and 55mph (instead of 40mph) coupled with considerable side wear on the leading driving wheels, the locomotive having run 57,000 miles and being due for repair at a mileage of 65,000, were the major causes thrown up by the inquiry into the accident. Points recommended for consideration included deeper wheel flanges, lubrication of check rails and increasing the strength of the bogie control springs.

In the course of the report it was stated that driver Chapman had had charge of this particular engine for the whole seventeen months of its existence; with the mileage given above it may be deduced that on average twenty round trips from London to Dover were made every month. No E853 was fitted with a six-wheel tender which had confined its use to the Eastern Section but on going to works for repair after the accident it parted with that tender and was furnished with a Urie-pattern bogie type instead. – *Maunsell's Nelsons*, by D. W. Winkworth.

The three-cylinder U1 2-6-0s derived from the rebuild of 2-6-4 tank No A890. That engine had conjugated valve gear for the inside piston valve, but the new 2-6-0s, while retaining the high front platform under which it resided, used a separate Walschaerts valve gear, driven by two eccentrics, for the middle valve.

Q Class No 530 was the first of Maunsell's updating of the archetypal British 0-6-0. Steaming was not entirely reliable and some were fitted with multiple jet blastpipes and large chimneys. The retention of Stephenson valve gear was a retrograde feature which affected mechanical reliability.

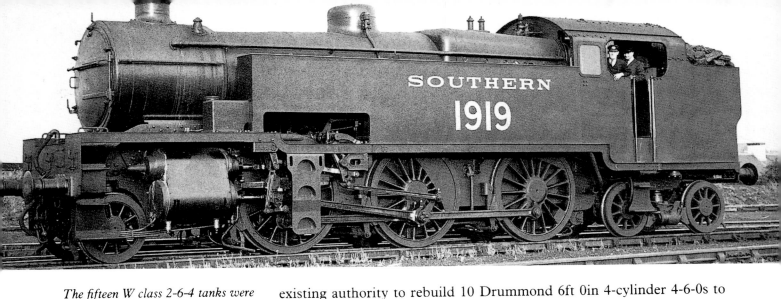

The fifteen W class 2-6-4 tanks were built for cross-London freight traffic and were three-cylinder machines similar in most respects to the N1 2-6-0s. The bogie wheels were also braked for handling loose coupled trains on the steep gradients of some of their regular routes. No 1919 was at Hither Green in August 1935.

Ironside at Guildford

At Guildford one gazed down at the locomotive shed gouged out of the chalk hillside, movements of dead locomotives in and out of the roundhouse being controlled by *Ironside*, a diminutive ex-Southampton Docks Company 0-4-0T which darted on and off the central turntable like a spider overseeing its web. Occasionally a class N 2-6-0 gleaming bright after repair and repaint at Ashford Works would call in at Guildford on its way home to far away Exmouth Junction or Okehampton. Its allocation also contained several Adams 'Jubilee' 0-4-2 tender engines for local goods work – R.A. Savill.

existing authority to rebuild 10 Drummond 6ft 0in 4-cylinder 4-6-0s to two-cylinder superheated engines, using the existing boiler shells with their shallow fireboxes and level grates. But at the behest of the traffic people, who knew full well their indifferent steaming, Maunsell decided instead to give them 6ft 7in wheels and new N15 boilers with sloping grates. Eastleigh was then set to work 'Ashford-ising' the N15 design and bringing it within the composite gauge; the valve gear was modified to give over 6½in travel, and the smokebox, superheater and draughting brought into line with approved Ashford practice. The outcome was the 'King Arthurs', inspired locomotives which soon took over the heavy Continental boat trains and Brighton line expresses in addition to West of England trains. They seemed to have a special affinity for the banks of the Salisbury–Exeter section, sweeping downhill at speeds into the eighties to rush the next sharp rise. Their steaming was impeccable but like most engines with two outside cylinders they suffered the characteristic roughness in the coupled axleboxes as mileage built up (and they were not fitted with adjustable horn wedges). There were diehards at Eastleigh who would not accept that they were any improvement on the original Urie design, but the running sheds put them on the hardest work to the exclusion of the Urie engines, which told its own tale. The S15 4-6-0 mixed traffic design with small wheels was given similar treatment.

Meanwhile, the new big passenger engine was progressing. The 4-6-0 layout was chosen rather than a Pacific as better suited to Southern conditions, and thinking crystallised on four cylinders with divided drive. Holcroft argued the merits of the unusual setting of cranks at 135°, and following comparative tests with a modified Drummond 4-6-0 his argument was confirmed. It resulted in eight exhaust beats per revolution. In 1926 the first Lord Nelson appeared from Eastleigh, the class later to be expanded to 16 engines. It was immediately hailed by the publicity people as the most powerful express passenger engine in Britain on the basis of its tractive effort, an 'honour' which it held for barely a year. The Nelsons rode well – indeed, in 1929 the leading coupled wheels of one of them derailed at Kent House for a short distance and then rerailed themselves at points without the driver realising that anything untoward had happened – and proved highly reliable and light on maintenance. Day-to-day performance could, however, be distinctly variable. Satisfactory steaming demanded good coal and a high standard of firing to keep the long grate suitably fed

Maunsell's Z class 0-8-0T was designed for hump and other heavy shunting and had three cylinders to provide uniform torque at low speeds. The class was later also used for banking trains up the severe 1 in 37 grade from St David's into Exeter Central station. Its shunting work was in the very field which was later taken over by the ubiquitous 350hp diesel shunter.

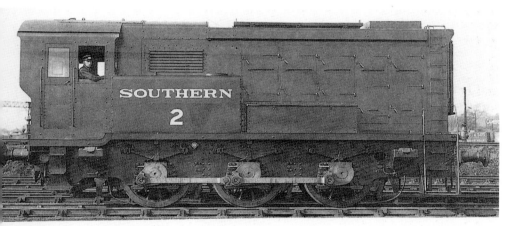

The Southern's variant of the 350hp diesel electric shunter, built in 1937, shows interesting mechanical differences from the comparable LMS pioneers. No provision was made for vacuum braking.

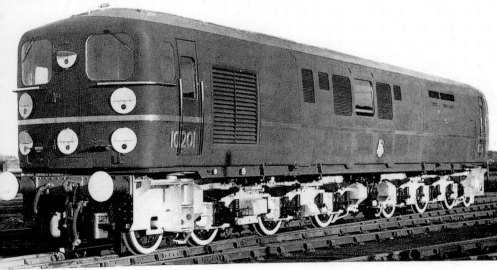

BR Southern Region's first main line diesel-electric locomotive, No 10201, came from Ashford in 1951 with English Electric engine and electrical equipment. The styling was rather disappointing and boxy, but the four axle centreless bogie was widely taken up by British Rail.

The second venture into electric locomotives, CC2, was built in 1945. While current pick up was normally via the usual third rail shoes – no fewer than four each side – a pantograph was also provided to collect from overhead wires specially installed in certain freight yards.

Ugly Atlantic. When Bulleid was working up the Leader class design, a guinea pig was needed to develop the difficult concept of sleeve valve cylinders. Brighton Atlantic No 2039 Hartland Point *had the dubious distinction of being selected. It received new fabricated cylinders and other modifications for a short remaining life.*

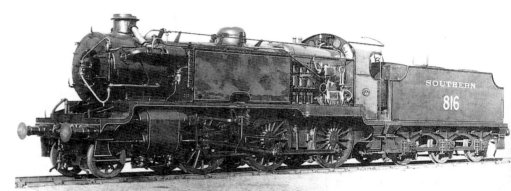

A Maunsell eyesore. In 1930 Maunsell fitted up one of his standard N class 5ft 6in 2-6-0s No A816 with the Anderson steam heat conservation equipment. It was a semi-condensing system, with draught provided by a fan driven by rotary steam engine in the smokebox door. It ran trials for about three years, with some success, before the makers of the system ran out of money. The engine was notable for its almost total silence.

Bulleid's Swansong. The first Leader *(and the only one completed) is seen outside Brighton works during trials. The coal bunker is adjacent to the nearest cab; the other cab was in over-close proximity to the hot smokebox! The large external boxes visible on the far bogie housed the coupling chains.*

A trio of Jubilees. Like the other grouping companies the Southern Railway inherited a large number of Victorian classes of locomotive, among them the ex LSWR A12 Adams Jubilee 0-4-2s dating from 1895. These three are seen coming off shed at Salisbury around 1930.

despite the hump over the trailing axle; a thick fire was a sure formula for a 'cold' run. The front end design and exhaust passages, too, left room for improvement. On a light rein a Nelson would run like the wind, but west of Salisbury their hill-climbing was hardly up to King Arthur standard. It took a range of modifications and a new CME to get rid of the rough edges, and even then they were never entirely at home in the post-war rough-and-tumble.

Maunsell himself certainly did not regard the Nelsons as the last word in Southern passenger power. In the early 1930s he contemplated a Pacific design, largely a Nelson with trailing truck and wide-firebox boiler, but its limited route availability killed it. An alternative three-cylinder 2-6-2 was offered, but the civil engineer's mistrust of leading Bissel trucks after Sevenoaks (paragraph following) lived on and made it unacceptable. Tentative plans for a heavy freight engine of 4-8-0 type from the same stable foundered on operating objections.

By complete contrast with these thoughts of large power, 1926 also saw the long-delayed emergence of a new 4-4-0 for the Eastern Section. It is not entirely clear why further E1s were not ordered; instead, the rather pedestrian Wainwright L class was selected, with its slightly larger boiler (but smaller grate) and the front end modified to improve the valves as far as the existing cylinder castings allowed. Clayton's influence was clear to see in the uncanny outward resemblance of the L1s to the Midland Class 2P 4-4-0s. Unlike the D1s and E1s which were rebuilt, the L1s were new engines.

On to this developing scene burst the traumatic derailment at speed of K class 2-6-4 tank No A800 at Sevenoaks on 24 August 1927, which resulted in serious casualties. It followed two other derailments of the class on running lines, and brought to a head complaints of rolling at speed on indifferent track, of which the Eastern Section had more than its fair share. It spelled the end of the use of 2-6-4 tanks on fast passenger work. The entire class of 21 engines was immediately taken out of service, and apart from riding tests on the Western Section and on the East Coast main line, never ran again. They were rebuilt as 2-6-0 tender engines, on the pattern of the new U class, and the one three-cylinder engine among them formed the prototype of the small U1 class. Their 6ft 0in coupled wheels made them ideal for a wide spectrum of secondary passenger services the length and breadth of the system. All these 2-6-0s – there were ultimately 157 Ns, N1s, Us and U1s – carried the same boiler and many other components. But the 2-6-4 tank was not to be wholly extinct, for in 1931 a new design, the W class with three cylinders and 5ft 6in wheels, was produced by Maunsell for the specific duty of freight transfer work between London yards. It too used the standard 2-6-0 boiler.

It was in the early 1930s that a number of Southern locomotive types

Away, you rolling river. One of the basic types built by Maunsell for SE&CR traffic, No A798 River Wey *was of thoroughly modern design. But their rough riding on the indifferent Eastern Section track culminating in the disastrous Sevenoaks derailment in 1927, led to rebuilding as 2-6-0 tender engines in class U, except for the one three-cylinder* River *as Class U1.*

Little lady with a big number! Drummond 0-4-0T No 3744 was originally built as a 2-2-0T for working push-pull trains, which, like steam railmotors, was underpowered. It was rebuilt as an 0-4-0T in October 1923, becoming a handy small shunter, Class C14, seen here at Eastleigh in 1947. It bore the highest number of any Southern Railway engine.

Beattie survivor. Three of the ex LSWR 0298 class well tanks, which had once worked London suburban services were sent down to the far south west to work the sharply curved Wenford Bridge china clay branch. They lasted well into the BR era, not being withdrawn until 1962. No 3329 became BR No 30586.

underwent – some would say, suffered – a visual change. Complaints from drivers of vision being obscured by drifting steam from short chimneys, with the short cutoff working made possible by long travel valves, led eventually to the adoption of smoke deflector plates beside the smokebox. This followed trials of various alternatives similar to those also tried by the LMS and LNE, which proved ineffective; wind tunnel tests were made on models to determine the most effective form. An unexpected spinoff was that the plates were effective in trapping the carcasses of any pheasants which might be hit en route!

Maunsell had a masterpiece still up his sleeve. A traffic request for a powerful 4-4-0 to work 400 ton trains and at the same time conform to the restricted Hastings line gauge was met by a scaled down mixture of Nelson and King Arthur practice; three Nelson cylinders were fed by an N15 firebox married to a shorter boiler barrel. At 67.1 tons the Schools were the heaviest 4-4-0s ever to run in Britain, powerful engines for a 42 ton adhesion weight, and they needed careful handling; the original dry sanding was replaced by steam sanding to help drivers avoid slipping. They first took over the Dover line expresses, showing themselves a match for 12-coach trains on the 80 minute non-stop timing to Folkestone, before also taking in the difficult Hastings road. But their sterling qualities were not fully realised until later batches were allocated to Fratton shed for the Waterloo–Portsmouth expresses, where they were allowed 350 tons on a 90 minute timing, including some heavy climbing at 1 in 80, and handled the work with seeming ease. When displaced by electrification they moved to Bournemouth, where their running became positively inspired, working expresses of up to 500 tons and keeping time. But they would not tolerate any attempt at thrashing; they liked a light hand and to be allowed to make their own pace. Bearing in mind that their tenders held no more than 4000 gallons of water to get them between Waterloo and Southampton, 79 miles non-stop, such treatment was de rigueur.

Ian Allan

Even in the days immediately after the end of the war, much of the spirit of Walker still pervaded the Southern. But in one respect the public relations department was very different from its early days, when John Elliot was told off by Walker for attending a cricket match in office hours. Now the whole department seemed to be 'freelancing' in one way or another.

This gave Ian Allan a chance that resulted in the formation of his transport publishing house, rival to the publishers of the present volume. Appointed a trainee in the department in 1939 and 'frozen' in railway work during the war, Ian saw a need for a book of Southern locomotives, the first of his famous ABC series. 2,000 copies were printed when it became clear that 'Mr Bulleid doesn't like it and it musn't be published'.

What to do? Ian sent a copy to R. Holland Martin, the chairman, and that did the trick. He congratulated Ian on his enterprise and described it as an 'asset to the SR'. Bulleid called him a 'crafty b.......' but Ian was on his way to a rapid sale.

We asked him what the Southern was like to work for. 'It was an exciting place, plenty of drama in the war of course, and absolutely no doubt it was the best run and best organised of the four railways.'

Urie tank. Another characteristic Urie design, the H16 4-6-2T of 1921. Only five were built for cross London freight work from Feltham yard and they only normally strayed from this work on Ascot race days – but this was enough to warrant painting them in passenger livery! No 516 is seen at Feltham shed in May 1939.

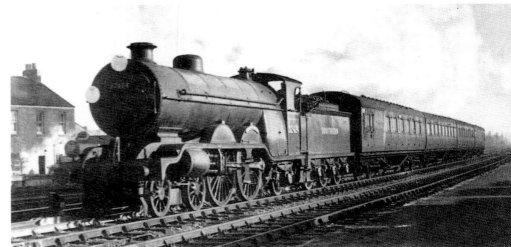

Marsh Atlantic. Strikingly similar to the Ivatt Great Northern Atlantics (hardly surprising when one considers that Marsh moved to the LB&SCR from Doncaster), the H2 class 4-4-2s were built at Brighton in 1911 for working the principal expresses out of Victoria. As BR No 32424 Beachy Head was the last of its class to be withdrawn – as late as April 1958. The photograph shows it working the 9.40am from Brighton to Bournemouth at Worthing on 21 January 1949.

Ugly Duckling. Drummond's four-cylinder 4-6-0s were ungainly looking beasts and superheating by Urie and some minor rebuilding by Maunsell did little to improve either their appearance or their performance. One was totally destroyed by a German bomb during World War II.

Maunsell, incidentally, was somewhat in advance of his fellow CMEs in constructing wooden 'mockups' of the cabs of several classes; while perhaps mainly for the benefit of enginemen, whose opinions were actively sought, they were also useful to the draughtsmen in planning pipe runs and to fitters to ensure accessibility.

Fourteen Arthurs and ten Schools were released by electrification to the South Coast, but not enough for the Western Section's insatiable demand for power. This led to two cheap class adaptations. The last ten remaining Drummond 4-6-0s, the T14 'Paddleboxes', were given treatment well short of a rebuild to improve their availability, and the big Billinton 4-6-4 tanks (redundant following electrification to Eastbourne) were rebuilt as 4-6-0 tender engines of class N15X. The latter may have superficially resembled the King Arthurs, but their performance fell some way short. New steam locomotive construction fell to tiny numbers (in 1937 no new engines were built) and only one Maunsell design, the Q class 0-6-0, remained to emerge after his retirement; even that was hardly regarded as a standard.

With Maunsell's departure, largely on grounds of ill-health, in the autumn of 1937 and the arrival of O. V. S. Bulleid in his place, things could only change. After a quick exercise in improving the draughting of the Nelsons, using a five-jet Lemaître-type blastpipe and large chimney (subsequently applied to other classes also) Bulleid started to consider a new locomotive for the heaviest express workings. Given his background under Gresley and the civil engineer's refusal to contemplate a 2-8-2, it was inevitable that it should be a 4-6-2, though there appears to have been no clear operating specification against which it was designed. The first Merchant Navy Pacific did not appear until 1941, and was then billed as a mixed traffic engine, on the basis of its 6ft 2in wheels, to get round government restrictions on building passenger locomotives in wartime, though the fiction was not sustained. It had a magnificent boiler which seemed able to meet any demand made upon it and

A pair of Nelsons. In 1939, Bulleid was leaving his mark on the Nelsons. Stewarts Lane depot was host to No 854 Howard of Effingham *in original condition apart from smoke deflectors and raised tender sides, and No 863* Lord Rodney *now fitted with Lemaître multiple-jet blastpipe and the early stovepipe large diameter chimney.*

introduced thermic syphons to Britain. There was some excellent design in the chassis, but the concept of three sets of chain-driven valve gear enclosed with the inside connecting rod in an oil bath between the frames, in order to overcome problems which were more illusory than real, produced quite horrendous difficulties which were never solved. Elsewhere, the need to keep weight down within a 21 ton axleload resulted in some flimsy construction which soon revealed its weaknesses.

The Merchant Navies could handle, with panache, virtually anything that the Southern operators could throw at them, and certainly made their mark during the Interchange Trials of 1948; but in the 1950s their availability was deplorable, and due to erratic cylinder performance their appetite for coal was, to say the least, extravagant. Thirty were built, and were followed by 110 similar but slightly smaller West Country and Battle of Britain Pacifics from 1945, numbers which were probably excessive to cover legitimate Pacific duties. In these smaller engines the axleload was kept below 19 tons.

World War II brought a need for an engine to handle heavy freight traffic, and Bulleid responded with a new 0-6-0, a sort of Super Q in 1942, and a somewhat curious wheel arrangement to adopt at that time. Its main feature, apart from the lamentable visual treatment, was a much larger boiler with bigger grate, using Nelson pressings and carrying a higher pressure. The Q1 was a powerful brute, able to accelerate rapidly through the electric services, but the continued use of Stephenson link motion restricted journal sizes on the crank axle and made the engine prone to heated axleboxes.

All this, however, was humdrum stuff by comparison with Bulleid's final product, to meet a need for large tank engines for both main line and heavier branch line duties. If the K class 2-6-4 tanks had still been in service, more might have been built in updated form to fill the breach;

Battle of Britain by night. Salisbury, once an almost universal engine changing point, became a mere pause for the Pacifics. This superb picture shows No 34060 25 Squadron on an up express, electric lights gleaming, safety valves showing a white feather.

instead, after a number of alternatives had been rejected, Bulleid set out to produce a new concept of the steam locomotive, double-ended, all-adhesion, and with some features of his Pacifics allied to a host of new and untried ones. They included two three-axle bogies each with three sleeve-valve cylinders, the axles coupled by chains, and an innovatory firebox with four thermic syphons and no water legs. Only one Leader was ever completed, in 1950. It weighed about 130 tons in working order, with considerably more weight on one rail than the other due to the boiler, tank and bunker being offset to provide a corridor the length of the engine. Its complexity doomed it to failure from the start, and its running was virtually confined to comparative dynamometer car tests hauling up to 325 tons between Eastleigh and Woking against a U class 2-6-0 (total weight 107.7 tons), which proved much superior in both performance and efficiency. The test report, incidentally, paid tribute to the fortitude of the test fireman, who worked in his centre cab in a temperature exceeding 120°F and with wet sacking tied round his legs to prevent his overalls being burned off. The next year it led its partly-built brothers to the scrapheap.

By the early 1950s a programme of something like 200 palliative modifications to the Pacifics, initiated by Bulleid, was being put in hand to overcome a long list of weaknesses. It included reduction in boiler pressure from 280 to 250lb/sq in to reduce firebox maintenance, which was proving heavy in spite of water treatment. Then in 1953 a Merchant Navy suffered a broken crank axle at speed, fortunately without serious consequences for its train. Thought at first to have been due to corrosion fatigue at the chain sprocket seating, it was found on closer analysis that the axle had been being stressed well beyond acceptable fatigue limits in an attempt to keep down weight. All the Merchant Navies had to be withdrawn until fitted with redesigned crank axles. The smaller Pacifics had these axles replaced at normal shopping.

Locomotive Exchanges. The Southern used both Merchant Navy and West Country Pacifics in the 1948 locomotive trials, with the locomotives performing well but with somewhat excessive coal consumption.

No 35018 British India Line stands at Waterloo with the down ACE trailing the Great Western dynamometer car. The engine is still in SR livery although with 'British Railways' on the tender and carrying the number 35018 in Southern style figures.

This experience was the catalyst for further major modifications to eliminate three very undesirable features which were causing serious loss of availability (about 40 per cent of Merchant Navy Pacifics were under repair in works or sheds at any time) and high operating costs. These were the chain driven valve gear, the inside oil bath and the boiler casing, which was prone to fire. The scheme, prepared by R. G. Jarvis, chief technical assistant (locomotives) at Brighton, was ingenious in using a very high proportion of the original locomotives, including boilers and outside cylinders, while providing three sets of conventional Walschaerts valve gear and a more conventional appearance by getting rid of the 'air-smoothed' casing. All the large Pacifics were rebuilt, together with 60 of the smaller ones, before the BR Modernisation Plan stopped further work. Argument among footplate staff as to whether the performance of the rebuilds was an improvement persisted to the end and beyond, but the accountants confirmed that the cost of the rebuilding was recouped within four years. By now Bulleid had gone to CIE across the Irish Sea and in retirement during the 'Indian Summer' of steam on the Bournemouth and West of England routes complained that his machines should have been scrapped rather than being so rebuilt.

Fitted with large type smoke deflectors West Country Pacific No 34004 Yeovil (renumbered, cab modified and with an LMS tender) attaches the Glasgow portion to the Edinburgh coaches at Perth on a train for Inverness on 5 July 1948.

Right. This view of Epsom Downs on Derby Day 1873 shows engines from the many special trains stabled around the yard awaiting their return workings.

In parallel with this steam locomotive development, three designs jointly with the electrical engineer must also be chronicled. Maunsell, impressed with what the LMS was pioneering with diesel traction, produced three 350hp diesel-electric 0-6-0 shunting locomotives in 1937 with English Electric engines. They were more than just yard shunters, being geared for a maximum of 45mph for freight transfer work. They hardly had the engine power for such duty, however, and were usually confined to Hither Green and Norwood yards.

The next development was a Co-Co electric freight locomotive for the Central Section, the first of which appeared in 1941, to be followed by two more on the same theme in later years. They were sufficiently versatile to work not only the intended freight trains but also boat trains to and from Newhaven.

Finally, the Southern dipped a toe into the stream of main line diesel traction. Though the first locomotive did not emerge until 1951, after nationalisation, development of the design in collaboration with English Electric had started back in 1946, contemporaneously with or even preceding Ivatt's work at Derby on 10000/1. The locomotives were of the 1Co-Co1 arrangement, lacking the compactness and happy styling of the LMS engines, but the centreless bogies proved sufficiently attractive to form the basis of four subsequent BR classes. The locomotives also demonstrated the progressive uprating of the English Electric 16-cylinder engine from 1600hp on 10000/1 to 1750hp on the first two Southern locomotives and to 2000hp on the final example. The three locomotives led a short and nomadic life between the LM Region and the South Eastern and South Western Divisions of the Southern.

Bulleid made one stab at the idea of a combined shunter/transfer engine, producing in 1951 a single 0-6-0 fitted with 500hp Paxman engine driving a jackshaft through fluid coupling and gearbox giving three steps in each of high and low ratios. The gear steps were its undoing, however, for it proved not really suitable for either duty, and its working life was brief.

In its 25 years of independent existence the Southern Railway built a little over 400 steam (about 17 a year), two electric and three diesel locomotives, not counting the wartime construction of LMS 2-8-0s for use elsewhere. It was a case of small but (with few exceptions) good – and sometimes very good indeed.

The Derby

The greatest event in the racing calendar has always been the Derby, and after the South Western's pioneer efforts, the London, Brighton & South Coast Railway secured a firm hold on this traffic with the opening of its line to Epsom Town in 1847, and to Epsom Downs in 1865. But the Brighton's monopoly was broken in 1901 when the South Eastern & Chatham Railway opened the Chipstead Valley line to Tattenham Corner in time for Derby Day, and handled 50 specials at the new terminus on top of the Downs alongside the course. Tattenham Corner Station was laid out even more spaciously than Epsom Downs had been. It had seven long platforms, extensive sidings, a turntable and locomotive servicing facilities. Only on the wooden station buildings was expense spared; these were said to be temporary but they survive today.

A feature of both the LBSC and SE&C routes used to be the tiny lineside signal cabins, some of them not even distinguished with names, which were manned for two or three days in the year merely to handle the intensive services provided for the big races. In 1937, as an example, 54 trains ran to Epsom Downs and 68 to Tattenham Corner during the morning and early afternoon of Derby Day, the customary electrics being supplemented by steam-hauled specials from Kent, and by Pullman trains from Victoria, Charing Cross and Cannon Street, which brought business men from their offices in time for the afternoon's racing. The steam-worked specials to Epsom Downs were usually double-headed by two tank engines while Moguls were used on the Tattenham Corner trains. After the war the Pullman specials were sometimes worked by electric locomotives, but rail traffic has declined in recent years, and the Royal Train from Victoria to Tattenham Corner broke the electrified uniformity of Derby Day.

Locomotive Allocation
December 1945

Ashford (Sub-shed Canterbury West): 801–6, 1010/69, 1147/58/74/91, 1218/39/61/2/8/9/74, 1305–7/22/73/85/90, 1400–5/26/77, 512/7/49/77/89/95–9, 1711/21/6/48/70–7, 2357/63–5/80/8. (62)

Barnstaple (Sub-sheds Ilfracombe, Torrington): 23/36/42/4, 247/50, 321, 670, 2094–6, 2608/10/96. (14)

Basingstoke: 244/8/65/78, 307/48/68, 407/18/26, 693, 706/8, 931, 1614/5/21–5/9/32–4. (25)

Bournemouth (Sub-sheds Swanage, Hamworthy Junction): 21/8/40/7/50–2/7/9/88/92/9, 100/4/6/7/11–3/31/6/61/5/8/9/73, 239/51/81, 305/18/45/63/79/93/4/8/9, 415/20/9/38, 548/9, 696, 700/19/28/72, 850–5/62–5, 928–30. (62)

Bricklayers Arms: 932–9, 1033/6/71/93, 102/9/62/3/6/75/6, 1217/23/51/3/70/5/7/80/7/94/7, 1315/24/6/8/88/9/95/7/8, 1410–4/25/8/9/53/4/9/60/91, 1500/4/6/7/33/41/2/6/7/50/81/4, 1685/7/93, 1723/31/2/53/4/7–9/82–9, 1817–21/3/43/50/8/9/62/75, 2097, 2113/28/51/65/6/8/70, 2453/4/8–62. (110)

Brighton: 423/8/30, 1178, 1557, 2038/9/43–5/52/62/7/71, 2122/7/53, 2255, 2337–41/68/72/6/85/97, 2421/2/4–6/70/80/6/91/6, 2505/10/3/23/8/43/6/66/7/83/7/92/7 – 9, 2606. (54)

Dorchester (Sub-shed Weymouth): 146/62/77, 221/3/9/33/84/6, 387, 410, 695. (12)

Dover: 767–9, 924–7, 1027/65, 1108/61, 1252/5/76/91, 1325, 1441/3, 1520/30–2/45/55/6, 1631/9/73, 1705/8/27/55/6, 1807/8, 2108/9. (37)

Eastbourne: 2042, 2215/29/34/59/74/84/99, 2358/61/77/91/5, 2402/4/6/85, 2548/74/88/95/6, 2605/99. (24)

Eastleigh (Subsheds Winchester, Andover Junction, Lymington): 1/2/4–6/8/16/29/48/53/82/3/7, 109/20/5/48/50/1/4/5/7/9/70/1/5/98, 200/13/25/31/40/2/61/4/7/72/4/5/7, 302/6/13/6/36/7/41/2/50/1/7/66/7/95/7, 463–7/9/71/7/9/95/7, 521–4/30/2/9/47/97/8, 600/6/9/12/23–5/7/9/36/7/42/8/58/74, 707/36/7/9–43/7–52/4, 952, 1827/9/65–7/70/4, 2133/47/60, 2609, 3101, 3397, 3509, 3741/4, C11–8. (131)

Exmouth Junction (Sub-sheds Seaton, Lyme Regis, Exmouth, Okehampton, Bude, Launceston): 24/30/4/7/9/46/9/55, 105/24/33/5/7/8/56/92/3/9, 207/24/30/2/45/52/3/5/6/82/3, 301/20/3/9/56/74–7/96, 402–4/8/9/11/3/4/36/9, 668/9/71, 722–5/30–3/8/53/87/9–92, 823–7/47, 954, 1406–9, 1635/8, 1795, 1828/30–8/40–2/5/7/51/3–6/69/71, 2124/35, 2695/7, 3029, 3125, 3520, 21C1–5, 21C101–19. (131)

Faversham: 1046, 1106, 1229/31/42/6/60/5/79, 1309/10/69/79, 1438/48/70/81/7/9/93/5/6, 1501/2/5/9, 1709/39/41. (34)

Folkestone Junction: 1047, 1107/27/8/54, 1323/37/40/78, 1558. (10)

Feltham: 9/25/31/2, 139/40/4/53/8/67/74/, 346/7/52/83/5, 473/4/8/92–9, 500–20, 687–9/97/8, 833-46, 2244, 3154/63/7, 3400/33/42/96, 3506, C19–40. (98)

Fratton (Sub-sheds Gosport, Midhurst): 20/7/45/54, 114/5/8/64/6/72, 287, 300/4/38/84, 400/1/17/24/5/41/80, 716/56, 1796/7, 2139, 2260/9, 2490, 2509/37/48/54/9/62, 2635/44/55/9/61/2/90/1/4. (45)

Gillingham: 1002/3/7/13/4/39/44/51/64/6/92, 1105/12, 1215/34/8/56/67/78, 1308/17/84/91, 1430/9/49, 1510/73/4/9/83/5, 1658–60/2/3/5/6/82/4/8/97, 1713/46/50. (46)

Guildford (Sub-sheds Bordon, Ash): 22/6/43/56, 108/10/21/7/8/41, 246/54/62/8–70, 308/9/11/24–8/43/9/78/81, 416/9/22/33/4/81, 545/6/99, 613–5/8/20/30/4/8/43/72/6, 704/5/26, 1798/9, 1800–6/9/68, 2487, 2500/4, 3083, 3155, 3436/9/58, C1–10. (80)

Hither Green: 950/1/3/5/6, 1018/28/31/54/9/61/8/90, 1110/3/23, 1205/43–5/8/57/8/71/98, 1374/7/81/6, 1480, 1572, 1689/95, 1822/76–80, 1911/3/21–5, 2239. (47)

Horsham (Sub-shed Bognor): 540–4, 2235/52/83, 2300/1/6–8/55/73/84/6/7/99, 2401/49/64, 2501/11/4/5/21/50/6/7/70/1/3/84/94. (35)

Isle of Wight (Sheds Newport, Ryde): W1–4, W8, W11/3–33. (27)

New Cross Gate: 2037/50/1/5/60/3/8/70/2–7/9/85/7/9/91, 2142/64, 2253, 2342–53, 2407–18/42/6/8/63/8/74, 2524/5/36/49/51/64/5/8/75/6/8/86/91, 2601/3. (68)

Newhaven: 2054, 2423/34/8/43/75/82/92/4/9, 2508/33/4/9, 2636/47. (16)

Nine Elms: 33/8, 119/23/30/2/42/9/60/79, 204/12/41/9/57/9/63/6/71/3, 319/22/53/4/80/6/90–2, 406/27/31/5/7/40/2–7/59–62/77/82–91, 667/73/92/4/9, 701/13/8/55/66/75/7, 856–61, 949, 1544/51–3, 1613/6/7/9/37/96/8, 2220/86/9, 2327–33, 21C11–20. (107)

Norwood: 1844/52, 1916–20, 2167/9, 2302/9, 2436/40/4/7/55–7/66/7/9/71–3/6–9/81/9/93/5/8, 2502/6/35/40/4/7/61/3/79, 81, Diesel 1–3. (46)

Plymouth (Sub-shed Callington): 3/7/35/84/91/4, 103/16/82/3/97, 201/16/36/80/9, 711/57/8. (19)

Ramsgate: 909–23, 1004/16/80, 1151/64/82, 1316, 1451/2, 1521–3/92, 1778–81. (32)

Reading: 258/60, 1042/3/60/2/78/9, 1140/56/83/8/95, 1610/1/20/7/8, 1857/60/1. (21)

Redhill: 531/3–8, 1157, 1273, 1587, 1728–30, 1814–6/49/63/4/90–9, 2008–10, 2359, 2435/7/41/50, 2507/17/22/6/41/58/60. (44)

St. Leonard's: 900–8, 1041/75, 1101, 1272, 1335/9, 1740/4/66–8, 2371/9/83/94. (24)

Salisbury: 10/3/41/60, 117/22, 237/43/79/85/8, 310/2/4/5/7/30–5/55/61/82/8/9, 405/21/32/48–57/75/6, 644/9/52/4/75/90/1, 709/15/21/7/9/44–6/73/4/84/5, 828–32, 957, 1612/8/26/30/6, 1839/46/8/72/3, 3441, 21C6–10. (83)

Stewarts Lane: 763–5/70/1/5/6/8–83/8/93–9, 800, 1005/19/67, 1109/45/60/5/77/9/84, 1247/59/63/6/93/5, 1302/11/9/31/9/80, 1434/45/6/50/92/4/7–9, 1508/11/4–6/48/54/75/6/8/82, 1602/4/61/81/3/90/4, 1706/10/2/4–9/22/35/6/43/5/9–65/9, 1810–24–6, 1900–10/2/4/5, 2081/2/90, 2100–7, 2325/6. (126)

Southampton Docks: 81/5/6/9/90/3/5–8, 101/2/47/76, 2112/56/62, 2689. (18)

Three Bridges: 2078/80/3/4/6/8, 2303, 2400/5/45/51/65/84/97, 2516/8–20/7/9/32/45/52/84, 400/1/17/24/5/41/80, 716/56, 1796/7, 3/72/7/85/9/93, 2602/4. (31)

Tonbridge: 1021/37/8/48/57/63/86, 1150/93, 1219/21/5/7, 1320/7/70/96, 1432/7/40/55/7/61/86/8/90, 1503/13/8/40/3/80/6/8/90/1/3, 1670–2/5/86, 1700/3/4/7/15/20/4/5/33/4/7/8, 2129/38/41/5, 2367/70/4/8, 2488, 2503/80. (66)

Tunbridge Wells West: 2001–7/21–3/5–30, 2366/89/90/3/8, 2512/82/90. (24)

Wadebridge: 181, 203, 703/17, 3298, 3314/29. (7)

Yeovil (Sub-shed Templecombe): 58, 129/34/43/5/52/63, 238/76, 303/40/4, 412, 702/10/2/4, 1790–4. (22)

Unallocated: 2240, 2678*, 3440*

*Loaned to Kent & East Sussex Railway.

Locomotive Stock at
Nationalisation

4-6-2 (90) Merchant Navy: 21C1–20 (20). West Country: 21C101–48 (48) (21C119 oil-burning). Battle of Britain: 21C149–70 (22).

4-6-0 (177) N15 King Arthur: 448–57, 763–806 (54). S15: 823–47 (25). Lord Nelson: 850–65 (16). LSWR H15: 330–5, 473–8/82–91, 521–4 (26). LSWR T14: 443–7/59–62 (9). LSWR S15: 496–515 (20). LSWR N15: 736–55 (20) (740/5/8/9/52 oil-burning). LBSC N15X rebuild: 2327–33 (7).

4-4-2 (9) LBSC H1: 2037–9 (3). LBSC H2: 2421–6 (6).

4-4-0 (372) V Schools: 900–39 (40). L1: 1753–59/82–9, (15). LSWR T9: 113–22, 280–9, 300–5/7/10–4/36–8, 702–19/21–33 (66) (113–5/8/21, 280/6, 303/5/14, 713/22/31 oil-burning). LSWR L11: 134/48/54–9/61/3–75, 405–14/35–42 (40) (148/54/57/70/2, 411/37 oil-burning). LSWR K10: 135/7/9–46/50–3, 329/40/1/3/5/80/2–6/9–94 (31). LSWR S11: 395–404 (10). LSWR L12: 415–34 (20). LSWR D15: 463–72 (10) (463 oil-burning). SE&C F1: 1002/28/31/42/78, 1105/51, 1215/31 (9). SE&C B1: 1013, 1217, 1440/3/5/6/8–55/7/9 (16). SE&C E1: 1019/67, 1160/3/5/79, 1497, 1504/6/7/11 (11). SE&C E: 1036, 1157/9/66/75/6, 1273/5, 1315, 1491, 1514–6/47/87 (15). SE&C D: 1057/75/92, 1477/88/90/3/6, 1501/49/74/7/86/91, 1728–34/8/40/4/6/8/50 (28). SE&C D1: 1145, 1246/7, 1470/87/9/92/4, 1502/5/9/45, 1727/35/6/9/41/3/5/9 (20). SE&C L: 1760–81 (22). LBSC B4X: 2043/50/2/5/6/60/70–3 (12). LBSC B4: 2044/51/4/62/3/8/74 (7).

2-6-0 (174) N: 1400–14, 1810–21/3–75 (80) (1831 oil-burning). U: 1610–39, 1790–1809* (50) (1625, 1797 oil-burning). N1: 1822/76–80 (6). U1: 1890–1910† (21). LBSC K: 2337–53 (17).

0-6-0 (322) Q: 530–49 (20). Q1: C1–40 (40). LSWR 700: 306/8/9/15–7/25–7/39/46/50/2/5/68, 687–701 (30). SE&C O1: 1003/7/14/39/41/4/6/8/51/64–6/80/93, 1106/8/9/23, 1238/48/58, 1316/69/70/3/4/7–81/4–6/8–91/5–8, 1425/6/8–30/2/4/7–9 (51). SE&C C: 1004/18/33/7/8/54/9/61/3/8/71/

86/90, 1102/12/3/50/91, 1218/9/21/3/5/7/9/ 34/42–5/52/3/5–7/60/7/8/70–2/7/80/7/91/3/ 4/7/8, 1317, 1460/1/80/1/6/95/8, 1508/10/ 3/72/3/5/6/8–85/8–90/2/3, 1681–4/6–95, 1711–25 (106). LBSC C3: 2300–3/6–9 (8). LBSC C2X: 2434/7/8/40–51, 2521–9/32/ 4–41/3–54 (45). LBSC C2: 2435/6, 2533 (3). LSWR 0395: 3029/83, 3101/54/5/63/ 7, 3397, 3400/33/6/9–42/96, 3506/9 (18).

0-4-2 (4) LSWR A12: 618/27/9/36 (4).

4-8-0T (4) LSWR G16: 492–5 (4).

4-6-2T (7) LSWR H16: 516–20 (5). LBSC J1: 2325 (1). LBSC J2: 2326 (1).

4-4-2T (47) LBSC I1X: 2001–10, 2595/6/8/ 9, 2601–4 (18). LBSC I3: 2021–3/5–30/ 75–91 (26). LSWR 0415: 3125, 3488, 3520 (3).

2-6-4T (15) W: 1911–25 (15).

2-4-0T (3) LSWR 0298: 3298, 3314/29 (3).

0-8-0T (9) Z: 950–7 (8). K&ES: 949 (1).

0-6-4T (5) SE&C J: 1595–9 (5)

0-6-2T (142) PD&SW 757: 757/8 (2). LBSC E1R: 2094–6, 2124/35, 2608/10/95–7 (10). LBSC E3: 2165–70, 2453–62 (16). LBSC E5: 2399, 2400/2/4–6, 2567/8/71– 5/83–5/7–94 (24). LBSC E5X: 2401, 2570 /6/86 (4). LBSC E6X: 2407/11 (2). LBSC E6: 2408–10/2–8 (10). LBSC E4: 2463–5/ 7–76/9–82/4–8/90–9, 2500–20/56–66/77– 82 (70). LBSC E4X: 2466/77/8/89 (4).

0-6-0T (124) USA: 61–74 (14). LSWR G6: 160/2, 237–40/57–79, 348/9/51/3/4 (34). LSWR 756: 756 (1). SE&C R1: 1010/47/ 69, 1107/27/8/47/54/74, 1335/7/9/40 (13). SE&C P: 1027, 1178, 1323/5, 1555–8 (8). SE&C T: 1602/4 (2). SE&C S: 1685 (1). LBSC E1: 2097, 2112/3/22/7–9/33/8/9/41/ 2/5/7/51/3/6/60/2/4, 2606/9/89–91/4, W1– 4 (30). LBSC E2: 2100–9 (10). LBSC A1X: 2636/40/4/7/55/9/61/2/78, W8, W13 (11).

0-4-4T (287) LSWR T1: 1–3/5/7–10/3/20, 361/3/6/7 (14). LSWR M7: 21–60, 104– 12/23–5/7–33, 241–56, 318–24/8/56/7/74– 9, 479–81, 667–76 (104). LSWR O2: 177/ 9/81–3/92/3/7–9, 200/3/4/7/12/3/6/21/3–5/ 9–33/6, W14–34 (48). SE&C H: 1005/16, 1158/61/2/4/77/82/4/93, 1239/59/61/3/5/6/ 9/74/6/8/9/95, 1305–11/9–22/4/6–9, 1500/ 3/12/7–23/30–3/40/4/6/8/50–4 (64). SE&C R: 1658–63/5–7/70–5 (15). SE&C R1: 1696–9, 1700/3–10 (13), LBSC D3: 2364–

8/70–4/6–80/3–91/3–5/8 (28). LBSC D3X: 2397 (1).

0-4-2T (18) LBSC D1/M): 2215/34/5/9/52/3/ 9/69/74/83/9/99, 2358/61, 2605/99 (16). LBSC D1: 2286, 2359 (2).

0-4-0T (29) LSWR B4: 81–103/47/76 (25). SE&C Crane Tank: 1302 (1). LSWR 0458: 3458 (1). LSWR C14: 3741/4 (2).

Diesel Locomotives (3)
0-6-0 Diesel Electric 350hp: 1–3 (3).

Electric Locomotives (2)
Co-Co 1470hp: CC1/2 (2)

Service Locomotives (9)
Steam:
0-6-0T (4) LBSC A1X: 377S, 515S (2). SE&C T: 500S (1). LB&SC A1: 680S (1)
0-4-2T (2) LBSC D1/M: 700S, 701S (2).
0-4-0T (1) LSWR C14: 77S (1).
Electric:
Bo-Bo (1) 74S (Durnsford Road Power Station)
Bo (1) 75S (Waterloo & City Line)

Miscellaneous Locomotives (not in locomotive stock)
Steam:
0-6-0T (1) LBSC A1: 82 *Boxhill*
Petrol Inspection Car: 346S (Engineer's Dept)
Petrol Shunter: 343S (Eastleigh Carriage Works), 49S (Broad Clyst Sleeper Depot)
Diesel Shunter: 400S (Dock Engineer's Dept, South-ampton)

Locomotives on Loan:
2-8-0 WD (from MOS): 70811/53/78, 77007/ 30/52/6/9/62/74/86/90/4/8, 77101/3/8/22/ 50/80, 77205/26/56/9/70/86/96, 77311/21/ 40/55/9/79, 77444/60/81/5, 78531/69/96/7, 78666/88, 78705, 79199, 79203/7/10/62/ 81 (50).

Locomotives Loaned Out:
0-6-0 (1) LSWR 0395: 3440 (to KESR).
0-6-0T (1) LBSC A1X: 2678 (to KESR).

*1790–1809 rebuilt from K 2–6–4T
†1890 rebuilt from K1 2–6–4T

Electric Multiple-Unit Stock at Nationalisation

3-coach Suburban Units (3-SUB): 1266/73/ 4, 1401/4/6/8/21/5/30/2/8/40/5/8/9/58/61/3/ 5/79/81/2/7/92/4/5, 1525/8/99, 1601/4/6/7/ 9/10/4/6/7/9/20/2/7/30–3/5/7–42/4/6/7/9– 51/4–7/9/60/3/6/8/9/72/4/8/81/3/5–91/3/4/7– 9, 1700/2–6/8/10–9/21/3/5–7/9/32–5/8–40/3/ 4/6–51/3/6–8/62–5/7/8/71/2/6/80/1/3–5/ 90–3/7/8, 1800.
(150 Units – 300 motor coaches)

2-coach Non-Lavatory Units (2 NOL): 1801–6/8–27/9–54/6–90.
(87 Units – 87 motor coaches)

2-coach Lavatory Units, lavatory in each coach (2BIL): 2001–13/5–99, 2100/1/3– 18/20–30/2–52.
(148 Units – 148 motor coaches)

2-coach Lavatory Units, lavatory in trailer coach only (2HAL): 2601–45/7–92.
(91 Units – 91 motor coaches)

4-coach Lavatory Units (4LAV): 2921–55.
(35 Units – 70 motor coaches)

6-coach Express Units with Pullman coach (6PUL): 3001–20/41–3.
(23 Units – 46 motor coaches)

6-coach Express Units with Pantry coach (6PAN): 3021–37.
(17 Units – 34 motor coaches)

4-coach Express Units with Restaurant coach (4RES): 3054–7/9/61/2/4–72.
(16 Units – 32 motor coaches)

4-coach Express Units with Buffet coach (4BUF): 3073–85.
(13 Units – 26 motor coaches)

4-coach Express Units (4COR): 3101–58.
(58 Units – 116 motor coaches)

4-coach Suburban Units (4SUB): 4101–84/ 95–9, 4200–14/6–21/3–32/5/51–5, 4300– 54/72–7, 4401–99, 4500–16/20/1/7/32/7/ 49/51/2/6/61/4/9/72/9, 4601–7/13/4.
(326 Units – 652 motor coaches)

Waterloo & City Line: Motor coaches: 51–62 (12)

Note:- The 5-coach *Brighton Belle* Pullman Units (5BEL) 3051–3 belonged to the Pullman Car Co and were not included in Southern Railway stock.

5
BOAT TRAINS AND PULLMANS

TRAIN FERRIES

Harwich

Dover

Zeebrugge.

Dunkerque

FOR TRADE WITH THE CONTINENT

Ask, in 1935, the man on the Clapham omnibus to name one of the Southern Railway's crack trains and the chances were pretty strong that the answer would come from the trio of *Golden Arrow, Brighton Belle* and *Bournemouth Belle*. All of these were Pullman trains with the distinctive liveried carriages which undoubtedly appealed to the public's imagination: Pullman cars, as they were termed, had a long history back into pre-grouping days, although not stretching so far back as boat trains, of which the *Golden Arrow* was the most distinguished member.

Railway development in the south of England was reaching the harbours used for cross-channel traffic in the period 1843–5 and the first boat trains – trains run to connect with specified sailings rather than trains generally to the port of departure – were to follow soon after. The South Eastern Railway arranged sailings to Boulogne from Folkestone in 1843 but passenger trains did not work down to the harbour until the beginning of 1849. However, by 1852 the SER's timetable advertised 'The daily Special Express Train to the Folkestone Tidal Steamer, besides seven ordinary Trains from London to Folkestone and Dover . . .' and 'The Tidal Train . . . passengers by this Train being conveyed direct to the Tidal Steamer'. In 1844 the London, Brighton & South Coast Railway was co-operating with a Shoreham–Brighton–Dieppe steamship service and likewise the London & South Western Railway in 1845 with services from Southampton to the Channel Islands, Le Havre and St Malo.

Eventually the railway companies obtained powers to operate their own steamships across the Channel and a regular pattern of routes evolved. Dover–Calais and Folkestone–Boulogne became established early on for the LC&D and SE respectively, while the LBSC, after flirting with services from Littlehampton (to the Channel Islands and St Malo among other places) from 1867 to 1882, settled down to the Newhaven–Dieppe run first started by its own steamers in 1863. The LSWR continued with the routes of 1845. The service to alter most was that to Flushing which had a variety of Kentish ports – Sheerness, Queenborough, Port Victoria, Folkestone and Gravesend.

Timings for the tidal train of the SER differed every day until 1885 when a fixed timetable came into force but it was an up tidal boat train, in which Charles Dickens was a passenger, that figured in the Staplehurst accident of 1865 due, in some measure, to a ganger misreading his timetable of the 'tidals'. For the Paris Exhibition of 1889 an elite *Club Train* was put on from London to Paris (via Dover–Calais) which consisted of Wagon-Lits stock; although one train sufficed between Calais and Paris the LCDR and SER each had a W-L train, the one to and from Victoria, the other Charing Cross. Starting on 4 June

1889, the service, after the first six months, did not prosper and ceased on 30 September 1893. A little later, at the turn of the century, Southampton started to expand as a port and the ocean liner services required trains in addition to those for the French and Channel Islands traffic.

After the grouping of 1923 the Southern Railway decided that the major alteration required was the concentration of all the short sea routes boat trains on Victoria as the London terminus. This was achieved that summer giving a total of seven services between the British and French capitals on weekdays. In France an all-Pullman first class service *La Flèche d'Or* was inaugurated on 13 September 1926 but the SR stayed its hand until not only an all-Pullman train could be introduced in England but also a new luxury steamship. With the completion of TSS *Canterbury* (which, with its 1,700 passenger capacity, gave exceptionally spacious accommodation for the 250 to 300 expected travellers for each crossing) the SR inaugurated its *Golden Arrow* on 15 May 1929, leaving Victoria at 11 o'clock and arriving in Paris at 5.35pm; the inward service ran exactly one hour later throughout, both services using Dover–Calais as the sea route.

For the next summer newly-renovated Pullman cars were placed on the service but, unfortunately, the trade slump gripped the country and

Dover Marine. The dignity of this splendid Continental passenger terminal is complemented by the grace of rebuilt SE&CR E1 class 4-4-0 No 163 and its all-Pullman boat express. E1s 160 and 163 of Dover shed were almost exclusively responsible for boat train workings in the 1920s, and 163 had the added distinction of six months as an oil burner during the 1926 miners' strike. Note the top-feed on the dome and fluted coupling rods which distinguished Class E1 from the otherwise very similar Class D1 rebuilds.

Brighton Pullman. Ex LB&SCR Marsh 4-6-2 tank as No 325, but carrying no name, heads the Southern Belle *just south of Quarry Tunnel in the late 1920s. This was one of two named tanks (325 Abergavenny, 326 Bessborough) built in December 1910 by the Brighton line to work its principal express trains.*

Boat Train

When the [Channel Islands] train comes down from Clapham at about 8.30pm, Waterloo Station always seems to be enjoying one of its few spacious and leisurely moments. Vast crowds are not there and so queues do not form. There is room to move, and the loudspeaker is dispensing more light music than announcements.

Although the train stops at Basingstoke and Winchester, few people use it except for those who are bound either for the Channel Islands or for Le Havre, and the language of the passengers is almost as likely to be French as English. The whole train in fact has a pleasantly continental and holiday air. Two vans at the back carry the mail, and the mail bag labels have half the towns in France stencilled on them. There is a dining-car, but not many have dinner. The hour is too late, and besides, the experienced traveller to Le Havre or St Peter Port knows well that the railway boats have an excellent restaurant, where they serve a far more ample and varied supper before the boat sails than can be had anywhere ashore.

At nine o'clock out into the darkness and round the double curve into Vauxhall the train runs behind its 'Lord Nelson' or its 'King Arthur' engine, and by Clapham Junction it has worked up to full speed. At Basingstoke it picks up a few passengers, and *continued opposite*

as from 15 May 1931 the ship had to carry all, rather than just first class, passengers. Then, from the summer of 1932, the *Golden Arrow* had to do the same, so losing its all-Pullman status. That year saw the nadir of the cross-channel passenger traffic which dipped by over a third to less than a million passengers yearly. Further economies had to be introduced in October 1935 when the French wanted to use just one Pullman set and so the inward service was routed via Boulogne and Folkestone, which meant that the *Canterbury* was confined to one leg of the sea crossing.

By the summer of 1937 the number of continental passengers was back to pre-1932 figures, so much so that Saturday 31 July saw 22,828 such passengers leave Victoria – an all-time record – which necessitated 50 *additional* boat trains. So heavy was the traffic becoming that agents' specials had to be diverted to Cannon Street which then saw Lord Nelsons entering its platforms for the first time.

Belatedly, perhaps, but, to its great credit, when the potential was realised in the depth of the slump, the Southern's board sanctioned the introduction of a train ferry for a night service between London and Paris. Difficulties in the dock delayed construction: the first public service left Victoria at 10pm on 14 October 1936 complete with its complement of Wagon-Lits sleeping cars. These were taken aboard one of the specially-built train ferries for the Dover–Dunkerque sea crossing and then on to Paris for an arrival there at about 9am. Ordinary carriages for non-sleeping passengers which did not go through were included in the train, christened *Night Ferry*, so although there was a through portion there was also, for the purpose of our definition, a boat train portion.

From the beginning of May 1932 the Tilbury–Dunkerque service changed to Folkestone and naturally, with the advent of the Dover–Dunkerque ferry this was discontinued.

Outbreak of World War II put a stop to all these activities. The *Night Ferry* was the first casualty, as from 26 August 1939, the *Golden Arrow* following a week later. The Lord Nelson class of locomotives, some of which were shedded at Stewarts Lane to power the *Golden Arrow* and other boat (but not *Night Ferry*) services, were transferred away and never returned. The Batavier Line service suffered likewise; this ran between Victoria and Gravesend West Street and is described more fully in a separate 'snippet'.

There were of course boat trains from Victoria to Newhaven for the Dieppe crossing, and the expansion of the docks at Southampton under the auspices of the SR based on various steamship lines deciding to make it their main port of call (Cunard in 1920, P&O in 1925 and North German Lloyd in 1928) saw the ocean liner traffic to and from London (Waterloo) increase with the trains usually in charge of King Arthur or lesser 4-6-0 types.

With the opening of the Imperial Airways terminal adjacent to Victoria station and the introduction of the Empire Air Mail Scheme special flying-boat trains between Victoria and Southampton Docks were run from June 1939. Although Imperial Airways had asked for sleeping cars (take-off was at dawn) the trains used Pullman cars and, there being no more than four coaches, were easily handled by T9 4-4-0s outwards via Balham, Tooting and Wimbledon and inwards via East Putney and Stewarts Lane. War intervened here, of course, but such trains operated at various periods to Bournemouth West or from Poole (the flying boats were then based at Poole Harbour) being discontinued in mid-April 1946.

The war over, the *Golden Arrow* was reintroduced in all-Pullman form again as from 15 April 1946 now in the charge of Bulleid Pacifics. In BR days there was a reversion to the Folkestone Harbour route outwards with a 1pm departure from Victoria, which lasted from September 1952 until May 1960. The all-Pullman concept had again been abandoned during this period and in June 1961 electric traction took over from steam. The end came on 30 September 1972.

The *Night Ferry* did not restart until 14 December 1947 because the ships were not demobilised. This service prospered for many years and from June 1957 a sleeping car was included for Brussels. Zenith of the train was about 1964 when, with electric traction, the 19-coach 850 tons trains became the heaviest on BR. Improvements in landing techniques in foggy weather at Heathrow finally spelt its doom. Very much a shadow of its former self, and long having been abandoned by politicians and other personalities of the day, it ran for the last time on 31 October 1980. The cost of replacing the dedicated stock running no more than 300 miles a day was just too great.

Over on the Western Section in BR days the boat trains for the French ports were named *Normandy Express* and *Brittany Express* in 1952 and 1954 respectively and many of the ocean liner trains received names about the same time such as *Cunarder, Statesman, South American* and, later, *Arosa Line, Springbok* and *Sitmar Line*. The ocean liner traffic suddenly collapsed – in five years the volume decreased to just five per cent of the total of 1957 – as the jet aeroplane took over. Nowadays there is occasional cruise traffic but little else but, as ever, the railway adapts as witness the 15-minute interval Gatwick Expresses between Victoria and Gatwick Airport. Shades of traffic to London's first airport at Croydon. You lose some and you win some!

Pullman cars first appeared south of the Thames in 1875 on the LBSC, not to dispense refreshments, but to offer superior accommodation on a railway which was scarcely famed for its rolling stock. 5 December 1881 saw the inauguration between Victoria and Brighton of the first all-Pullman train in the country although this neither ran non-stop nor in

continued
those waiting for it at Winchester hear the most stirring announcement of the day there, 'Channel Islands Boat Train. Only passengers for Jersey, Guernsey and France travel by this train. The next stop will be inside Southampton Docks.' They enter and the train sweeps on, working up again to full speed before Shawford, and rushing through the maze of lines at Eastleigh at nearly seventy miles an hour. Not for another mile or two, when it comes to St Denys, does it begin to slacken speed, and for me this is the signal to find a corridor window looking out on the right-hand side of the train, and to lean out of it for the rest of the way. We slow down steadily until Southampton Terminus station comes into sight, where a tank engine is shunting rolling stock ready for the morning trains, and it seems almost as if we were going to enter it, but at the last moment we lurch to the left, and slowly glide round the outside of it. By now we are crawling at no more than walking pace, and we go across what is in daytime a very busy road, our passage being guarded by a man with a bell and a red lamp. Then the train passes through the dock gates, and grinds round a left-hand curve so sharp that one wonders so large an engine can negotiate it. In less than a minute more we pass out of the darkness and into the glaring, metallic light of the dock shed, where at last we come to rest. – Roger Lloyd, The Fascination of Railways, 1951.

The Night Ferry

Two photographs of this sadly extinct service between London (Victoria) and Paris (Nord) via Dunkerque which lasted from 1936 (excepting the war years) until 1980. The first train, seen here entering Victoria, was hauled from Dover behind L1 class 4-4-0 No 1758 double heading another L1, a classic combination which lasted until the arrival of the Bulleid Pacifics. Even then the train was normally double headed using a 4-4-0 and a 4-6-2!

The stock for the Night Ferry comprised Wagons-Lits sleepers specially built for this service to the smaller British loading gauge clearances to allow use over the old South Eastern & Chatham system. Dining car services were provided between Victoria and Dover by the Southern Railway and later BR, and by Wagons-Lits in France. It was perhaps the last civilised way of journeying from London to Paris. The photograph shows the train being shunted on to the Saint Eloi at Dunkerque.

70

the hour. That was to be left to the Sundays-only *Brighton Limited* which first ran with a title on New Year's Day 1899, having been introduced on 2 October the previous year. In many ways it was the precursor of the *Southern Belle* which started on 1 December 1908 as a daily service at 11am from Victoria and 5.45pm from Brighton. There were seven first class cars, the first all-Pullman train to be constructed in England (previous ones had been assembled from American kits), of unsurpassed Edwardian opulence which justifiably became advertised as the Most Luxurious Train in the World. Eastbourne got the old *Brighton Limited* stock cascaded (as 1980s parlance has it) as a Sundays-only all Pullman train but chose to ignore it: day trippers, especially on the Sunday, were not what Eastbourne wanted.

The LSWR dabbled with a few Pullman cars in trains on the Bournemouth route while in Kent cars were used in various services, especially some of the business trains from Ramsgate to London. It was on 10 July 1921 that an all-Pullman train appeared in Kent although confined to Sundays in the summer: this was the first-class only *Thanet Pullman Limited* which left Victoria at 10.10am and ran non-stop to Margate West in 90 minutes, then called at Broadstairs and terminated at Ramsgate Harbour. Return was at 5.30pm and, with similar calls as the outward service, Victoria was reached at 7.15pm.

So the newly-formed Southern Railway in 1923 inherited three all-Pullman trains. After the vicissitudes of the war years the *Southern Belle* had resumed its all-Pullman nature from 1 December 1921 and, in due course, the SR allocated new King Arthur class locomotives to be responsible for its haulage displacing the distinctive Brighton Atlantics or Baltic tanks. The *Thanet Pullman Limited* continued for a time but eventually it fizzled out as a train in its own right on 30 September 1928 and as a combined service on 30 June 1929. The third all-Pullman train, the *Eastbourne Sunday Limited*, had had a chequered career. It had been christened *Eastbourne Pullman Limited* on 6 June 1909, but on 1 June 1913 *Pullman* was altered to *Sunday* because a non-Pullman slip coach portion for the west coast line was carried in the formation: the war put a stop to even this at the end of 1916 but the train was revived as from 4 December 1921. As it was doing no harm and brought in some revenue the SR saw no reason to discontinue it but enlivened proceedings with a good variety of motive power including T9 'Greyhounds'.

As already noted, the *Golden Arrow* was introduced in 1929, to be followed (at a not very propitious time in the national economy) by the *Bournemouth Belle* on 5 July 1931. For the summer of 1931 it left Waterloo at 10.30am and served Southampton and Bournemouth daily and on weekdays Poole, Wareham, Dorchester and Weymouth in addition. Arrival at Weymouth was at 1.45pm and the return from there was 4pm with the London arrival at 7.18pm. This was an all-Pullman train and when serving Weymouth half of the ten cars went forward the other five concluding at and returning from Bournemouth West. For the winter of 1931–2 the train ran on Sundays to Bournemouth and for the resumption of the daily summer service of 1932 this remained the terminus. Weymouth, not surprisingly, had had its day doubtless because the 2¼ hours stay was hardly sufficient to entice excursionists (those mainly attracted by the Pullman) such a distance. This point was

Bilingual West Street

Whenever there was a stranger among the few passengers on the lightly-used two-coach pull-and-push terminating at what it seemed was the end of civilisation at Gravesend West Street, he or she must have wondered why the small station was so lavishly signposted in two languages. The Southern, with its usual efficiency, had of course smoothed the path for 'boat train' passengers.

The story goes like this. Until 1914 – and even into World War I as far as 1916 – the Zeeland Steamship Company ran day and night crossings to Holland in conjunction with the LC&D, but on restoration of services after 1918 eventually went only by day. To preserve an overnight service, the SECR entered into an association with a sister steamship operator the Batavier Line. Its ships sailed from the Pool of London, leaving during the afternoon for Rotterdam. So that passengers, especially businessmen, could have a few more hours in London before setting out, a boat train ran from Victoria, via the LCDR route, to Gravesend West Street, adjacent to Gravesend Pier, where the steamer called especially.

The boat train was a mini-version of the Dover/Folkestone ones, three or four coaches of boat train stock complete with roof boards and hauled by a C class 0-6-0 or H class 0-4-4T, quite an oddity and happily photographed by H. C. Casserley who lived by the line below Bromley South, the train's only intermediate calling point.

The steamer ceased with the outbreak of World War II, of course, and though it resumed in 1945 it called at Tilbury instead of Gravesend. West Street (latterly known more simply as Gravesend West) remained fully signed in the two languages though only used by the pull-and-pushers until the station closed to passengers in 1953.

The Thanet Belle. *This service begin operation in the summer of 1948, the first year of the nationalised British Railways system. The photograph shows the train near Herne Bay during that year hauled by (then) unnamed Bulleid Battle of Britain Pacific No 21C162 in SR colours. The engine was later named 17 Squadron.*

The Devon Belle. *Two scenes of this Pullman train to the south west which was inaugurated in the summer of 1947 – the last year of the Southern Railway – running for only eight short seasons with 1954 as its last year.*

West Country Pacific No 34041 Wilton *takes the Ilfracombe section over the River Taw at Barnstaple on 1 September 1949.*

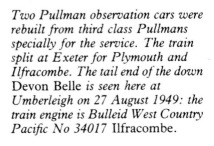

Two Pullman observation cars were rebuilt from third class Pullmans specially for the service. The train split at Exeter for Plymouth and Ilfracombe. The tail end of the down Devon Belle *is seen here at Umberleigh on 27 August 1949: the train engine is Bulleid West Country Pacific No 34017* Ilfracombe.

clearly recognised even for Bournemouth because the revised timing now had an 8.30pm arrival back at Waterloo. Difficulty was encountered in striking the right time to get back to London because 9.40pm and 6.55pm were tried until 6.45pm (weekdays) and 8.45pm (Sundays) were settled upon. From 1 January 1936 the train ran daily summer and winter until World War II ended it.

Over in Sussex electrification was in full flood. Some of the electric multiple unit stock ordered for these services included a Pullman car in the sets although it has never been explained satisfactorily why Littlehampton could sustain Pullmans yet Bognor Regis, six miles away as the seagull flies, could not. Be that as it may, the SR certainly considered the *Southern Belle* should continue and introduced three five-car sets for the service, these working singly or in pairs. Although it

SOUTHERN RAILWAY

SUNDAYS!
NEW CHEAP FARES
BY
"BOURNEMOUTH BELLE"
ALL-PULLMAN EXPRESS.
LONDON TO SOUTHAMPTON AND BOURNEMOUTH.

Commencing Sunday August 30th and every Sunday thereafter until further notice :—

CHEAP DAY RETURN TICKETS from Waterloo :—

	1st Class.	3rd Class.
To SOUTHAMPTON WEST	20/-	12/6
To BOURNEMOUTH CENT. and WEST	25/-	15/-

(Fares include Pullman Supplement)
Excellent Catering available *en route.*

OUTWARDS		RETURN		Until Sept. 20th inclusive.	Sept. 27th and until further notice.
	a.m.			p.m.	p.m.
WATERLOO .. .. dep.	10 30	BOURNEMOUTH WEST dep.		4 50	6 35
SOUTHAMPTON WEST arr.	11 59	,, CENT. ,,		5 10	6 46
	p.m.				
BOURNEMOUTH CENT. ,,	12 39	SOUTHAMPTON WEST ,,		5 48	7 24
,, WEST ,,	12 52	WATERLOO .. .. arr.		7 18	8 52

CHILDREN UNDER 14 YEARS OF AGE. HALF-FARE.
TAKE TICKETS IN ADVANCE AT WATERLOO.

NOTICE AS TO CONDITIONS.—These tickets are issued at less than the ordinary fares, and are subject to the Notice and Conditions shown in the current Time Tables.
No luggage allowed except small handbags, luncheon baskets or other small articles intended for the passenger's personal use during the day.
On the RETURN journey passengers may take with them, free of charge, at Owner's Risk, goods not exceeding in the aggregate 60 lbs. which they may have purchased for their own use (not for sale).

Waterloo Station, S.E. 1.
August, 1931.

H. A. WALKER.
General Manager.

C.X. 3302/20/25831

* Waterlow & Sons Limited, London, Dunstable & Watford.

Sleep on

The passengers with the most superior feeling coming up to Victoria must have been those travelling in the massive (though kept to British loading-gauge restrictions) Wagon-Lits – over fifty-five tons each – on the *Night Ferry* from Paris. But exactly how they felt as British commuters were starting their daily cycle of course depended on what kind of night's sleep they enjoyed.

A lot of shunting was inevitably involved in getting the blue sleepers off their express from Paris onto the two centre tracks of the train ferry. Screeching was inevitable round sharp curves, even if the attaching and detaching of the locomotive caused no jolt. There was also some tilting, sideways and longitudinally, on the long, articulated link between shore and ship. Once on board, weight was taken off the bogies by powerful jacks, and the main frames anchored down by chains, bound with rope to muffle the noise, in which they were only partially successful. Even though the men on the job moved stealthily to reduce any sound, a curious passenger banging his compartment door might wake neighbours. The curious, or those suffering from insomnia, could of course alight on the centre platform and walk up to the saloon deck.

It was a hard process to achieve silently, yet most passengers swore by the train, especially enjoying the comfort of lying out in privacy if the sea were rough. More usually it was a gentle motion of the waves that induced sleep that lasted while the train was reformed on English soil for the trip up to London, usually double-headed by 4-4-0s though later sometimes by a single Pacific, a string of vans leading.

The Golden Arrow. *A 1947 photograph of this, one of Britain's most famous trains, running under the even better known White Cliffs along the coast approaching Dover headed by a then unnamed Bulleid West Country Pacific No 21C134 built in July 1946. It was a Stewarts Lane engine at the time and was renumbered into the BR series in July 1948 carrying the name* Honiton.

could have advertised the train as being the first all-electric all-Pullman train in the world, the Southern contented itself by saying it was the 'Finest Train in Britain'.

For its introduction on 1 January 1933 the services were stepped up to three each way daily (two on Sundays) and on 29 June 1934 the name was changed to *Brighton Belle*. When electrification reached Eastbourne the *Eastbourne Sunday Limited* ran for the last time on 30 June 1935.

The average net yearly receipts to the Pullman Car Company for the years 1935–7 for operation of its cars on the SR was approximately £47,500 and naturally it wanted to restart as soon as possible after the war. Both the *Bournemouth Belle* and the *Brighton Belle* were resurrected (literally so in the case of one of the latter sets damaged by bombing), the Bournemouth service on 7 October 1946, the Brighton service a year later. An innovation, in the shape of an all-Pullman service to the West Country, was made in the *Devon Belle* which ran, at extended summer weekends, to Ilfracombe and Plymouth starting on 20 June 1947. With its full complement of 14 Pullmans in the charge of a Merchant Navy class locomotive it was a stirring sight but was in the nature of a stop-gap service to get passengers to West Country resorts in comfortable conditions. The Plymouth portion did not operate after 1949, days of operation were curtailed and the last run of all was made on 19 September 1954.

Nationalisation did not stop another all-Pullman service from being launched – the *Thanet Belle*. This ran between London (Victoria) and Ramsgate during the summer, with one daily return trip, starting 31 May 1948. For the Festival of Britain year of 1951 a portion also served Canterbury (detached/attached at Faversham) and so the train was renamed *Kentish Belle* and, although such a portion never operated in subsequent summers, the train retained that name until 14 September 1958, the end of the summer service before electrification.

In the same way the *Bournemouth Belle* was swept away by electrification, the final run taking place on 9 July 1967. The *Brighton Belle*, despite being tarted-up in BR blue Pullman livery, could not last for ever with its 1933 stock and, as replacements were not sanctioned, it went out in a blaze of glory on 30 April 1972, the last all-Pullman train on the Southern Region.

The Southern Underground

Take the list of longest British railway tunnels (excluding purely underground routes) and those of the Southern Railway barely make the top ten; just one, Sevenoaks, manages tenth place with a length of about 70yd short of two miles, and hardly in the same league as the three milers through the Pennines, and the Severn Tunnel which tops the list at just over 4¼ miles. Yet tunnels feature large on several Southern routes, far more so than on the main lines to the north and west of London.

On the northern main lines from London all have tunnels as they climb out of the Thames basin through the Northern Heights and the Chilterns, but after that they are few and far between. Indeed on the West Coast route to Scotland, after Kilsby Tunnel, through the Northamptonshire Heights, and Shugborough Tunnel, south of Stafford, there is nothing but a long bridge for 300 miles to a little way north of Stirling. On the Great Western, trains travel for 100 miles on the Bristol line before reaching Box Tunnel, and 125 miles on the Berks & Hants line to Somerton Tunnel.

But on the Southern, certainly on the lines to the south and south east, the tunnels are met not only soon after journey's start, but on and off all the way to the coast. The prime reason is the great chalk belt of the North and South Downs, running from west to east almost from Salisbury Plain to the Sussex and Kent Coasts, with the High Weald in between, and interspersed with river valleys, some of which run parallel with the chalk ramparts and some which break through forming gaps in the hills. Thus lines going with the hills or along the valleys could have gentle grades and no tunnels, but those going in other directions had to cut across the hills, either going up and over, or tunnelling through them.

The most extensive tunnelling is on the former South Eastern line from Charing Cross to Dover via Tonbridge. It takes in two of the Southern's longest, Polhill and Sevenoaks, but first trains will have passed through the long bridge at New Cross, and the tunnels at Elmstead Woods and Chelsfield. After Sevenoaks there is a respite, for the line turns east at Tonbridge for the almost straight run to Ashford but beyond Sandling there are more tunnels, Sandling, Saltwood, Martello, Abbotscliffe and Shakespeare Cliff, the last three on that remarkable coastal section mostly through chalk as the line runs alongside the English Channel between Folkestone and Dover, and now the area under which the longest of European tunnels, the Channel Tunnel is being bored. Between London and Dover the total length of tunnels is around seven miles, ten per cent of the total mileage, the highest proportion of any British main line.

Not far behind comes the Brighton line, with five or six tunnels depending which tracks are taken. Trains missing Redhill travelling on the Quarry line between Coulsdon and Earlswood go through six – Quarry (Merstham), Redhill, Balcombe, Haywards Heath, Clayton and Patcham. Those calling at Redhill travelling on the original South Eastern route to that point miss out on Redhill tunnel. Until the 1950s there was another tunnel on the Quarry line. Perhaps tunnel is not the right word, but to passengers it seemed every bit like one. This was the Cane Hill covered way just south of Coulsdon as the Quarry line passed through the grounds of Cane Hill hospital between the two bridges carrying the line first over and then back again across the Brighton road. Rather than an open cutting it was decreed that the line should be hidden under a cover, possibly to deter the hospital patients from trying to reach the track. Maintenance costs outweighed the continuing need to keep the line covered, and so today's passengers see open cutting walls.

Clayton tunnel is remarkable for it not only has castellated towers on the northern portal but includes a house right on top of the arch over the tracks. Another of the SR's tunnels was originally a canal tunnel. Strictly speaking the Higham–Strood tunnel on the South

The first tunnel. The first railway to be built which became part of the SR, the Canterbury & Whitstable, included Tyler Hill tunnel, a very small bore not originally intended for locomotives since trains were cable hauled through it. Later, locomotives replaced the cable but had cut down cabs and chimneys like this R1 0-6-0T No 124 photographed at Whitstable.

Eastern line between Gravesend and Strood is two tunnels linked by a gap in the middle, where it was intended that the barges on the original canal should pass. In the mid 1840s the Thames & Medway Canal Company built a single track railway on the towpath alongside the canal through the tunnel but in 1846 the South Eastern bought out the canal company, drained the canal and laid a double track railway on the canal bed which, with links through Dartford to London, formed a new Thames-side route from London to the Medway towns.

Another Southern tunnel, although on a minor route, has a claim to fame for it was the first on a railway that later became part of the Southern system, Tyler Hill Tunnel on the Canterbury & Whitstable Railway, opened in 1830. In relation to the loading gauge of later 4ft 8½in gauge lines Tyler Hill was very small with a height limit of just 11ft at the crown. It was not originally intended for locomotives since much of the line was cable worked from stationary engines at first, but, later, small locomotives with cut down chimneys and cabs were allowed to work through it.

Many of the tunnels on the South Eastern Railway had tight clearances which have imposed the much-known and tiresome restrictions on the width of rolling stock. The line between Tonbridge and Hastings was, of

Above. Heading west. One of the few tunnels on the West of England route is Honiton between Seaton Junction and Honiton and approached from the east by a seven mile climb, mostly at 1 in 80. Here, Merchant Navy Pacific No 35014 Nederland Line *emerges from the tunnel with the down* Atlantic Coast Express *in August 1964.*

Top right. South Eastern at Reading. Two ancients at Reading South shed in August 1937. Foremost is ex SECR 4-4-0 of Class F1 No 1043 for use on the Reading to Redhill trains while in the rear is SECR Class R 0-6-0 tank No 1070 in original condition with Stirling cab, domeless boiler and tall chimney.

Right. Auto tank. Ex LWSR M7 class 0-4-4 tank No 51 in spotless olive green on Bournemouth shed during the summer of 1939. This was one of the many members of its class fitted for push-pull working (1930). It was a Bournemouth engine for many years.

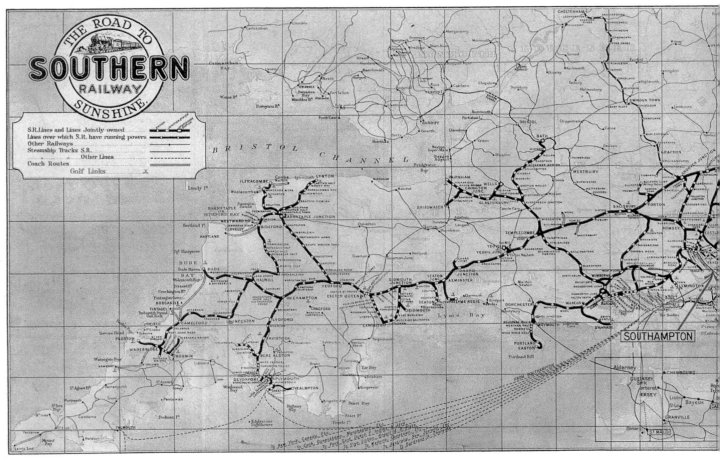

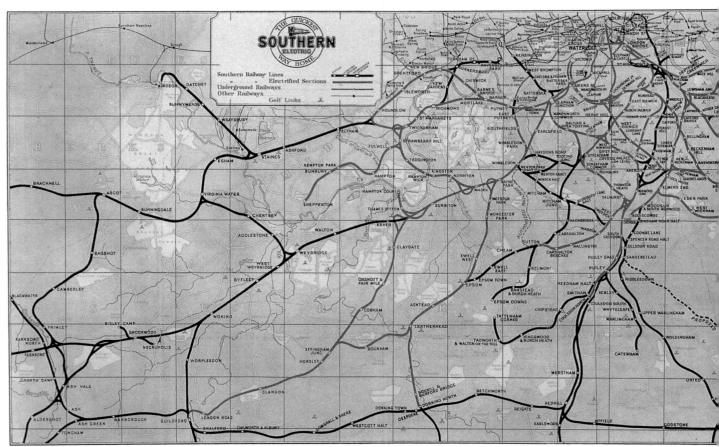

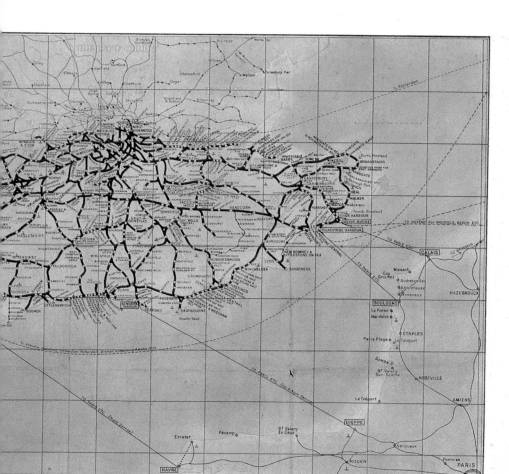

Southern all-line system map.

*London area lines showing the
Southern suburban electric network.*

course, especially notorious. The clearances between Tonbridge and Tunbridge Wells were slightly easier than those south of Tunbridge Wells. One of the problems arose soon after construction when the contractors were found to have skimped the tunnel linings and additional brick courses had to be added, reducing the space for trains. This is why until the 1980s narrow locomotives and coaches no more than about 8ft wide were required for trains running from Tonbridge to Hastings via Battle, not a problem in SECR days when the general carriage width over bodies was about 8ft but a handicap for the SR in building the 8ft 6in and 9ft wide stock allowed on most other routes. The problem was overcome in the last few years by singling the former double track through the Hastings line tunnels to allow unrestricted use by normal width stock as part of an electrification scheme.

The Southern's largest constituent in terms of mileage, the LSWR, broke the mould of the other SR companies so far as tunnels were concerned, at least on its West of England main line, for it was much like the northern companies and had only a few tunnels. Trains from London run 80 miles, much further than the whole distance to the Kent and Sussex coasts, before traversing the short Fisherton Tunnel just before Salisbury. This is followed by Buckhorn Weston Tunnel at the hump between Gillingham and Templecombe, a short one at Crewkerne, and just one more on the climb from Seaton Junction towards Honiton, just four tunnels on the 173 miles to Exeter. Beyond, the lines mostly went up and over for there were few tunnels on the Withered Arm, one between Exeter Central and St Davids, one on the drop down to Ilfracombe and three between Tavistock and Plymouth.

The LSWR routes to Bournemouth and Portsmouth in a tunnelling sense were as well as literally somewhere between the West of England line and Sussex coast lines of the LBSC, for they went up and over but could not avoid some tunnelling. On the Bournemouth line there was the short Litchfield Tunnel at the top of the six-mile climb from Worting Junction followed by the two short Popham tunnels before Micheldever, and Wallers Ash Tunnel between there and Winchester. After that just one short tunnel at the approach to Southampton Central, for in Southern Railway terms Bincombe Tunnels on the steep drop through Upwey Wishing Well Halt (delightful name) to Weymouth do not count as they were Great Western, although in today's Network SouthEast reign they are now firmly part of Southern Electric territory. To Portsmouth it was not possible to get out of Guildford towards the south without tunnelling, the first of two tunnels almost at the platform end being through chalk and second through sandstone. From there the line was built on the cheap with a sawtooth profile and largely 1 in 80 grades with the main summit at Haslemere and a second at Buriton but in the latter case needing the short Buriton Tunnel.

Further east along the Sussex coast route, trains leaving Brighton were faced with a short but horrible tunnel at London Road while Kemp Town branch trains ran most of the way to the terminus through the tight and foul Kemp Town tunnel; often enginemen had to lie on the footplate to breathe when working a heavy freight. Hastings, too, was surrounded by tunnels, four in all, Bo-Peep and Hastings tunnels flanking Warrior Square station, Mount Pleasant between Hastings and Ore, and the almost mile long Ore Tunnel on the climb from there on the way out towards Ashford.

Whatever some of its hard up promotors might have done to avoid tunnels, overall tunnel maintenance costs still figure substantially in the Southern Region's budget.

Top left. King Arthur at Templecombe. N15 class 4-6-0 No 789 Sir Guy in Bulleid light green livery leaves Templecombe with an up express in the summer of 1939. Sir Guy is trailing an eight wheeled bogie tender for use on the West of England main line, for the Southern had no water troughs. At that time the engine was stationed at Exmouth Junction shed. It was one of the batch of N15s built by the North British Locomotive Co. (23285/25).

Left. Pacific tank. Ex LB&SCR Class J1 4-6-2 tank No 2325 in olive green livery at Eastleigh in April 1938. Built by Marsh in December 1910 this engine was originally named Abergavenny and stationed at Brighton for use on the principal London expresses. After electrification it moved to Eastbourne performing at the head of the Sunny South Express until the outbreak of World War II. It is seen here with modified cab and boiler fittings to bring it within the SR's composite loading gauge. No 2325 finished its life at Tunbridge Wells and was withdrawn in June 1951.

6
STATIONS GREAT AND SMALL

Ignominious Impotence
Thankfully, not all accidents are destructive and appalling in loss of life; most are disruptive and the all too few amusing. The last two elements were present for an accident on the first Saturday of the summer timetable of 1950.

Porter Sell at Christchurch station had already dealt with the last up Friday night/Saturday morning train and there just remained the 10.30pm from Waterloo to attend to when it called at a few minutes after 2am. A heat-wave was in progress and so the presence of a good quantity of moisture on the up track just after the Hamworthy–Eastleigh goods had gone through at 12.25am puzzled Porter Sell and, as his nostrils detected the aroma of what he though to be creosote, he advised the signalman who, in turn, arranged for the train to be examined when it arrived at Brockenhurst. There, in darkness, nothing untoward was found. But on arrival at Bevois Park (Southampton) it was noticed that a wagon end was heavily splashed with tar, and closer examination disclosed that the wagon in front, a tank car, had its outlet missing as well as its contents. Meanwhile the 3.25am up freight from Bournemouth had gone through Christchurch without incident.

When dawn came it was found that the outlet valve had come off just after the train had crossed the bridge over the river Stour west of Christchurch and, because the internal valve was not properly closed, about 3000 gallons of compound had discharged itself on the climb up through Hinton
continued opposite

Since it was essentially a *passenger* line, the Southern's stations were a vital part of the railway corpus and generally very busy. Commuters in their thousands flowed daily through many of them, mostly men, grey-faced, black-coated, clutching rolled umbrellas and little suitcases containing their thrifty sandwich lunch, and perhaps a detective novel to read after the newspaper had been finished. At the suburban and 'residential' country and seaside stations, kept as tidy as the minds of their season ticket holders, from eight o'clock or earlier, regimented rows stood along the platforms, knowing from long experience exactly where to stand for the carriage of their choice. Reaching the great London termini, the trains disgorged, the crowds surging blindly forward to the ticket barriers in a flood, their feet taking them automatically along the most direct route to Underground or street.

Far less organised, and indeed often in a state of bewilderment or near panic, were the more variously garbed holidaymakers and excursionists of July and August, queueing and waiting eagerly at Victoria and Waterloo. And at London Bridge, each September, the Southern accepted (welcomed is not quite the right word) lively and indisciplined Cockneys making for their working holiday in the Kent hopfields, seeking to wangle as much free travel as possible for their numerous offspring and many belongings.

Crowds were indeed a characteristic feature of many Southern stations, nowhere more so perhaps than at Clapham Junction, with its countless steps, sooty-windowed and wooden-floored gallery and its grim subway, always bustling with people, most of whom were changing trains rather than moving in and out to and from the street. The traffic at this station, which had great variety, was virtually continuous throughout the twenty four hours and although the LSWR and LBSCR shared its platforms, the segregation was very apparent, long after the alleged 'amalgamation' of 1923. The vast spread of platforms, seventeen in all, passed by well over 2,000 trains daily, covered almost twenty eight acres, making it the largest station in Britain in area, an appropriate 'first' for a railway company dominated by passenger business.

Perhaps the most 'typical' Southern stations were those serving the holiday resorts. In memory at least, their platforms seem always bathed in sunshine, and their atmosphere welcoming and relaxing. Brighton, Bexhill Central and West, Bournemouth West, Eastbourne, Bognor, Worthing, Margate . . . all had a certain dignity, all were built for crowds. Summer, spring and autumn, often in winter too, through their large entrance halls and across their spacious concourses, passed a constant procession of holidaymakers, and day excursionists, not to mention lovers, illicit and otherwise.

Sunny south bound. Sunlight and shadow at Victoria Brighton side. Three-cylinder 2-6-0 Class U1 No 1908 heads an Eastbourne train before electrification. The leading vehicle is a South Eastern & Chatham birdcage brake.

continued
Admiral. By Sway the wagon had emptied.

The normal passage of the 3.25am freight probably gave false assurance. The sun rose and quickly its heat caused the compound to act as a lubricant so that the driving wheels could not grip the rails. The first victim was the 5.38am Poole to Southampton passenger train: seven more trains were to suffer before a light engine was sent through to apply sand and the effects wore off. Bulleid's Pacifics were, at the best of times, rather light on their feet, and with this added lubricant the wheels fairly spun round on the incline up from Christchurch. The locomotives' sandboxes were quickly depleted; firemen were throwing ballast and dirt under the driving wheels in an effort to obtain a grip.

The worst-affected service was the 7.20am from Bournemouth West to Waterloo which had to have the engine off the 4.20am down freight from Eastleigh attached to assist it to Brockenhurst. A loss of 41 minutes by this train contributed to a total loss of 155 minutes by the eight trains, discounting disruption to other services. Coming at the start of a summer Saturday, Control was not amused. But some bystanders were hard put to conceal their amusement at Bulleid's powerful creations being reduced to ignominious impotence.

Quieter and more demure were the little seaside and country stations west of Salisbury, known only to the middle class holidaymakers and the local population, many of whom were retired members of the same breed. Reached after what seemed, at least to a child anxious for the beach, interminably long journeys, stations like Sidmouth, Bude, and Mortehoe & Woolacombe, all too often some distance from the town, but well-attended by cheap taxis and helpful staff, were associated with nothing but happy memories and sunny days. To such outposts of the Southern, in North Cornwall, the train carried the young and observant John Betjeman, who wrote in his *First and Last Loves* (1952):

Green Southern Railway engines came right into the brown and cream Great Western district of Cornwall, to reach Padstow, Launceston, Egloskerry, Otterham, Tresmeer, Camelford – and so on down that windy single line. I know the stations by heart, the slate and granite-built waiting rooms, the oil lamps and veronica bushes.

Victoria, Chatham side. A down Kent Coast train leaving the SE&CR station behind Bulleid West Country Pacific No 34033 Chard in the summer of 1949. The engine is in SR green with full British Railways lettering on the tender. On the right is ex SE&CR H class 0-4-4 tank No 1321 with, as yet, no cast numberplate on the smokebox door. A very Southern scene, the 0-4-4 tank being used for empty stock workings in and out of the terminus and in banking departing trains up the 1 in 62 gradient on to Grosvenor bridge.

For the Frocks

Once there were a staggering number of race specials to Royal Ascot, which country station was only a very short walk down a footpath from the course. Quite easily the dressiest of race meetings and the Southern *really* catered for the frocks! Entire special trains of nothing but first class carriages from LSWR and SE&C sidings which had far more room for tails or pretty dresses than the then modern ones, which could not be spared anyway. Non stop to Ascot – a steady procession of special trains from Waterloo. And, to haul them, even Urie's short distance heavy express goods 4-6-2 tanks were pressed into service, the only time they were ever seen on passenger trains. And what passenger trains; and what engines, for, because they did this work once a year, they were painted in passenger green and fully lined out! They always ran forwards except on empty stock, returning from Ascot via Bagshot and round the curve onto the main line between Farnborough and Brookwood. They rode like heavy army tanks but *looked* impressive. Nowadays, without first-class-only trains, the glamorous part of the traffic has disappeared.

How sad he must have been when Beeching wrenched away the 'Withered Arm' and these little stations he loved so much.

Thanks to an inheritance from four smaller companies in varying states of financial health, the Southern acquired stations of great variety and varying quality, from the decrepit and muddled to those offering some architectural elegance as well as convenience for both passenger and operator. Despite John Elliot's gallant efforts to publicise and decorate them with green and white enamel signs and populate them with Sunny South Sams, many of the smaller stations remained decidedly dreary and drab, although a great many on the LBSCR system, and a fair number on the LSWR, were always adequate, pleasing and serviceable, with reasonable, even quite lavish, provision for passengers' comfort. Of those passed on by the SECR, little good could be said, though, as we shall see, there were some exceptions to this generalisation.

Arguably the finest on the Southern and one of the best large stations in the United Kingdom was the rebuilt Waterloo, whose reconstruction, interrupted by World War I, the LSWR only just managed to complete in time to hand over to its successor. It made a fitting flagship for the new Southern, providing a grand, almost Imperial setting for its predominantly upper and middle class clientele, which included senior civil servants, army and navy officers, the denizens of the Surrey and North Hants 'stockbroker belt', and the cream of 'society' on their way to country house parties and other social occasions such as Ascot Week, not to mention statesmen, film stars, authors and other famous people travelling on the Southampton boat trains. Whilst the vast panoply of factory-type ridge-and-furrow roofing of the new train shed might seem dull against the great arched roofs of the great Victorian stations north of the Thames, the sweeping spaciousness of Waterloo's gracefully curving concourse and the elegant range of offices that flanked its north side were impressive, adorned as they were with the great War Memorial steps and entrance at the west end, the cab road arch and many other design features contributed by the LSWR's architect J. Robb Scott. Alas, outside, Scott's work could not be properly appreciated, since the new building was thrust tightly up against the SER viaduct into Charing Cross. This, and Walker's penny-pinching decision to retain the North Station of 1885 with the minimum of alteration considerably reduced the architectural impact of this important building.

For many of its early stations the LSWR enjoyed the services of the notable architect Sir William Tite, who provided classical façades at Nine Elms (1838) and Southampton (1840), the latter still surviving. His severely plain intermediate buildings for the London & Southampton Railway included Micheldever, which can still be studied. Gosport (1841), also by Tite, with its fourteen-bay Tuscan colonnade in Portland stone, fortuitously provided suitable dignity for its later use by Queen Victoria, who preferred the privacy of this route for her journeys to and from Osborne, her summer home on the Isle of Wight. Other notable early stations by Tite still with us include the 1846 Tudor Gothic Barnes, a red brick station house with black lozenges, mullioned windows and tall Tudor chimneys, sole survivor of a series after the widening of the Windsor Lines. In the same style, Tite's Windsor (1851) is also a delight, with its handsome royal waiting room and entrance, its series of doors down the side large enough to pass mounted guardsmen and its little watch tower from which the departure of the royal entourage from the Castle could be glimpsed and warning given to those below. Only the curiously amateurish monograms and date in black bricks seem

Empty stock train. Charing Cross station on 3 April 1954 with Class L 4-4-0 No 31770 about to leave on a train of empty coaches possibly for Cannon Street. This is one of twelve locomotives built by Beyer Peacock & Co. in 1914. The other twelve were built in Germany by A. Borsig & Co, some of the very few German built locomotives ever to run in England.

Double Standard

105. (a) Motor drivers or carters, whilst on duty, must not stop at public houses, coffee houses, or any other premises except on the business of the company;

(b) Employees of the Company are strictly forbidden to consume intoxicating liquor whilst on duty.

Note:- For the purpose of paragraphs (a) and (b) of this Instruction, the expression 'on duty' does not include any interval which a driver, carter, attendant or vanguard may be required by law or authorised by the Company to take for rest and refreshment during his period of duty in connection with a vehicle or its load.

136. Motor drivers and carters must not divulge any information or show delivery sheets to any of the public other than those to whom the goods are consigned.

The addresses of packages on the vehicle must be turned inwards or away from the public gaze.

158. Particulars of any traffic conveyed by other carriers which might be conveyed by the Company, and particulars of any traffic lost or gained, must be reported at once.

Extracts from Southern Railway *Instructions to Motor Drivers, Carters, Vanguards, Shunt Horse Drivers, Stablemen and others concerned in Cartage Operations or with the care of Horses*, 1946.

incongruous, though some might say they add to the period charm. Today's electric trains seem out of place as they slide in and out of a station redolent with royal associations.

As the most important seaside resort on the LSWR, Bournemouth received a suitably impressive station in 1885. Bournemouth East (now Central) was dominated by a 40ft high glass and lattice girder overall roof set between glazed weather screens and supported by massive side walls. Alas the glass has long since gone (a railwayman once told an enquirer that it had been blown out by steam locomotives!) and the somewhat shabby though still awesome mass seems doomed to disappear under a commercial partnership redevelopment scheme. Rather less impressive was the clock-towered rebuilding of Southampton West of 1895, although this was better than what subsequently took its place in BR days.

Good if sometimes uninspired buildings were provided for the main line widenings out of Waterloo at the turn of the century but more satisfying and pleasing are the standardised red-brick tiled-roof stations of the 1885 New Guildford line and the similar ones of the same period on the Ringwood–Christchurch line. Perhaps the best of the small stations of the LSWR late period were the standardised batch for the 1903 Meon Valley line between Alton and Fareham. Very well-finished in the delightful Arts and Crafts style, with gables and mullioned windows, these were laid out in a manner that was to prove over-lavish for the traffic, in tone with the whole line (did the War Office or Admiralty play a secret hand ?). In the 1950s, just before closure, one found them very evocative of the final optimistic flush of railway monopoly.

A curiosity among stations on the LSWR was that provided by the London Necropolis Company alongside Waterloo (rebuilt when the main station was improved), from which special trains carried funeral parties to the Necropolis at Brookwood, where there were also two little stations solely devoted to the last earthly journeys of London's middle and upper class dead. At the inner end there were neat arrangements to ensure the mourners did not see the coffins being loaded.

The LBSCR indisputably provided a high general standard of station construction across its area. That it cared for its passengers was evident in the extensive platform canopies, front entrance canopies or generous gabled porches and covered footbridges at lonely rural stations – and in the cosy little refreshment rooms to be found at such isolated spots as Horsted Keynes. Indeed, in the late 19th century and the Edwardian years, expense seemed no object for this company, even at quite small stations in areas where traffic was likely to be light for many years, if not always. The LBSCR also sought to pamper the upper crust at play, as is shown by the erection in 1881 of a spacious four-platform layout at Singleton on the Midhurst–Chichester line, together with engine turntable, a glass covered way and a beech-bordered carriage drive, all for a few days of Goodwood race traffic each year. At Lingfield, another horse racing centre, around 1890 the company erected a three-platform station, complete with special footbridge and quarter mile-long covered way to the racecourse. Ample horse dock facilities were also installed. Lavishness was also stimulated by other factors, at Christ's Hospital for

Waterloo in the 1930s. Schools class 4-4-0 No 930 Radley *about to leave with a Portsmouth Direct (via Guildford) express in September 1936. Semaphore signals are still much in evidence; note the boarded third rail in the vicinity of the locomotive and the branded carriage set number on the train to the right of the picture.*

South Western country station. Alresford station on the Alton to Winchester line in September 1951. Happily this is still there, being part of the successful Mid-Hants tourist railway which uses mainly ex Southern engines and forms part of the living history of the railway. The station abounds with items of ex LSWR characteristic infrastructure.

Sussex junction. Lewes in 1947 showing a fascinating mixture of steam and electric services in the last year of the Southern Railway. The Marsh Atlantic No 2426 St Alban's Head *is at the front of the Victoria–Newhaven Harbour boat train, the leading coach a typical example of the SECR Continental stock.*

Get Me to the Course on Time

Ascot, Epsom, Lingfield, Kempton Park . . . the Southern was deeply into the sport of kings, not only in handling the race crowds – sometimes augmented by the kings themselves to add to the operating difficulties – but also the runners.

A small winter race meeting at Sandown Park, alongside Esher station, on a Wednesday and Thursday in January 1939, illustrates some of the special arrangements involved. The first race on each day was at 1pm, the last at 3.30.

Esher station had a goods and coal yard on the down side, including a horse loading dock, and three special race platforms on the up side separate from the station proper, of which No 1 was on the up local line. All was controlled by two ex-LSWR signalboxes, West and East, the latter being usually switched out and only opened for race meetings. On these two days East box was opened from 10.45 to 17.45 in order to bring additional fast/slow and up/down crossovers into use and to ease the free acceptance of trains. At this time all running signals were lower quadrant semaphores except for Hampton Court Junction's up colour-light distant signals. A real curiosity was the 'temporary' up starting signal from No 1 race platform; it comprised a permanent slotted post with a lower quadrant semaphore arm usually hidden vertically in the slot, which was only made operative as West box's No 47
continued opposite

Almost the end of an era. Petersfield station on 10 June 1937 just before the full electric service between Waterloo and Portsmouth Harbour was inaugurated two weeks later. Limited electric working for specials and on Saturdays had started at the end of May. The train is the 3.50pm Waterloo–Portsmouth headed by Schools class 4-4-0 No 927 Clifton.

example, by the arrival of the public school from London and planned housing development ('West Horsham') which never in the event even started. These produced in 1902 a substantial villa type station building with decorative brickwork and barge-boarded gables admitting passengers to no less than seven platform faces at the junction of the Mid-Sussex and Guildford lines, a white elephant if ever there was one. It was all razed to the ground in 1972 to be replaced by a 'bus stop' type halt. In return for right of passage through some of the best of Surrey's scenery at Norbury Park in 1867, the LBSCR commissioned the architect Charles H. Driver to design an ornately-gabled station at Box Hill with a small tower reminiscent of a French chateau. Driver also produced charming stations either side, at Leatherhead and Dorking, of which only the first survives. In later years, the LBSCR continued its policy of providing good stations; when the main line was widened in the early 1900s, handsome and substantial neo-Georgian structures appeared at Horley, Earlswood and Three Bridges.

The large seaside towns on LBSCR all finished up with ample and often impressive stations consonant with their importance as traffic generators. Brighton's main glory was its fine overall roof of 1883 by the engineer H. E. Wallis, though this and a new accretion outside sadly obscured David Mocatta's original Palladian elevations of 1841. Eastbourne, rebuilt in the late 1880s, received a spacious building adorned with a corner clock tower and displaying a fine eclectic conceit; one can detect Italianate, gothic and French Renaissance treatments. The rebuilt station at Bognor (1902) was very stylish and impressive but that at Worthing (1911) was unremarkable, if adequate. Bexhill, lavishly reconstructed in 1901 in response to the threat of SER invasion, although also mundane in style, was well capable of handling large crowds in full protection from the worst of seaside weather.

For all that, even the LBSCR was not perfect. Its London Bridge terminus possessed a pleasing overall roof with a central crescent-trussed section but little else by way of charm or convenience. Victoria, as originally built, had no proper frontage apart from J. T. Knowle's heavy and oppressive 1861 Grosvenor Hotel at its north west corner. Inside, it

became increasingly congested and inadequate until 1901–8 when it was rebuilt to the plans of the company's engineer, Sir Charles Morgan. This not altogether successful exercise was achieved by extending the site lengthwise towards the Thames and adding a much more impressive frontage in the form of an extension of the hotel. At the same time an ornamental screen wall penetrated by a new royal entrance and cab arch was erected along Buckingham Palace Road, a thoroughfare which, with the LCDR station on the other side, had prevented a more passenger-friendly lateral expansion. Discreditable LBSC stations included wooden Shoreham by Sea, and Littlehampton and Chichester, the two last having to await the BR era for their much-needed rebuilding.

The SER had some pleasing stations, including the early ones by Samuel Beazley at Canterbury, Gravesend, Erith and New Cross. William Tress designed a delightful Italianate building for the 1846 station at Tunbridge Wells, which has been handsomely refurbished for the recent Hastings line electrification and this was followed in 1851–2 by a series of Italianate and Gothic buildings by the same architect between Tunbridge Wells and Hastings of which the delightful Battle is the crowning glory. Nor should we overlook the pretty *cottages ornés* on the Reading, Guildford & Reigate Railway, though the best of these, at Dorking, was insensitively demolished in 1969. There were also one or two good later ones of merit, like the quietly dignified Domestic Revival style Nutfield (1883) which has now gone, the similar Sandling (1888) and the well-mannered and restrained High Brooms of 1893. But these were exceptions. There were some very dull single-storied brick stations such as Orpington and, worse still, numerous slate covered, hip-roofed clapboard sheds with sash windows, erected from the 1840s onwards, which, with smelly lavatories and creeping dry and wet rot, were allowed to live on through SR and BR days. Many, alas, are still with us. Curiously this almost standardised form was continued when the company was also erecting much more creditable stations, the last being an enlarged version, with gable, built for race traffic at the terminus of the new Tattenham Corner branch in 1901; no attempt was made to rebuild when a new suburb developed around it in the 1930s.

The SER's London Bridge station was something of a muddle and boringly drab, no credit to the City of London which supplied most of its traffic. John Hawkshaw's transpontine termini at Cannon Street and Charing Cross were rather better, if a little cramped, fronted as they were by E. M. Barry's elegant hotels and roofed by arched trusses springing from high side walls. When the roof at Charing Cross collapsed in June 1905, with some loss of life, it was replaced by the more mundane ridge-and-furrow covering with decorated end girder still to be seen today. As for Cannon Street, it is now but a poor thing, left with only its side walls and Baroque water towers, all the rest having suffered wartime damage and unsympathetic rebuilding to provide office warrens in the late 1950s and early 1960s. Without the roof it was their purpose to support, the lonely walls hardly merit listed status which prevents BR from redeveloping its highly valuable property.

The LCDR's original stations tended to be plain and cramped, displaying mean canopies and narrow platforms; typically their brick-

continued
lever from 15.30 until the last departure on race days, after which it was 'put to bed' again.

Three other special steps were authorised to assist in handling the traffic. A block was put on coal and 'rough' freight traffic for Esher until the Thursday evening to keep the yard fairly clear for horseboxes. Down trains were permitted to approach the platform starting signals at danger with no more than 100yd clearance beyond instead of the usual 440yd; handsignalmen with red flags and detonators were employed to reinforce the message. Then, in readiness for the punters' return to Waterloo, the inspector in charge was empowered (though it does not appear to have been done on this occasion) to close the up local line from Walton to Esher and use it for berthing empty trains.

Horses started to arrive on the afternoon prior to the meeting, with trains from Clapham Junction (collecting from Newmarket and northern stables) and from Lambourn and Newbury via Reading and Chertsey. Clearly some trainers insisted that their horses rested overnight before their exertions. These trains were unloaded respectively at the down side horse dock and No 3 race platform, and stabled for cleaning. During Wednesday four more trains of horses arrived from Clapham Junction, Guildford and the GWR, and the place must have been looking fairly full. By the Thursday, however, the traffic had become two-way; trains for the GWR and Clapham Junction went off in the morning, to be replaced by incoming Clapham and Guildford trains. The last animals were got away to Clapham and Newbury and Lambourn on the Friday morning, and peace descended once more.

On the passenger side, the two race days saw specials from Waterloo and special stop orders at Esher for passengers on early

continued overleaf

continued

trains from Exeter and Weymouth. (Curiously, no provision
was made for West Country passengers to get home; it was a case
of getting to Waterloo or by local
train to Woking and catching a
train from there.) Only one of the
Waterloo–Esher specials was an
electric working, stabling at
Woking before the return service,
but after the racing it was supplemented by two more electric
trains using spare stock before
taking up peak hour services.
There were also two steam-hauled
specials, shown in the working
notice as for 'Members and 1st
Class'. The empty stock, probably
kept specially for such events,
came up from Barnes. Having
unloaded at Esher and cleared the
empty stock right across the main
lines into the race platforms, the
engines went off, coupled, to turn
on the Weybridge/Byfleet triangle, returning to stand on their
trains and keep them warm ready
for departure at 3.48 and 4.0pm.
Not very productive work for the
train crews – 28 miles of passenger
working and 22 miles light engine
in a shift!

The working notice severely
commanded that 'No unauthorised person must be allowed to
travel in the driving cabs or
guards' vans of electric trains, the
doors of which must be locked
and windows closed', as were the
doors of first class compartments
on the platform side. 'It is important that the return special trains
from Esher to Waterloo . . .
should start punctually. They
must not leave Esher before their
booked times' for these were vocal
clients who would not hesitate to
bemoan the inadequacies of the
Southern Railway after a hard day
of also-rans.

The following two days were
Windsor Races.

work was parti-coloured and pierced by arch-topped windows. Some of the larger ones such as Canterbury, Sittingbourne and Dover Harbour boasted overall pitched roofs of iron. For sheer boldness of siting without regard to environmental effect the candle was taken by the 1863 Ramsgate Harbour; convenient if intrusive, its arch-roofed bulk lay alongside the beach, over which the smoke of the locomotives drifted; more smoke billowed from the mouth of the tunnel which penetrated the chalk cliffs just beyond the end of the platforms. Another noteworthy LCDR asset of more dubious commercial value was Edward Barry's 1865 station at Crystal Palace, which lay alongside and below the glistening bulk of its dominating namesake. At each end of a building totally enclosed by roof and high walls were capacious exits and stair-cases, and a cavernous pedestrian approach leading under the road into the Palace. Most of the time the station's empty halls echoed only to the scuttling of rats beneath its dusty wooden boards but occasionally crowds came, crowds with which it was well able to cope, since they were only very rarely as large as those foreseen by its designers. The LBSCR had a rival and less ambitious establishment a little down the hill. Not so spacious, and opened in 1854, this possessed a French Renaissance frontage, large dark staircases and a windy train shed enclosed by high walls. Frightened by the Charing Cross collapse, the LBSCR removed all of its overall roof except the brick built portion at the Palace end.

In line with the rest of the LCDR stations, the metropolitan termini were unremarkable, or worse. St Paul's (later Blackfriars), Ludgate Hill and Holborn Viaduct, close together, small and mean, jointly just managed to distribute the company's City commuter and long-distance traffic. St Paul's enlivened its dreary frontage by announcing in letters incised into its quoin stones that it was a departure point for Petersburg (later Leningrad), Vienna, Dresden, Cannes and Florence, amongst other foreign delights, as well as for the more prosaic Bromley and Westgate on Sea. At Victoria, Sir John Fowler's fine 1862 roof of two tied lattice-arch spans was fronted by nothing better than a sagging single-storey wooden shack which resembled a whisky saloon thrown up in a day in the Yukon goldfield. The main entrance building, a decent but plain structure, was hidden away in a side turning off Wilton Road. This disgrace was remedied in 1908 when Alfred William Blomfield, the SECR's new architectural assistant (appointed at age 26 in 1905), provided flamboyant French Second Empire style elevations across the end of the train shed and along Wilton Road. It was a matter of keeping up with the Jones's, though not following their architectural style, since the LBSCR next door had just completed their new frontage in Edwardian Baroque. Blomfield's work was embellished with sculpture by Henry C. Fehr and the main (north) elevation was pierced by a graceful cab road arch which became the scene of many sad and all too frequently final farewells as soldiers left for the hell of northern France in 1914–18.

Blomfield was also responsible for several buildings which the SECR's Joint Managing Committee somehow managed to finance after its formation in 1899. For the new station of Eltham Park on the Bexley Heath Railway in 1908 he designed a pretty entrance pavilion in pebble dash, red bricks, and red tiles. This station was partly financed by

Cameron Corbett, who was at the time filling up the surrounding area with substantial houses, mostly to be taken by lower middle class commuters. Blomfield's hand is also seen in the four major rebuildings achieved under the SECR regime: the Queen Anne domestic style Rochester Bridge (1908), the clock-towered and ebullient Tunbridge Wells Down Side (1911), Whitstable & Tankerton (1913) and the majestically Imperial glass-roofed Dover Marine (now Western Docks), completed just in time to play a major part in World War I troop and supply movements across the Channel.

On the SER system in 1902, the SECR made a competitive lunge at Bexhill. Although the rebuilt station at Crowhurst was workmanlike and lavishly spacious, its plain appearance suggested the design originated in the engineer's office. Sidley, the intermediate station on the new line, and the terminus at Bexhill were quite different; in red brick and terracotta, their exuberant Edwardian baroque exemplified the blind optimism of the management. Bexhill, with its four platform layout and vast tracts of unused or under-used land, was never completed as intended, since two platforms and run round roads sufficed for the traffic it attracted. In 1897–1900 the SER and SECR also completed pleasingly-gabled outer suburban stations at Chipstead, Kingswood, and Tadworth on the new Tattenham Corner Branch, substantial structures well calculated to satisfy the egos of the affluent middle class families who began to settle in this pretty valley around the time the railway came.

In its short lifespan of twenty five years the SR erected forty seven new stations and thirty one new halts. Some thirty five stations were also completely rebuilt, the opportunity being taken to improve signalling and rationalise layouts. In this new construction much use was made of prefabricated concrete units for lighting posts, platform edging and posts and panels, fencing and nameboards and some halts consisted of little else. Major rebuildings were often associated with the operational needs of electrification and the greatly increased train services and new traffic it was expected to attract. Many of the new stations were in the constantly expanding electrified area, where, between the wars, housebuilding for

Station in concrete. Very much Southern Railway 1930s 'Odeon' type architecture – the new station at Malden Manor.

91

Approach to Ramsgate. A photograph taken in 1958 showing Ramsgate shed and station. The shed is on the left of the photograph with a BR Standard Class 5 4-6-0 standing outside, an ex SE&CR D class 4-4-0 as washout engine on the left of a U class 2-6-0 (just in front of the water tower) and various unidentifiable ex SE&CR 0-6-0s of ancient vintage. The train entering the station has an LMS Ivatt 2-6-2 tank; leaving on the right is L class 4-4-0 No 31780.

Coaling
The Church wanted coal for the office fire. 'The Church' was a thin, lugubrious-looking elderly clerk in the goods office at Portsmouth Town station, almost under the High Level lines to the Harbour. He always wore his hat, in and out of doors. If the office had run out of its allowance of coal, The Church would take the scuttle and stand below the point where, sooner or later, a gleaming Schools class 4-4-0 would come to a stand with a twelve coach restaurant car train for London. He would call up to the enginemen and start abusing them for the smell, the smoke, the noise, their personal appearance – anything that came to mind. At first astonished, they would reply in kind and then, goaded beyond endurance would throw lumps of coal down at him in fury. When he had enough – it only took two or three throws, he produced his scuttle, thanked them and gathered up the coal as the express, under barely a breath of steam (the 1 in 60 down from the High level was enough to accelerate the train to the 30mph limit through Fratton) slipped off on its non-stop run to Waterloo: 'Waterloo – Portsmouth – Isle of Wight'.

the middle classes was proceeding apace (no less than thirty three of the new station sites were in and around London, many of them partly financed by estate developers).

There appears to have been no central or indeed any rational policy as to station design. An architectural contribution was invariably deemed essential for the larger and more important buildings and from the late 1920s some architectural treatment began to be applied to some smaller stations. The responsibility for this lay with J. Robb Scott, who had moved to the SR from the LSWR as company architect. He had of course to work closely with the chief engineers, A. W. Szlumper till August 1927, then George Ellson, who were responsible for the overall layout and all other design to meet the operational requirement. This was a situation capable of generating conflict, in which the engineer, as the more senior officer, would have had the final say and against whose decisions there was no appeal since unlike the Underground, with its Frank Pick, the Southern had no industrial and architectural design enthusiast at the top. Three broad styles for Scott's Southern work can be identified: the restrained neo-Georgian of the 1920s and early 1930s; the plain brick or stone frontages (sometimes with modest art deco touches) of the same period; and the unsure attempts of the 1930s to apply the international modern style to railway structures. Charles Holden and other architects for the Underground were in general far more successful with the contemporary style since they were allowed free reign everywhere, detailing right down to the clocks, a policy which produced fully integrated designs; in contrast the Southern had no firm overall design direction.

Scott provided what might be regarded as an intermediate 'modern' design for the rebuilt Wimbledon in 1929, a plain façade of Portland stone blocks carrying the railway's name in bold letters above an art deco metal grille and wide entrances which led into his capacious and airy ticket hall. More revolutionary was Wimbledon Chase, opened in the same year on the new Wimbledon to Sutton electric line. This was given a low, curving flat-roofed street frontage of white glazed blocks which carried the words SOUTHERN RAILWAY in large letters above a canopied and generously wide entrance. The smooth flowing simplicity of the lines owed much to contemporary cinema architecture but the effect was totally spoiled by an ugly lift tower and the engineer's workmanlike but incongruous platform canopy on the embankment above. It may well have been intended as a pattern for the other stations on this line but in practice what was built showed little or no evidence of an architect's hand; someone had screwed down the budget. However the stations for the new Chessington branch (1938–9) were clearly developed from the Wimbledon Chase prototype and also featured attractive platform work with their cantilevered 'Chisarc' concrete canopies lit by an early version of fluorescent tubes. The latter were a stunning innovation for Southern passengers, who were often obliged to wait for electric trains in gas or even oil lamp lighting. The best of this group, the nearest the SR came to an integrated design, were the two Chessington stations, since the street level buildings at least were completed in brick, which maintained its appearance over the years far better than the concrete and cement used at Tolworth and Malden Manor and on the platforms at all four stations. Larger buildings were also attempted in the new uncluttered style, notably the rebuilt Richmond (1937), a steel-framed, Portland stone structure of three storey height, and the rather more flashy reinforced concrete Surbiton (1938) with its flat-topped square-section clock tower and lofty booking hall block with finned windows looking for all the world like a contemporary cinema until one read the inscription above. Again the engineer had his way on the platforms, although here the architect seems to have designed the footbridge. Unfortunately the impact of this, perhaps the best of all Scott's international modern stations, has in BR days been reduced by the erection of an unsympathetic and taller office slab at right angles to its frontage. Bricks and Portland stone were used for other intermediate or international modern style work in station rebuildings including Haywards Heath (1932), Falconwood (1936), Seaton (1936), Horsham (1938), Havant (1938), and Bishopstone (1938) although all these designs, except perhaps the last, showed little inspiration.

Scott seems to have been happiest with neo-Georgian classicism, as he shows in the heavy massing of his spacious brick and stone Ramsgate and Margate of 1926, his elegant little Bromley North of the same year, his brick-built Hastings of 1931 with its low pitched-roof wings each side of a huge flat-topped entrance hall, and above all in the confident and handsome two-storey pitched roof Exeter Central of 1933. All these have his graceful large round-arched windows and doorways. All possess innate dignity, if showing little originality. Exeter, which replaced shoddy wooden buildings of 1860, was a fine addition.

So it was still a hotchpotch that was passed on to British Railways. But if many lacked grandeur or even architectural merit, and some were inconvenient for passengers, most were as well maintained as they were well used, reflecting the more prosperous and civilised parts of England that they served, country stations often being graced with floral displays and topiary, luggage barrows neatly lined up, litter notable for its absence, disinfectant regularly used on the booking hall floor. When in 1950 Sir John Elliot was moved from the Southern to head the London Midland, he could scarcely believe the neglect and decay from which many of its stations, even serving London commuters, suffered. Paucity of ideas and resources may have affected the Southern as its predecessors; it could never have been accused of neglect, and certainly passengers were not turned away by the disintegration and grime that characterised many stations north of the Thames.

Station change. Devonport Kings Road was originally built as a terminus for trains on the LSWR route from Waterloo, which arrived in Plymouth over the mixed gauge Great Western Tavistock and Launceston branch, entering the city from the east. In 1890 the independent Plymouth, Devonport, & South Western Junction Railway opened a new route from Lydford via Bere Alston to the Tamar Valley approaching Devonport from the north west which meant that the original end wall had to be opened up to allow the new tracks into what then became a through station, with LSWR trains continuing to North Road and later a new terminus at Plymouth Friary.

Signalling and Safety

Whatever else might have been lacking in the Southern's constituents it was not in the field of signalling. All three had been in the forefront of signalling developments.

From the earliest times the South Eastern had been among the pioneers in the introduction of the block telegraph so that by the 1850s the block system was in operation throughout between London and Dover, nearly 40 years before it became a legal requirement for passenger lines. And in the 1870s a famous employee of the London, Chatham & Dover, W. R. Sykes, had invented the lock-and-block system: train wheels activated treadles on the line, which switched on electric circuits to locks in signalboxes connected to block instruments and levers. Trains could be proved to have passed through a section and the signals placed to danger behind them before another train could be accepted. It was a system adopted widely on London suburban lines of all the Southern's constituents and in some instances extended down the main lines as well – to Balcombe on the LBSC, and to Southampton on the LSWR.

In the first few years of the present century the LSWR had tried out power operation, using the low pressure pneumatic system which within a few years, with track circuits, brought automatic semaphore signalling between Woking and Basingstoke. At Victoria, just as World War I came to an end, the SE&C completed resignalling with track circuits, power operation and a complete installation of American built three-position upper quadrant semaphore signals, the only large installation of its type in Britain. The arm was horizontal for danger and showing a red light at night, inclined up at 45deg for caution, showing a yellow light at night, and vertical for clear showing a green light at night. It was controversial, as was the use of a yellow light for caution, since the normal caution colour on distant signals at the time was still red. Drivers were expected to know the line sufficiently well to distinguish between stop signals and distant signals, both displaying a red light in the danger and caution position respectively. (All the southern lines helped their drivers by adding an illuminated white > alongside the red light of distant signals, known as the Coligny Welch distant signal indicator.)

A signal engineers' committee was set up to examine the future of what was called 'three-position signalling'. It reported in 1924, the year after the Southern came into existence and when planning was well under way for more electrification. The closer headways envisaged were clearly going to require something more flexible than semaphore signalling and Sykes lock-and-block. The committee's members happily included W. J. Thorrowgood, who had been the LSWR's signal and telegraph engineer and who was now the Southern's signal engineer. So it was no surprise that the report found no future for three-position semaphores but recommended the adoption of colour-light signals, not merely three-aspect where every signal could act as the distant for the next signal ahead, but a possible fourth, double yellow, meaning 'attention, run at medium speed.'

The report laid the foundations for British signalling development from then on, and with detail changes in meanings – the double yellow now implies 'preliminary caution, be prepared to pass the next signal at caution' – survives not merely today but seems likely to survive so long as there is a need for lineside signals.

Thorrowgood and his signalling staff, with the backing of general manager Walker lost no time in pressing on with the new colour-light signals, including the fourth aspect, as part of the resignalling allied to suburban electrification on former SE&C lines, (redesignated the Eastern Section) starting with the line from Holborn Viaduct to Elephant & Castle, followed by Charing Cross, Cannon Street and London Bridge. Many of the signals on multi-track sections were carried on overhead gantries with cluster-style signal heads having the four lights arranged at 90deg round a circular head with the two yellow lights at top and bottom, the red light to the

All three of the Southern's main constituents were in the forefront of signalling developments. At the end of World War I the SECR installed three-position upper quadrant semaphore signals at Victoria, seen here at the platform end as Class L 4-4-0 No 1761 arrives with a train from Dover in 1938 just before the SR resignalled with colour-lights.

left and the green light to the right, contrasting with the more normal vertical arrangement. At junction signals each route had its own signal head just like the separate semaphore arms of mechanical signals, for the white light route indicator of today did not appear until the LNER adopted it in the 1930s. Three-aspect signals were of the usual vertical pattern with the red lens at the bottom and green at the top; the four aspect signals at that time had the second yellow light at the bottom, below the red, but in more recent years on BR the second yellow has been at the top to leave the bottom light free from any possible obstruction such as snow building up on top of the hood of the bottom light.

The Brighton main-line electrification of 1932 involved resignalling from Coulsdon to Brighton via the Quarry route, avoiding Redhill, with full track circuiting and colour-light signals. Control was mostly through existing signalboxes which could be switched out when not required to work points, and the signals left to work automatically. Gradually new signals and in some cases new all-electric signalboxes were extended to other suburban and main lines although not in continuous sections, and some areas, (Croydon for example) had to wait until after World War II for new signalling, and others (Redhill for one) until the 1980s for colour-lights and power operation. In Redhill's case it was a full half century after the parallel tracks on the Quarry line had been resignalled in the 1930s. Moreover they were resignalled a second time as part of the Three Bridges 1980s scheme.

Although the Southern adapted some of the existing signalboxes for operating the new colour-light signals from the old mechanical levers through electric contacts, the new signalboxes were given miniature lever frames, originally with mechanical interlocking between levers and electric lever locks from track circuits. Behind the levers were signal repeaters showing the indication displayed by the signal and whether points were standing normal or reverse. As in mechanical practice, one lever performed one function. Miniature lever frames remained the Southern standard for power signalling until the development of one-control-switch panels in the late 1950s and the entrance-exit push-button panels which followed soon after; a few miniature lever frames survive today on the Southern and one at least from SR parts on a preserved railway at Churston on the Torbay & Dartmouth Railway.

With its intensive services the Southern pinned its faith in multiple-aspect colour-light signals just as its predecessors had done with Sykes lock-and-block working. Yet the Southern had its share of tragedies when signalmen managed to defeat the security of the Sykes system, and drivers somehow ran past colour-light signals at red. Although the Great Western had developed its automatic train control which gave audible warnings to the driver of signals at caution, the Southern felt that the widespread adoption of colour-light signals brought far better value for the limited money it could spend and that add-on audible warnings were not required or indeed desirable. The view of course

The SECR introduced power operation on the approach lines to Charing Cross. At St John's, between New Cross and Lewisham, 'B' cabin, controlling the junction from the main line towards Lewisham, had power operated semaphore signals and mechanically controlled points. It had Sykes lock and block equipment and rotary train describers.

Soon after the turn of the century the LSWR introduced power worked semaphore signals at Grateley, using the low pressure pneumatic system, and developed it into automatic signalling between Woking and Basingstoke. These are pneumatically worked signals at Basingstoke.

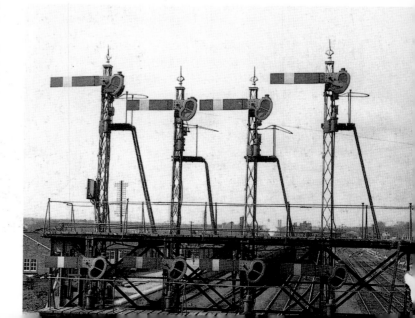

survived well into BR days when the automatic warning system was being installed elsewhere. The Southern's main worry, apart from initial technical problems in overcoming stray traction current effects on aws magnets, was that with trains often approaching London termini on a succession of double or single yellow aspects, aws caution warnings to be cancelled every time would become repetitive leading to unconscious cancellation at a vital red signal with dangerous results. In practice there have been major Southern accidents both with colour-lights and no aws, and – in recent years – with aws.

Two of the worst accidents on the former SE&C main line, though, had nothing to do with signalling and arose through track defects. The first was near Sevenoaks on 24 August 1927 when a River class 2-6-4T developed a roll at speed and eventually derailed approaching Sevenoaks station. An overbridge was caught by the train which piled up and 13 passengers were killed. Although the design of the locomotives was under suspicion, on trials on the Great Northern line of the LNER riding was good and seemingly the engines were sensitive to South Eastern track. Still, they were rebuilt as 2-6-0 tender engines. Although history did not repeat itself 40 years later nevertheless South Eastern Division track caused the worst derailment ever on Southern lines when a broken rail derailed a Hastings line diesel multiple-unit which overturned at speed approaching Hither Green on 5 November 1967, killing 49 passengers. Again the trains were said to be rough riders but as before trials down the former GN line with another Hastings dmu showed riding to be acceptable suggesting that once again SR track with its by then almost total domination by multiple-units with heavy unsprung weights on the motor bogies, needed a higher standard of upkeep.

But inevitably the operating accidents on the Southern reflected that whatever protection was afforded by the Sykes lock-and-block system – which with the Southern's very intensive traffic had given a high standard of protection – it was capable of being over-ridden by a release key kept for emergency use. Thus signalmen thought that a locked signal had failed when actually it was telling them that a train was present which they had overlooked, usually in fog. Three major disasters were caused when signalmen released the Sykes locking to accept or signal forward a second train: at Battersea Park, in 1937 when nine passengers were killed (but not, remarkably, the driver of the colliding train who was this author's great uncle); at South Croydon, on 24 October 1947 (the last major accident in Southern Railway days when 31 passengers and a driver were killed as an up Tattenham Corner train ran into the back of an up Haywards Heath – London Bridge train) and at Barnes Junction, on 2 December 1955 when an electric train, formed of old LSWR converted wooden bodied coaches, hit the back of a goods train and burst into flames, killing 11 passengers and two staff. There were others from the same cause, fortunately by no means as serious in terms of casualties.

The Southern Railway, and more recently the Southern Region, had pressed on with the installation of colour-light signals and full track circuiting, with a philosophy that said colour-light signals were easier for drivers to see and interpret. As the BR automatic warning system was extended round other regions, the Southern Region still resisted. The one thing that the Sykes system did not do was give protection from drivers' errors. Yet the need for some aid was all too clear certainly in BR days as SR signalling practices became widespread. In the early 1970s there was a trial of signal repeating aws which identified each aspect, but it was expensive and not pursued. There were of course the occasional over-runs of semaphore signals as well but certainly in the three decades of the 1950s, 1960s and 1970s accidents from signals passed at danger on the Southern and with Southern style signalling seemed to form a high proportion of all accidents, many more than during the Southern Railways days. Undoubtedly the worst was at St John's, Lewisham, on 4 December 1957, when in fog a steam-hauled down Ramsgate train missed caution and danger colour-lights and rammed the back of a standing electric train, bringing down a heavy girder rail overbridge on to the wreckage and killing 89 passengers, the highest casualty list ever in a Southern accident. Waterloo, London Bridge, Borough Market Junction, and Cannon Street all saw collisions, in some, more than one, and Waterloo with its awkward curving approach was the scene of several collisions mainly through drivers mis-reading signals across the layout.

Brake failure or mismanagement was the root cause of a number of accidents involving Southern electric stock. At Guildford in November 1952 a train approaching the station simply had no air to operate the brakes as a compressor fuse had blown, and it hit a light engine. This accident showed the need to prove the braking system was operative before power could be applied. But less than a year later an electric train with the brakes fully working ploughed into the stationmaster's office at the end of a bay platform at Guildford; the driver mismanaged the brake. Much the same thing happened at Sheerness in 1971 when a train went through the buffers and over the concourse.

Perhaps as a last defiant fling against old Southern methods there were two collisions on the Brighton line, one near Patcham in 1978 when a train passed a signal which should have been at red but which was showing no light – the old Southern signalling circuits here dating from the early 1930s did not prove the red light to be working as would be done today – and at East Croydon in 1982 with a straightforward run by, but without track aws.

During the late 1970s and into the 1980s the Brighton line was resignalled again, with just three signalboxes, at London Bridge, Clapham Junction and Three Bridges taking over the whole line. It had all the modern features including aws, and reversible working over parts of the double track section south of Balcombe. On 31 May 1985 a Gatwick express push-pull train of air conditioned coaches proved that possibly the old Southern thinking was right, for its driver, running under a succession of caution aspects from Clapham Junction cancelling the aws warning at each signal, pressed the button to stop the warning for the red signal approaching Battersea Park, failed to look at the signal and hit the back of an Oxted line diesel just opposite the site of the 1937 collision. Later in 1985 there was another collision at Copyhold Junction a mile or so north of Haywards Heath when the last late night services in each direction booked to run in the 'wrong' direction over the double line sections met head-on as the up train was about to cross to the down line. The down train could not stop before over-running the protecting signal at danger because leaf fall had made the rails greasy. What would Sir Herbert Walker have done about that?

Mechanical lever frame at Portsmouth & Southsea signalbox controlling the terminal platforms and the through high level tracks to the Harbour. The short handled levers control power worked signals and points. Unusually the signalman is not using a cloth to hold the lever. This box was replaced in the late 1960s by a new power signalling centre at Portsmouth.

Major Train Accidents on SR and BR (SR)

Date	Place	Type	Cause	Killed	Notes
24 Aug 1927	Sevenoaks	Derailment	Locomotive unstable on indifferent track	13	a
25 May 1933	Raynes Park	Derailment & collision	Locomotive unable to ride over unfinished lifting of track by PW staff. Derailed train hit by another on adjoining track	5	a
2 Apl 1937	Battersea Park	Collision	Sykes lock & block irregularly released	10	b
27 Jun 1937	Swanley	Buffer stop collision	Train ran into siding	4	
24 Oct 1947	South Croydon	Collision	Sykes lock & block irregularly released	32	b
5 Aug 1951	Ford Junction	Collision	Signal passed at danger	9	c
8 Nov 1952	Guildford	Collision	Brake failure – no air	2	e
18 Sep 1953	Guildford	Bufferstop collision	EP brake mishandled	2	e
2 Dec 1955	Barnes	Collision & fire	Sykes lock & block irregularly released	13	b
4 Dec 1957	St John's Lewisham	Collision & bridge collapse	Colour-light signal passed at danger	90	d
25 Aug 1958	Eastbourne	Collision	Signal passed at danger	5	c
5 Nov 1967	Hither Green	Derailment	Broken rail	49	a
4 Jan 1969	Marden	Collision	Colour-light signal passed at danger	3	d
11 Jun 1972	Eltham Well Hall	Derailment	Driver failed to slow for severe speed restriction	6	f
19 Dec 1978	Hassocks	Collision	Colour-light signal passed showing no light	3	d

Possible prevention for the future

a   Southern track maintenance was criticised on several occasions, particularly after the Sevenoaks derailment in which the train had been rolling badly before the accident, but the formation may have been weakened by long rainy spells. At Raynes Park permanent way men had been lifting and packing and had not finished the work, which was not properly protected, when the train approached. It was suggested that the 0-4-4T locomotive type involved was more susceptible to track irregularities. At Hither Green, maintenance standards were again criticised.

b   The Sykes lock & block system provided added safety for the block telegraph and gave signalmen the automation to prevent them from making mistakes. Its loophole was the release key which could unlock the system intended for genuine failures and to be used only under laid down procedures. These and other accidents on the SR were caused when signalmen thought that the system had failed and jumped to the conclusion that the line was clear when it was in fact occupied by a forgotten train.

c   Semaphore signals passed at danger. The automatic warning system as installed at BR today would not provide protection in these instances since aws is not installed at purely stop signals. Only full cab automation would provide protection.

d   AWS would probably have prevented these accidents, but the Southern Region of BR set its face against aws until recent years, on the grounds (still much discussed) that many trains habitually ran under double or even single yellow lights, necessitating the driver cancelling any aws protection which would be done so repeatedly as to become automatic. At Hassocks the colour-light signals were of the old Southern Railway system which did not include proving of the red aspect as being alight when it should be. The bulb had failed, and even though the previous signal was at caution the train failed to stop at the unlit signal in the dark.

e   The first Guildford accident showed the need to prove the brake system was operative before a train could move, a now standard feature. The second Guildford accident demonstrated the need for better training in driver's braking methods and one which needs to be highlighted since brake mishandling is still a cause of bufferstop collisions at terminal stations, or signal over-runs.

f   AWS and precise marking of speed limits. Even though BR has introduced better marking of speed limits, with aws, the guidelines mean that there are inconsistencies. Eltham Well Hall did not qualify even after the accident and signal restrictions were applied instead.

Victoria Central signalbox. A typical Southern Railway power box of the late 1930s with all electric miniature lever frame, signal and point repeater lights behind the frame, the track circuit diagram above, and the magazine train describers on top of the frame seen on each side of the signalman.

The Southern had a variety of signal structures including lattice masts as seen here at Lewes.

Signal variety on the Southern. Left, a wooden post lower quadrant LBSCR bracket signal at Midhurst; centre, even for signals the SR was adept at making do by constructing signal posts from old rails as in this upper quadrant distant at Southwater; right, Southern Railway four-aspect colour-light junction signal with three routes diverging to the left. The white light route indicators only display three lights as against the five lights standard on BR signals today.

7
COACHES:
OLD, REBUILT AND NEW

Here is a story of economy, of rebuilding and generally making do and mending, inevitably with a lot of detail and few clear trends apart from a universal desire to serve the public as efficiently as possible with the minimum of capital expenditure. The lack of clear policy was inevitably contributed to by the fact that the three officers primarily responsible for rolling stock each came from a different pre-grouping constituent: R. E. L. Maunsell the chief from the SE&C; Surrey Warner, his assistant mechanical engineer for carriages and wagons, from the LSWR; and A. H. Panter, the latter's deputy, from the LBSC. No one of the three companies had set a major lead over the other. Indeed, if you were to ask what had happened toward the introduction of modern corridor coaches, the answer would be not a lot.

Certainly the LSWR had introduced corridor trains during the decade leading to World War I, but the others had nothing but oddments including Pullmans and a few SE&CR multi-class corridor brake composites for through workings to other companies and a handful of corridors of the 1920s for a boat train set. Thus even the best expresses were almost entirely non-corridor. On the SE&CR this meant journeys of two hours or more, particularly on the leisurely Reading–Redhill–Tonbridge cross-country service. Not that that meant an inevitable lack of a lavatory. All three of the constituents had made extensive use of what was delightfully known as a non-corridor lavatory carriage – a non-gangwayed coach equipped with between-compartment toilets, or in some cases with internal corridors linking two or more compartments with the toilet. The problem for passengers, especially those joining at intermediate stations with short stopping times, was to identify which compartments gave access to a lavatory. There was no indication on the outside. The scene at New Cross or Clapham Junction, with parents herding large families bound for the coast into the appropriate door, especially of trains being divided en route for different destinations, just has to be left to the imagination.

The Southern of course also inherited large quantities of plain non-corridor non-lavatory stock, mainly for suburban use but in fact appearing widely on the Kent and Sussex coastal services. And by no means all were bogie coaches, for the SECR and LBSCR had been building four- and six-wheel coaches in quantity until the early years of the new century, mostly for specific suburban services and often in long rakes of block trains, that is fairly fixed formation permanently-coupled sets. They, too, were often appropriated at holiday times for extras or excursions to the coast, or for hop-pickers' specials. The Southern not merely inherited many of them but in a different guise passed them on to BR a quarter of a century later.

Last Slip Coaches

With the end of April the last survivors of the once numerous slip coach services of the Southern Railway and its constituent companies were withdrawn. They were the Horley slip (running through to Forest Row) on the 5.5pm express from London Bridge to Eastbourne, and the Hayward's Heath slip (slow portion for Brighton) on the 5.8pm from London Bridge to Worthing and Angmering; also, on Saturdays only, the Three Bridges slip of the 5.20pm from Victoria to Eastbourne. In each case a stop has replaced the slip, and in order that the Horley stop of the 5.5pm shall not delay the 5.8pm from London Bridge, the two trains have been transposed, the Angmering express now leaving at 5.4pm and the Eastbourne train at 5.8pm. The overall journey times of the two first-mentioned trains have been increased by 4 min. Up to the war 21 slips were detached daily on the Brighton line and eight on the South Eastern and Chatham, all of which have now been abandoned.
– *Railway Magazine*, June 1932.

The Southern's carriage inheritance, 1. The Southern took over an immense variety of stock in 1923, most of it non corridor, with and without lavatories. As such it lasted the SR for its entire existence to an extent that it did not build any new non-corridor coaches for steam haulage. Top, not all LBSCR stock had low arc roofs and some coaches built for main line duties and for push-pull working in the years before World War I had 'balloon' roofs which in Southern days made them out of gauge for some routes, particularly former SECR lines; centre upper, former SECR second and third class lavatory brake composite from a 60ft trio C set. The two second class compartments on the left and the next two third class compartments had access to the toilets by short side corridors; centre lower, commuter luxury – an SECR lavatory first with saloon compartment built in 1908 for boat train service which finished its days on that roundabout service, the 5.25pm London Bridge to Reading via Redhill, in the 1950s; bottom, one of the SECR 60ft ten-compartment thirds, built with the aim of later conversion to electric working, not in fact carried out. They survived until the early 1960s on cross country trains, excursion duties, main line strengthening at holiday times on Kent Coast services and branch workings.

The Southern's carriage inheritance, 2. Top, LSWR 'ironclad' corridor third, a design which appeared just before the Grouping and perpetuated by the SR for its first two years; centre upper, LSWR lavatory third rebuilt and lengthened on new 58ft underframes by the SR in the 1930s and used widely on cross country, main line stopping services and excursions; centre lower, former SECR boat train brake first of the so-called 1922 'Continental' stock. Even they included a small saloon and were unusual in having gangways only at the inner end; bottom, former SECR first and second class lavatory composite with part side corridor, built for boat train service in 1908 which lasted to the late 1950s on excursion and special traffic duties.

Opposite:
The Southern's carriage designs. Top, Standard restriction 4 corridor composite of the 1920s, with three third class and four first class compartments; centre upper, the 8ft wide restriction 0 narrow bodied version of the Southern standard corridor coach built specifically for the restricted tunnel clearances of the Tonbridge–Hastings line; centre lower, the post war Southern corridor stock by Bulleid showed marked changes compared with the pre-war Maunsell stock. Gone were the side doors, the coaches were longer, the steel panelled bodies had a continuous curve and the windows had sliding ventilators in the upper part. This is a Bournemouth line six dining set; bottom, the Southern only built two batches of new suburban electric stock before World War II. This is the motor coach of the 1925 stock built for the Eastern Section.

That then was the situation when Richard Maunsell and his carriage and wagon team took over the reins in 1923 with what amounted to a blank sheet of paper to prepare new Southern Railway main line corridor stock designs which would bring comforts for long-distance rail travel already enjoyed elsewhere in the country. At the same time the new corridor stock would upgrade existing services already provided with, by then, rather outdated LSWR corridor coaches on the Bournemouth and West of England routes. These – and, indeed, most of the coaches inherited from the LBSC and SECR – were antiquated in appearance. They had a small body profile, usually no more than 8ft or sometimes 8ft 6in wide, with low roofs – a plain arc in the case of the LBSC and a flattened ellipse on SE&CR and LSWR vehicles. Nearly all had timber

Hop Pickers

I have for the past 33 years done duty dealing with the outward and homeward hop-pickers' traffic at London Bridge and Paddock Wood. But what a difference has been brought about during the past few years in regard to the cleanliness and behaviour of these passengers. Twenty-five to thirty years ago, on the outward traffic, women wore shawls over their heads, and dozens of children were without shoes. Unfortunately the public houses were open till mid-night and they were generously patronised. The heaviest night for passengers travelling to the hop-district usually fell on a Saturday, 18 to 20 special trains being run from London Bridge, despatched from 10pm till 7am.

The booking of tickets commenced at 10pm, the first special left about 10.30pm and others left as soon as loaded; at 6.30 in the morning the mass of people in front of the station was nearly as great as it was at mid-night, and it was found necessary to send for extra Metropolitan Police to clear the front of the station. All people that were not travelling by train were forced to go over London Bridge, or down the Borough High Street, and it was not until 8.30am that all was clear. The company's dust cart, after cleaning up the front of station, was filled with rubbish, pram wheels, smashed boxes, clothing, etc.

It was a common practice for hoppers to put their youngsters, which were chargeable, in sacks and box wheel carts to pass the barrier. In most cases they were detected, and their parents made good the fares. If they escaped at London Bridge they were then told to get under the seats in the train. On arrival at Spa Road Station the collecting staff would find them and the parents made to pay.

What a great difference exists now to that of years past. Special trains now run to time in convey-

continued overleaf

103

continued
ing these passengers home. Years ago these trains ran as required from Paddock Wood and district. Farmers paid off their pickers at any time of the day and they did not care what became of them, they were all a necessary evil. The company had to convey them home, after the farmers had done with them. What a chaos it was! Some of the special trains were sent main line to London via Sevenoaks, others via Maidstone, Gravesend. The latter route was hated by the hop-pickers and they would shout out of the windows 'Where are we going, round the world, governor' when a train was sent that way. The roughest stations in the hop district were East Farleigh, Marden, Horsmonden, Yalding, and Paddock Wood. The worst evil, I think, was the public house being open all day. The hoppers, coming from the farms, had in some cases to pass two or three on the road to the station and these pubs were 'red lights' to them; after having a good drink up you may guess the condition of a good many when they arrived at stations. Beer was cheap and strong; there was fighting among them all day. – Henry Thrower, chief travelling ticket inspector. *Southern Railway Magazine*, January 1936.

bodies with full mouldings. There were the exceptions, as for example the balloon roof stock of the LBSC which formed a small proportion of the total, the slab matchboarded sides and much higher roof profile of the one SE&CR corridor train for continental services, and the steel-sided elliptical roof LSWR corridor coaches known as the ironclads. They were though very much the exceptions. One remit which Maunsell and his staff did not have was to produce new non-corridor stock – at least not for steam haulage – because so many coaches were taken over, and through its entire 25 years the Southern Railway did not build any new locomotive-hauled non-corridor coaches.

But Maunsell's blank sheet of paper had one word written on it: restrictions. Beset by loading gauge limitations on many of its routes, the Southern could not adopt just one set of standard designs for coaches that would run anywhere – at least not without sacrificing valuable internal space. Most severely restricted was the Tunbridge Wells – Hastings line as far south as Battle which was limited to coaches generally no more than 8ft wide over the bodies, 8ft 10½in overall, resulting from tight tunnel clearances which meant that tracks were laid slightly closer than normal and even then the tunnel arch encroached closely to cantrail level where the roof joined the bodyside. Other restrictions were imposed historically by tight spots at bridges or other structures and in South Eastern days until the 1920s meant that the SER main line via Tonbridge to Dover was limited to coaches no more than 8ft 6in wide. But here the odd tight spots were eased later in Southern days to allow 9ft wide stock. The Hastings line restriction survived until 1986 when lines through the affected tunnels were singled to allow full width stock to be used. The line between Tonbridge and Tunbridge Wells was also restricted but less severely and this has also been eased.

Thus Maunsell's team had to think in terms of coaches with three widths, 8ft for the Hastings line, 8ft 6in for certain of the other South Eastern lines and Eastbourne services, and 9ft for other routes not subject to restrictions, later known as Restriction 0, 1, and 4 respectively. There were other restrictions which died out in later years; 2A, for example, stopped certain Pullman cars from running over specified branches, while restriction 6 limited the coaches concerned – the Brighton balloon roof stock, for example, to former LBSC and LSWR lines. While the drawing boards were being prepared and Eastleigh, Lancing and Ashford Works were being geared up to build the new standard SR coaches, as an interim measure further batches of pre-grouping corridor coaches were built by the SR, particularly the 57ft 'ironclad' stock from the LSWR and additional 62ft continental stock from the SE&CR.

When the new SR stock appeared it was to a new length, 59ft over body 58ft over the underframes, and by the late 1920s three different body widths were used, 9ft for Portsmouth, Bournemouth, West of England and Brighton line stock, 8ft 6in for Eastbourne and Kent Coast services, and 8ft for the Hastings/Bexhill via Battle trains, the latter two straight sided. The coaches were what might be called conventional to the extent that they had side doors to each compartment, and on the corridor side the initial designs had wide windows between the doors which faced alternate compartments. The intermediate compartments

Contrasts in SR suburban electric stock. Top left, the final version of Bulleid's suburban stock (although not produced until early BR years) the 4EPB version of the 4SUB but with electro-pneumatic brakes, buck-eye couplers, detail variations in the driver's cab and mainly open saloon interiors; bottom left, original LSWR – one of the trailer composites with saloon, built around World War I, and lengthened by the SR; right, comparison between the narrow bodied pre-Grouping 8ft wide stock – in this case LBSCR – and the 9ft wide Bulleid all-steel stock.

did not have an external door on the corridor side but did have a droplight window exactly like the door windows. These were provided to give symmetry but tended to fool passengers who thought there was a door.

The wide corridor windows were originally no higher than the compartment windows, but within a year or so Maunsell coaches appeared with the wide corridor side windows extended up to the top of the bodyside which gave them a distinctive 'Southern' look, quite unlike coaches from the other three groups. Bodies were timber framed, but with steel exterior panels which, but for the wooden edging strip surround to the fixed windows, would have given a flush sided coach. Soon after the grouping, the Southern, in common with the LNER, decided to adopt Pullman style flexible end gangways, slightly wider than the British standard gangway used by most of the pre-grouping companies and by the LMS and GWR after the grouping. Adaptors had to be fitted to the British standard gangways to allow them to be coupled to the Pullman style gangways. Buckeye couplers were also to be the future Southern standard but with a drop-head arrangement to allow the screw coupling and side buffers to be used with non-buckeye stock.

Even though the new coaches were designed with three widths there were still limits, for the 9ft wide coaches with brake ends had the body alongside the guard's and luggage compartment recessed to allow a side ducket lookout to be fitted so that the guard could look out as required by the rules. (Until recent years guards were required to look out for signals in certain instances.) On the 8ft 6in and 8ft wide stock there was not room for a side lookout because of the tight clearances on former South Eastern lines. The South Eastern and then the SE&CR for years had roof lookouts, known as birdcages, above the main roof line. This was one reason why the SE&CR continued with the low flattened roof for so long; it survived on SE&CR stock on BR almost until 1960. Only after World War I with the continental corridor train and the small batch of ordinary corridor stock did the SE&CR coach roof extend to a full ellipse to the maximum height of the loading gauge. As it was dangerous for guards to put their heads out of the windows, in later years the Southern adopted the periscope roof lookout which protruded in a small housing no higher than the roof ventilators so that the guard seated at his desk in

Interior of Bulleid's 9ft wide 4SUB steel bodied stock of the 1940s. There was hardly any bodyside, just the thickness of the steel panels, the steel framing being seen only around door spaces and at partitions.

the van could see through the periscope mirrors along the train roof, just as he could have done seated high up in the birdcage observatory; this was fine provided the periscope front glass was kept clean.

Most of Maunsell's new corridor stock was of the side-door compartment type but open coaches were introduced on a limited scale for steam services although by no means as extensively as on the LMS. They were primarily, but not exclusively, for dining but were occasionally scheduled on certain trains for ordinary use. The open thirds were end door vehicles but there were several batches of open stock with doors at intervals along the sides, and known as nondescripts – that is they were used for first, second, or third class as occasion demanded with the class in use denoted by a removable board. Seats were basically of first class standard, two-and-one on each side of the off-central passageway; when used as second or third class it was luxury indeed. Usually for race trains they were designated as first class, for boat trains as second class and for other traffic as third class.

It might be wondered why the Southern clung to three classes. On ordinary trains second class survived on the SE&CR later than on the other constituents, the Southern abolishing it in its first year, when second class compartments generally became third. But to match Continental practice, boat trains continued with three classes until 1956. Then third class in Britain was renamed second and the old boat train second and third classes were simply merged into the new second. This is why some SR (and also a few BR) coaches actually carried second class branding on doors, adding yet another complication.

A feature which the Southern inherited from all of its constituents was set numbering of basically fixed formation coaching sets. The coaches intended for each basic group of services were marshalled into permanently formed sets with all the coaches of the set usually carrying the set number painted on the solebars and in large figures on the outer ends of the brake coaches at each end. Indeed new coaches were usually ordered, built, operated and maintained in sets, although there were also large numbers of loose (non set) coaches for strengthening or emergency use. The use of set trains applied right across the board from the two

Bulleid's notable double deck experiment, actually a 1½ decker with the upper compartments neatly interlaced between lower compartments to which they were linked by a staircase. The upper compartments had no opening windows and were pressure ventilated.

coach formations standard on the Devon and Cornwall branches to the three- and four-coach trains for main line, cross country and other general use (with due regard to the width limitations), six-coach Bournemouth dining sets, up to the 'long sets' of eight, nine or ten coaches for specific trains, such as the *City Limited* from Brighton to London Bridge. There is no doubt that the Southern was head and shoulders above the other railways in its operating discipline in keeping trains in their set formations. That is not to say that the Southern was as good as it might have been in coaching stock economics for some steam sets marshalled for specific workings were not suited to other duties and were not intensively used. And large numbers of sets, usually but not always formed of older stock, were kept for special traffic with specified stabling points, but often did not venture into revenue earning service more than one or two days a week, if that, on such trains as summer Saturday reliefs, excursions, school trains, hop-pickers specials (the very oldest of stock for those trains) or using the best coaches available, ocean liner boat train extras. But in those days not having enough rolling stock and having to turn traffic away would have been unthinkable.

Despite the introduction of new Maunsell corridor stock, many long distance services, particular summer Saturday reliefs, or strengthening coaches on otherwise corridor trains, were still formed of non-corridor coaches even well into the 1930s; indeed excursions to the Kent coast in the 1950s still saw non-corridor stock at times, and non-corridor coaches were still widely used on all-stations main line and cross country services. To the end of the 1950s, passengers on the Reading–Redhill–Tonbridge, or Tonbridge to Eastbourne and Brighton lines would not know whether to expect a corridor train (still the 8ft 6in wide restriction 1 stock) or an SE&CR Trio set of non-gangwayed lavatory stock with the birdcage roof brakes and often a saloon compartment in the firsts with armchair seats. Again, all this non-corridor stock was pre-grouping. The Southern actually rebuilt large quantities of LSWR non-corridor coaches, usually short 48ft vehicles on new steel 58ft underframes sometimes combining bits of different coach bodies in the one new unit almost like a kit of parts. In some cases old bodies were extended, as for example some old lavatory thirds which became brake thirds with the addition of a new guard's and luggage compartment. Similarly when the Isle of Wight lines needed new (new in Isle of Wight terms has always meant other people's cast offs) stock to replace the antiquities of the last century still running in the 1940s, former SECR birdcage Trio sets and LBSC coaches were rebuilt, with old lavatory compartments being merged into adjacent compartments as saloons, and to provide large luggage van space in brake coaches marshalled at the Ryde end of trains to allow quick transfer of holiday luggage and parcels between the ferry and the train at Ryde Pier.

The Southern was a pastmaster at making do. The suburban electrification schemes of the 1920s and 1930s mainly used coaches from existing stock: old bodies were mounted on new standard 62ft underframes. Almost from the Grouping the Southern of course embarked on what became one of the most ambitious electrification schemes in the world, gradually converting the London suburban lines

continued

the 04.20 empties to London Bridge Low Level to form the 05.45 passenger and vans to Ashford via Hastings. It then formed the 09.30 to Tonbridge. The other set was attached to the 14.00 empties the previous day to Charing Cross to form the 15.25 to Hastings, returning thence on the 19.30. Finally it formed part of the 10.50 to Wadhurst returning to Tonbridge on the 00.20 empties. The two sets are then re-united to work the 11.28 to Hastings and the 12.59 on to Ashford.

We left the four 'swingers' berthed at Tonbridge. It might be thought they would be kept together, but no. The BCK, FK, and one SK were attached next morning to 8 coach set 939 which formed the 07.38 from Hastings to Cannon Street. The empties were taken to Grove Park sidings. The BCK was transferred to Rotherhithe Road on the 11.16 empties and attached to the 18.40 empties forming the 19.34 Charing Cross to Ramsgate, the BCK being detached at Ashford.

The diagram of the FK was more complicated. It was transferred to the 16.10 empties to Cannon Street to form the 17.40 to Dover Priory. Next morning it was attached to the 04.55 to Ashford (one wonders how many first class passengers patronised that train). It then went up to Cannon Street on the 07.24, and thence to Rotherhithe Road. The third morning it went to London Bridge on the 04.55 empties to form the 07.24 to Margate via Dover. From Margate it reached Ashford on the 13.40 to Maidstone East.

The SK went up from Grove Park to Cannon Street on the 16.40 empties forming the 17.18 to Hastings, from which it was detached at Tonbridge. It resumed the transit to Hastings on the 20.07. The third day of the cycle it formed part of the 06.19 stopping train to Tonbridge, where the whole train was

continued overleaf

continued
attached to the following 06.58 to
Cannon Street. It was then taken
to Rotherhithe Road. Re-united
with the other SK, they form part
of the empties to Charing Cross
and thus reach Ashford on the
11.44. Because of the pooling
system referred to, the story of
how the other SK reached Rotherhithe Road from Tonbridge
proved too difficult to trace.

Thus all the components of the
18.22 have reached Ashford.
They were assembled to form the
16.10 from Ashford to Charing
Cross, due 18.03. After loading it
would leave as the 18.22 and the
cycle would begin again. And all
this before the computer age.

Belles

The new 1st Class and composite
1st and 3rd Class Pullman cars
that are now operating on the
'Southern' electric services between London and Brighton and
Worthing are all adorned with
names. For the 1st Class cars of
the three 'Southern Belle' units
the chosen names are:- 'Doris'
and 'Hazel'; 'Audrey' and 'Vera';
'Gwen' and 'Mona'. On the other
express services, 23 composite
cars are engaged and these bear
names as follows:- 'Alice'; 'Anne';
'Bertha'; 'Brenda'; 'Clara';
'Daisy'; 'Elinor'; 'Enid'; 'Ethel';
'Grace'; 'Gwladys'; 'Ida'; 'Iris';
'Joyce'; 'Lorna'; 'May'; 'Naomi';
'Olive'; 'Peggy'; 'Ruth'; 'Rita';
'Rose'; and 'Violet'. – *Meccano
Magazine*, May 1933.

in the 1920s and into the 1930s and moving on out into the country with the Brighton main line in 1932, Eastbourne and Hastings in 1935, to Portsmouth via Guildford 1937, Portsmouth via Horsham and the coastal routes 1938, Reading early 1939 and Maidstone East later in 1939. There was ever a demand for more electric trains.

The LSWR had started the conversion ball rolling by turning four-coach steam trains (known as bogie block sets) little more than a decade old into three-coach electric trains with a trailer coach between two motor coaches. These LSWR trains were distinguished by V shaped nose ends but the passenger accommodation was in normal compartments except for a few first class saloon compartments. Nothing came of the SE&CR's pre-1923 electrification plans but the railway built large numbers of what were known as ten-compartment thirds, 8ft wide, initially as steam stock but with the aim of later conversion. They seated 100 passengers and were quite austere inside. At 60ft in length they were not quite as cramped as Great Northern and Great Eastern suburban stock, but were classic examples of 'people movers', the cram-as-many-passengers-in-as-possible philosophy that the Southern was forced to adopt on some of its overcrowded routes. In the event the 100-seat thirds were never used for electric working but they lasted into the 1960s on steam branch and cross country trains and excursions, and were often rostered to strengthen otherwise corridor trains.

For the early Southern's own electrification schemes there were different solutions. On the South Eastern lines, most of the stock was converted from old SE&C coach bodies placed on new underframes, but there was also a batch of new coaches, 62ft in length, as non-corridor versions of the then newly-emerging steam stock. Similar but slightly shorter sets were built for the Guildford line but had many LSWR features including a V-nose like their LSWR predecessors, a curious feature since all other Southern electric stock had almost flat fronts with just a slight bow end. The short-lived extension of the Brighton's overhead electrification to Coulsdon used trains of pure LBSC style unusual in having motor luggage vans in the middle of five-coach formations, with of course driving trailers at each end. Three years later many of these were converted for third rail dc operation, but some of the driving trailers were converted back to steam use for push-pull trains. Among other things that meant replacing the Westinghouse compressed air brake used by the LBSC generally and by the Southern for electric trains (and on the Isle of Wight) with vacuum brake equipment.

Electrification to Brighton in 1932 brought a need for better class accommodation and indeed a distinct division of electric stock into three categories: suburban, semi-fast, and express. If all but two batches of suburban stock had been created by rebuilding old steam coaches the stock for semi-fast and express duties in contrast were, with one exception, all newly built. For a journey time of just an hour for the fastest non-stop London – Brighton trains some might say the Southern went overboard in the provision of full corridor trains with refreshment facilities and even Pullman cars, which had had a half century history on that line. Certainly the Southern was out to woo the fashionable South Coast towns with something far better than the other three groups did for towns a similar travelling time out from London.

For the express services on Brighton, Eastbourne, Hastings and Worthing lines, six coach trains were built with an open saloon motor brake third at each end having end doors, with one third class and two first and third class side corridor trailers, together with a first and third class Pullman car which provided a wide range of Pullman refreshments. For the electric successor to the *Southern Belle* all-Pullman service, the Southern accepted three five-car Pullman multiple-units including two motor brake parlour thirds, a trailer parlour third and two kitchen firsts, normally two units being in service and one spare. For many years the *Brighton Belle* worked three return services on weekdays and two on Sundays but there were timetable variations over the years. Although the *Belle* sets often worked in pairs and the ordinary trains ran as two six-coach sets to form 12 coaches on peak services, there was no access between the two units since the motor coaches were not gangwayed at their outer ends; neither were later six coach units with an ordinary pantry coach instead of a Pullman built for the Eastbourne electrification.

For the Portsmouth electrification schemes of 1937 and 1938, however, the express units were marshalled in four-coach units, fully gangwayed so that in the usual peak 12-coach formation passengers had access right through the train to the restaurant car normally included in the centre unit. The Portsmouth line did not have Pullmans and normal restaurant car facilities were provided on most trains from the start. For the Bognor line however it was deemed that a full meal service was not needed and refreshments were served from a new style art-nouveau buffet car marshalled in one of the four-coach units of each train; indeed these cars were known for much of their lives as the Bognor Buffets, even though in later years they strayed from the mid-Sussex route to Bognor. Nevertheless the Bognor Buffets sowed the seeds for the refreshment revolution on British trains which over the following 50 years saw the move away from set or à la carte meals to snacks and fast food.

For the semi-fast services the Southern opted for that traditional style of vehicle for the longer cross-country or main-line stopping services, the non-gangwayed lavatory carriage. Unlike their old-time predecessors the

The neat lines of the Southern's express electric units are clearly brought out in this photograph of a 6PAN motor brake third of 1935. They were the half way development between the 6PUL stock (in which the whole passenger window could be lowered as they did not have the upper draught free sliding ventilators) and the 4COR stock (which had through gangways at the driving end).

109

The buffet cars of the express sets for the Bognor and Portsmouth electrification of 1938 were a departure from what had gone before and counter self service was a foretaste of things to come.

Reverse Sparks Effect

In the early post-war years, having to go to the west side of Bexhill, quite close to Collington station (then classed as a halt), it seemed natural to get an electric Hastings express from Victoria, changing at Eastbourne into the half-hourly stopper. It was not a happy experience; the riding at speed of the 6PAN set was diabolical. Reading was out of the question, and it was impossible to enjoy the passing Downland scenery. It would have been a safety hazard to try to drink a cup of tea.

Next time it was by express from Cannon Street via Tonbridge, soon after five. Despite the narrower coaches the journey was very comfortable, and it was pleasant to listen to the six-to-a-bar beat of the St Leonard's 'Schools' clambering up the very steep rise out of Tonbridge to the tunnel. At Crowhurst the Bexhill West push-pull was waiting, two coaches with a Wainwright 0-4-4 tank. The four miles were in a period piece saloon, almost a club car, in which one sat facing across the coach to one's fellow travellers in an atmosphere which seemed to positively encourage discussion of the issues of the day. The journey took 15 minutes longer, but – as Toad of Toad Hall would have enthused – it was the only way to travel.

Southern's version included a full length internal corridor so that the whole coach had access to toilet facilities. For the Brighton line semi-fast and stopping services, the four-coach units included three non-corridor compartment coaches, the outer ones being motor brake thirds, plus one of these corridor non-gangwayed composite coaches. The third class non-corridor compartments were unusual in having armrests to divide the seats for five-a-side even though with 9ft wide bodies, like all the newly built semi-fast and express stock, the thirds could have seated six-a-side.

For the other 1930s main line electrification conversions of the Sussex coastal services, the Portsmouth routes, Reading, Camberley and Medway lines, three types of semi-fast stock were produced – all two-coach trains with a third class motor coach, and driving trailer composite. In one type both coaches had internal corridors and toilets; in the second only one coach had toilets and a corridor; and in the third neither coach had toilets and all accommodation was in compartments with no access to anywhere. Indeed these latter two-coach non-corridor units were again rebuilds on new underframes of old LSWR bodies. As such they were only 8ft wide and were not really different from ordinary suburban stock.

With all these detail variations in semi-fast stock, and its other electric trains the Southern had fun in coining short descriptions for telephone and telegram purposes, also for carriage working notices. It adopted a code made up of a figure (for the number of coaches in a set) and three letters denoting its make up or duty. Hence suburban electric sets, then usually in three-coach units were designated 3SUB, the six-coach express sets with Pullman car as 6PUL, the five-coach *Brighton Belle* sets as 5BEL, the six-coach pantry car units as 6PAN, while the Portsmouth/Bognor four-coach ordinary corridor units were 4COR, with restaurant car 4RES and with buffet car 4BUF. As for the semi fast sets what else could they have been but 4LAV, 2BIL (bi- or both with lavatories) 2HAL (half the unit, that is one coach with a lavatory) and 2NOL (no lavatories). In BR days as further variations occurred the codes were extended to denote units fitted with electro-pneumatic brake so that codes included the letter P, sometimes as a variation of the original SR code (2HAP for example) but sometimes a total break, 4EPB (four-coach suburban unit with EP brake) and the four coach corridor express unit as 4CEP. While a BR 4REP included a refreshment car, it was not a straight replacement for a 4RES, for it was applied to the Bournemouth line motor units which were twice as powerful as most other SR electric units.

As World War II plunged the country into conflict again the development of purely Southern Railway semi-fast and express electric stock had reached its climax, for further electrification had to wait until well into BR days and the stock for it was purely a BR concept even though internal layouts owed something to Southern practice. More pressing was the development of suburban stock, for overcrowding was hitting SR commuters hard. Until the early 1940s suburban electric trains were formed as three-coach motor sets, two of which were coupled at peak hours usually with a two-coach non-driving trailer unit coupled in between. It was a clumsy arrangement and involved shunting the two-coach units in and out in some cases. In 1941 Bulleid, then chief mechanical engineer, produced a glorious sardine can: a suburban train with the highest seating capacity ever seen in Britain, 468 in four coaches. It would have been even higher but for the fact that one coach was originally designed to include first class. The coaches were built with 9ft wide bodies with a noticeable curve from top to bottom, with steel body frames and external panels. As such they seated six-a-side, the first wide-body SR suburban stock to do so, and with nine compartments in the motor coaches and eleven compartments in the third class trailer they increased the seating capacity of a typical narrow-bodied equivalent set by over 50 per cent. Distinguishing features were well rounded window corners and top lights in doors. Eventually after the war further sets were built but then the Southern gave passengers a little more room and opened out trailers to ten compartments and motor coaches to eight compartments, all in the same 62ft length. Another feature was the introduction of open saloon seating with two-plus-three astride the off centre passageway but retaining side doors to each seating bay, for the Southern was addicted to side swing doors until recent times. Another distinguishing feature was the abandonment of the domed roof ends over driving cabs so that cab fronts were carried up to the top of the roof line. Body side panels were also taken right into the roof so that there was no obvious cantrail join between side and roof.

At the same time the old three-coach 3SUB units were augmented to four-coach units either by adding new wide body coaches or old style narrow body stock, and the trailer units disappeared. Gradually in the 1940s and on into BR days the SR produced more wide-body Bulleid-style suburban stock, in due course fitted with electro-pneumatic brakes to replace the older pre-grouping coaches. But the Southern had not done with the old stock for those very underframes of the 1920s which had carried pre-grouping bodies to form the 1920s electric trains were not discarded. They were given the new style Bulleid bodies to form the stock of the 1950s and many are still in service today.

Bulleid had one more attempt to increase train capacity, in the late 1940s, with his ingenious double-deck suburban train. Only two four-coach trains were built and they remained unique. They were not true double-deckers – the BR loading gauge saw to that – but the upper compartments were remarkably interlaced between the lower deck so

One of the more way out coach types of early BR days was this attempt by Bulleid to liven up catering vehicles by making them as much like a pub as possible. Known as the tavern cars they featured painted brick and half timbered livery externally at one end, and inside the bar was timber panelled. The restaurant section, not illustrated, had seats back to the sides facing inwards and only ventilator windows at the top of the sides were provided so that passengers could not see out when seated. They were not popular and were soon modified. The cars bore pub style names.

The Dyke branch

Several relatives were, conveniently, resident on Southern territory, and by the sea into the bargain, so that your observer – mother being a fervent believer in the power of sea air – would frequently be despatched to Hove or Broadstairs. In the former, the fresh air of the beach was often subjugated to Brighton station – especially the west end of the sweeping platform used by the Portsmouth-line services, which provided an advantageous view of the motive power depot. Brighton station was a spacious and dignified edifice, with a vast roof which echoed and reflected loudly the various steam and electric whistles from below. It was always full of interest, not only in the variety of locomotive power but also its operating intricacies. A favourite was the Dyke branch, a journey of great fascination as, in the height of the season, a Class E4 0-6-2T laboriously heaved its load of holidaymakers some 400ft up to the small terminus just below the summit of the Devil's Dyke – 3½ miles at 1 in 40. Hardly a viable proposition – short, capricious seasonal and expensive – it was not surprising it closed at the end of the 1938 season, a reminder that the Southern runs in the end a business like any other – R.A. Savill.

Top right. Pullman in isolation. For the Brighton electrification of 1933 (and the Eastbourne of 1935) the Southern built a series of six car sets without gangways at the outer ends. The original Brighton trains included a Pullman car and were classified 6PUL; the Pullman was manned by Pullman staff. 6PUL Unit No 3041 is seen here at Ore in an unusually clean condition in April 1966.

Right. Portsmouth electric. An immaculate 4COR unit working over the Waterloo to Portsmouth line near Haslemere in April 1966.

that the upstairs seats were more or less where the downstairs luggage racks would have been. A staircase linked each lower and upper compartment. But the double deck train took too long to load and unload and the Southern Region had to adopt longer trains with consequent lengthening of platforms and signalling alterations to cope with the heavy traffic.

As for steam stock Bulleid staged more or less a complete revolution, largely ignoring what had gone before. Again no more non-corridor stock was needed, at least not in Southern Railway days, but his main line corridor stock was of a completely new pattern mostly on longer 63ft 5in underframes giving 64ft 6in bow ended bodies, with steel sides, although retaining composite timber and steel construction, wide deep windows having sliding ventilator windows in the upper part, end and centre doors (apart from a few early side door sets similar to Maunsell vehicles in layout). There was also much more open saloon stock, some coaches having part open and part side corridor accommodation, particularly some handsome some semi-open brake thirds. Set formations, though, continued, ranging from general purpose two- three- and four-coach sets, to Bournemouth line six-coach dining sets. Much of what was in the Bulleid corridor stock was transformed into BR standard stock, particularly in lengths and layouts and continuously curved body side, although BR never adopted the part open/part side corridor style. On BR it was all or nothing – and all-steel construction.

Over the years naturally Southern Railway stock changed, but it changed to no great extent, with occasional rebuilds for push-pull workings and revised formations. Much of it survived well into BR days until the electrification schemes of the late 1950s and 1960s ousted most of the SR's steam stock while the SR's electric stock lasted until the 1970s. But the pre-grouping coaches had remarkably long lives. On parts of the South Eastern, even up to the Kent Coast electrification of 1959–61, some areas (Tonbridge for example) looked like a rolling museum with pre-Grouping locomotives and coaches well in evidence, especially at bank holidays. Fortunately a few Southern coaches, but perhaps never enough, have survived for preservation, including electric units, but then where are the preserved electric railways for them to run on other than rare outings on BR?

SR ELECTRIC TRAIN STOCK CODES
(Does not include some short lived formations made up during stock replacement periods)
Units with Westinghouse brakes and screw coupled at outer ends
3SUB Three-coach suburban unit
4SUB Four-coach suburban unit
4LAV Four-coach semi-fast unit with one corridor lavatory coach
2BIL Two-coach semi-fast unit with both corridor lavatory coaches
2HAL Two-coach semi-fast unit with one corridor lavatory coach
2NOL Two-coach semi-fast unit with no lavatory facilities
6PUL Six-coach corridor express unit with one Pullman car
      (No gangways at outer ends)
6PAN Six-coach corridor express unit with pantry car
      (No gangways at outer ends)

IM TAKING AN EARLY HOLIDAY COS i KNOW SUMMER COMES SOONEST IN THE SOUTH

SOUTHERN RAILWAY

Poster superb. Perhaps one of Britain's best known railway posters. The Southern Railway publicity department's inspiration speaks for itself. Its approach has never been bettered.

Five posters produced by the Southern Railway's publicity department, two from their 'Progress Poster' series and three by famous artists: shipping, docks and holiday routes. The 'Progress Posters' show the attention given to locomotives (not as much as the GWR but they did produce an excellent illustrated booklet in conjunction with the Locomotive Publishing Co) painted by R. D. Kerr in 1925 with electrification publicity showing emus en mass by the same artist at the same date.

The three 'famous artist' pictures are encouragements to travel (probably by special excursion) to Chatham, Portsmouth and Devonport dockyards by Leslie Carr, the glories of a trip by the Golden Arrow service (London Victoria dep. 11.00am, Paris Nord arr. 5.40pm, Paris Nord dep. 12.00 midday, London Victoria arr. 7.00pm) – and the introduction of car ferries, by Kenneth D. Shoesmith (Dover dep. 11.00am, Calais arr. 12.45pm, Calais dep. 2.15pm, Dover arr. 4.00pm), together with a flamboyant painting by the artist Shep of continental resorts served by the Southern depicted by the flags of 'all nations' including Japan, the USA and Nazi Germany.

STEAM!

THE "KING ARTHUR" CLASS, WEST OF ENGLAND EXPRESS

- 91 OF THE MOST POWERFUL -
ENGINES ARE BEING DELIVERED
TO THE SOUTHERN RAILWAY THIS
SUMMER, COSTING OVER £600,000.

SOUTHERN

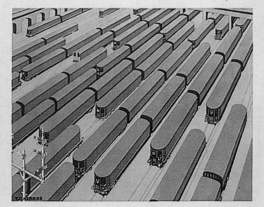

ELECTRIFICATION!

700 MILES OF SOUTHERN RAIL·
WAY WILL BE ELECTRIFIED BY
SPRING NEXT YEAR ~ 3 NEW
SECTIONS OPEN THIS SUMMER
~3 ELECTRIC FOR EVERY STEAM
TRAIN NOW RUNNING - - -
~ TOTAL COST £8,000,000

WORLD'S GREATEST SUBURBAN
ELECTRIC

SOUTHERN

The "GOLDEN ARROW" Service and the "MOTORISTS" Service, leaving Dover

LONDON (Victoria).. dep. 11.0 a.m.   PARIS (Nord)... dep. 12.0 noon   DOVER....dep. 11.0 a.m.   CALAIS......dep. 2.15 p.m.
PARIS (Nord)... arr. 5.40 p.m.   LONDON (Victoria).. arr. 7.0 p.m.   CALAIS...arr. 12.45 p.m.   DOVER......arr. 4.0 p.m.

SOUTHERN RAILWAY

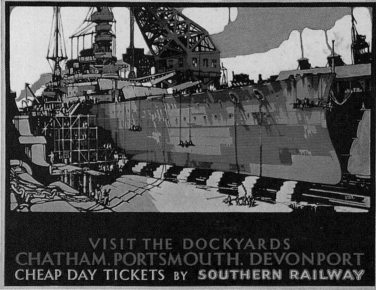

VISIT THE DOCKYARDS
CHATHAM, PORTSMOUTH, DEVONPORT
CHEAP DAY TICKETS BY SOUTHERN RAILWAY

5BEL Five-car Brighton Belle all-Pullman unit
    (No gangways at outer ends)
6CIT Six-coach City Limited unit with higher proportion of first class
    and Pullman car (No gangways at outer ends)
4COR Four-coach corridor express unit, gangwayed throughout
4RES Four-coach corridor express unit, with restaurant car,
    gangwayed throughout
4BUF Four-coach corridor express unit with buffet car, gangwayed
    throughout
4GRI Four-coach corridor express unit with griddle car, gangwayed
    throughout

Units with electro-pneumatic brakes and buckeye couplers
(from late 1940s)
4EPB Four-coach suburban unit
2EPB Two-coach suburban unit
4DD Four-coach suburban double-deck unit
4PEP Four-coach suburban unit with sliding doors (1970s) (Prototype
    of Class 508)
2PEP Two-coach suburban unit with sliding doors (1970s)
2HAP Two-coach semi-fast unit with one corridor lavatory coach
2SAP Two-coach semi-fast unit with one lavatory coach, converted to
    second class only
4CEP Four-coach corridor express unit, gangwayed throughout
4BEP Four-coach corridor express unit with buffet car, gangwayed
    throughout
4CIG Four-coach corridor express unit gangwayed throughout
    (The IG in the code is the old LBSC telegraphic code for
    Brighton, for which line these units were built)
4BIG Four-coach corridor express unit with buffet car, gangwayed
    throughout
4REP Four-coach corridor express unit, double-powered for Bourne-
    mouth line, with restaurant car, gangwayed throughout. To
    work with TC units
4VEP Four-coach semi-fast unit, open suburban type seating, with two
    lavatory coaches, gangwayed throughout (the V indicating
    vestibuled)
4VEG As 4VEP but adapted for Gatwick Airport – Victoria service and
    fitted with extra luggage racks
4TC Four-coach unpowered corridor express unit for Bournemouth
    line (to work with 4REP or locomotive, push-pull)
MLV Single motor luggage van
4VEC Four-coach ex-London Transport Underground unit for Isle of
    Wight
3TIS Three-coach ex-London Transport Underground unit for Isle of
    Wight (Vectis, the Latin name for the Isle of Wight)

Longest Passenger Train
At 10.50am on 4 May first 16-coach train left Waterloo for the West of England drawn by engine No 21C9, *Shaw-Savill*. This train, the longest ever worked on the Southern, now runs on Tuesdays, Wednesdays and Thursdays for the West Country. It will cover the service requiring two separate trains on other weekdays and has been introduced with a view to saving fuel, engine- and manpower. The innovation has only been made possible by the additional power of the recently built Merchant Navy class engines, which are able to work such exceptionally long trains over the difficult gradients of the Southern main line, including the steep five-mile climb up Honiton bank, where the gradient averages 1 in 80. – *Southern Railway Magazine*, May/June, 1943.

Waterloo station in War and Peace. Helen McKie's twin posters specially painted for the centenary of Waterloo station in 1948. Apart from the predominance of military uniforms in the wartime picture the Merchant Navy Pacific is clearly shown in black – evidence of the charade of its production as a 'vital wartime mixed traffic locomotive'.

8
FROM KENT COAST TO ACE: THE HOLIDAY TRAINS

Tales of the Trains

The Southern published a remarkable booklet in 1925, entitled *Tales of the Trains*, forty pages, by one E. P. Leigh-Bennett, who from the Introduction one gathers was a journalist commissioned (like S. P. B. Mais, who wrote a booklet on rambles in SR country) to describe railway operations in lay language from behind the scenes. (The railway's technical mind, he writes, views with an amused tolerance the entry of the layman into its province!) The booklet is packed with useful information, statistics, and anecdotes, presented in a wry, humorous style, and well illustrated.

From page seven we learn that the Southern Railway's new steamers *Isle of Thanet* and *Maid of Kent* cost a mere £200,000 each, and had lounges and promenades with glass sides like an Atlantic liner.

Page nine contains a fascinating description of London Bridge 'B' manual signal box in the rush *continued opposite*

Allhallows-on-Sea to Exmouth and Padstow to Ilfracombe were the lengths of coastline over which the Southern Railway held almost undisputed sway and to which Sunny South Sam exhorted the public to go for Sunshine.

Prior to World War I it was the day excursion traffic which was predominant, family holidays being confined to the upper strata of the middle classes and above. The pre-grouping railways encouraged the one-day traffic and some of the resorts, such as Brighton and Margate, welcomed it; others, like Eastbourne, tried to discourage or ignore it. In very early days great caravans of trains wended their way from London Bridge and New Cross Gate down through Croydon and the Downs to Sussex-by-the-Sea so that the working class of South London could take, among other things, the ozone: families spending a longer holiday at the seaside utilised the regular services which had no difficulty in accommodating traffic offered.

Kent Coast Express. An up Chatham line train hauled by Class L1 4-4-0 No 1783 approaches Bickley Junction in the summer of 1938. The carriages have roof destination boards and there is a Pullman car which purveyed refreshments third from the engine. By deduction from the timetable this was probably the 2.53pm Saturdays Only Margate to Victoria or the 2.55pm Saturdays Excepted from Ramsgate. The line coming in from the left is the connection from the down South Eastern line at Chislehurst to the down Chatham line.

After 1918 there was a steady shift in emphasis. The lower orders of the middle class, especially the commercial people, now played a greater part in the period traffic, while the large families with accompanying servants were less numerous. By Grouping in 1923 this was becoming more marked and during the thirties the vast numbers of cabin trunks sent Passengers' Luggage in Advance were silent witness to the revolution. The board residence establishments and the smaller hotels geared themselves up to a Saturday tea to Saturday breakfast stay. When the family arrived, the trunk collected from home on Wednesday was ready for unpacking in their bedroom. That does not mean that the one-day traffic collapsed: especially on Bank Holidays and Sundays within 100-mile radius of the metropolis, it continued to grow, but now tended to be looked upon much more as Excursion business (with all that entails) rather than holiday traffic.

The trend became much more marked after 1945 and holidays-with-pay became universal, while the five-day week (at first Saturday mornings had to be worked every second or third week but its effect was the same) was gaining ground rapidly. All this nearly overwhelmed the railway with its loss of stock and general run down in maintenance. While the soldier had been prepared to endure stoically a stand in the corridor from London to Barnstaple while serving His Majesty, he was far less tolerant about having to do the same thing in civvy street on holiday with his family.

After the Grouping the legacy of the awkward layout in Thanet was rationalised by the SR in time for the summer of 1926 with the old Ramsgate Harbour station abandoned in favour of a new station at the back of the town, complete with carriage sidings, which catered for traffic from the Margate as well as the Minster direction. This helped the operating staff immensely although, so far as the public was concerned, it was the introduction of corridor stock in 1924 which was perhaps the greater boon. The main thrust of traffic to Thanet had always been from London along the Kent Coast line through the junction of Faversham and had included for many years regular business trains – some of which had been graced with names, such as *City Express*, which titles the SR dispensed with early on – all of which was catered for by about twenty trains in each direction daily with one or two extras on Fridays and Mondays for weekend business. On summer Saturdays well over double this service had to be provided, some of the extra trains serving selected suburban stations to save passengers the toil of a change at Bromley South or travelling into Victoria. The *Sunny South Special* from the LMS and the LNWR before it provided a through service to and from the West Midlands and South Lancashire finding its way from Willesden Junction via Addison Road, later renamed Kensington (Olympia) to Bromley South. A service to Birkenhead, via the Great Western route, went via Canterbury, Ashford, Tonbridge, Redhill, Guildford and Reading. Only the LNER lacked a regular service to Thanet, although excursions formed of that company's stock were not unusual.

From Charing Cross traffic was not so heavy. Apart from Hastings, the resorts served were not so popular: Folkestone, Dover, Walmer and Deal and those on the New Romney branch. The Hastings route

---

continued

hour. ('The three men do not speak to each other, or to you. Signalmen acquire the inhibition of silence, ingrained through long years in small boxes by themselves. They are self-contained entities, taut upon the job in hand. A long line of shining bayonet-like levers confront them. Rows of glassed dials covered with green hieroglyphics which tell them rapid stories are above their heads. Engines roar beneath their feet. Coloured discs shiver and drop. Miniature signal arms flick up and down. Bells tinkle. A foot shoots out, a body is bent to the strain, a signal a hundred yards away flops down . . . and another . . . and again. Eyes glance keenly through the windows at departing tail lamps on rear coaches – a hand is wiped on cotton waste – a body is bent to the strain again – 'clunk' – and again . . . The whole maelstrom of movement below is an open book to them, whose pages are turned by the staccato motions of their legs and bent back bodies. The duration of the job is limited to an eight hour shift. The responsibility is illimitable.')

'Oyez! Oyez! Oyez!' cries the Guildford Town Crier on 12 July 1925, in language dating from 1256: 'Be it known unto all ye Burgesses of this ancient Borough of Guildford that your Mayor and his brethren and divers other persons have this day travelled by the first train on the new electric railway from Waterloo to Guildford. And I hereby declare that the line will be open to all people on Sunday next. God save the King!' The booklet informs that the run is thirty miles, the longest by electric train in the country.

Eastleigh works erecting shop evokes a fascinating description, including the masterly if dated: 'Other engines are undergoing major surgical operations upon their "innards" – half their intestines are scattered about the place with horrible men hammer-

continued overleaf

continued

ing them and *singing music hall songs*, if you please, while perpetrating their atrocities'.

Derby Day on 27 May 1925, we learn, required a 'Working Notice' of ninety-six pages (a typical page is reproduced), and 115 special trains were run to Tattenham Corner alone.

'The Way of Progress' on page 38 sums it all up: 'A vital and exceedingly complicated suburban system is being changed from steam to electrification, involving track, station, and equipment alterations that run into millions of pounds; bridges all over the Southern system are being rebuilt or strengthened on a scale not before contemplated. Locomotives, of larger dimensions and greater power, are being put into service every week; rolling stock that is old is being replaced by stock that is new just as fast as the shops can turn it out; a new signalling system is being installed over a wide suburban area; more steamships of new design are nearing completion for the cross channel services.'

The same E. P. Leigh-Bennett, in the same style and with the same theme, namely to help the travelling public realise that the railway staff are not mechanised, but are sympathetic human beings, doing their utmost to serve the public faithfully and well, was responsible for a quarterly publication sent to First Class Season Ticket holders, entitled 'Over the Points', a practice at that time unique in the railway world.

diverged at Tonbridge about 30 miles from London, and so the line through Ashford was generally able to give priority to the Continental traffic at Dover and Folkestone.

How well was traffic moved? By all accounts, well enough. The staff were highly versed in the operations and had years of service behind them Points failures were unknown; engine failures not common; signal failures could be overcome easily by flagging and there was no shortage of manpower. As an example, of the 52 movements through Tonbridge on August Bank Holiday 1938 between 10.30am and 3pm, there was but one train running as much as ten minutes late – the 11.10am Charing Cross to Ramsgate in the charge of L1 class 4-4-0 No 1784. Of the more noteable workings, the 10.15am Denmark Hill to Hastings was made up of 9 set 905 headed by T9 class 4-4-0 No 300, the 10.40am Bricklayers Arms (the goods depot was used for passenger purposes at holiday times) to Deal was headed by N class 2-6-0 No 1821, and another T9 class – No 310 – hauled the 11.01am Nunhead to Hastings.

On another occasion a 9-coach train from Charing Cross arrived at Hastings behind schedule on an August Saturday detrained its passengers, was partly cleaned, entrained returning holidaymakers, detached the locomotive at the front and acquired another at the rear and was leaving for London within 4½ minutes of arrival. When necessary, operations could be slick. Masses of figures could be quoted for these summer Saturdays but the most eloquent testimony of public reliance on the railway was demonstrated in the patiently-waiting crowds solidly packed on the concourses of Victoria and Waterloo stations.

After World War II it was the same but of course more so. The all-Pullman *Thanet Belle* – later *Kentish Belle* – was introduced in 1948 to give a quality veneer to the service and from 1950 made two runs in each direction between London and Ramsgate each Saturday but the sheer volume of traffic precluded it being really fast. Passengers spent the time in a modicum of comfort – the envy of those on trains to places such as Wolverhampton, Mansfield and Derby (Friargate). The variety was great, including via Strood originating at Blackheath or Gravesend, requiring a banker (an O1 or C class 0-6-0 or diesel shunter) from Strood up to the main line. On 26 July 1958, 66 Kent Coast trains were recorded and, although everyone knew that the Southern was awash with Pacifics, the most common locomotive type was the 2-6-0 (12 N class and 15 U1) followed by 20 4-4-0s (15 Schools, one L class, one E1 class and three D1s), 13 4-6-0s (6 King Arthurs, five BR Standard Class 5 and two BR Standard Class 4) with just six light Pacifics making up the total. Other classes would put in an appearance from Saturday to Saturday such as L1 4-4-0s, T9 4-4-0s (just after the war) and N1 2-6-0s. Because of congestion at Stewarts Lane shed it was very often the case of first available engine out for the next train rather than waiting for its proper duty. So it would not be surprising to see the afternoon *Kentish Belle* hauled by a 2-6-0 or even an L 4-4-0. One got there eventually! By the time electrification arrived the crowds had diminished, for the next change in holiday patterns had taken root, family car ownership, to be followed by the plebian delights of the package tour to the Costas.

Over on the Charing Cross–Folkestone–Dover–Deal route matters were still a little less hectic. There were the Saturday 'rounders' which

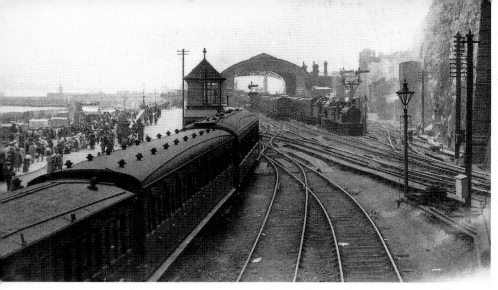

Last years of a station. On the Isle of Thanet the South Eastern and London, Chatham & Dover companies had their own stations at both Margate and Ramsgate, which despite the 1899 working union remained until Southern days. This is the LCD's Ramsgate Harbour station, with a train of mixed bogie and six wheel stock, including a Pullman, about to leave for Victoria, double headed by a former LCD Class M3 4-4-0 and SEC rebuilt 4-4-0 of Class D1 or E1, just around the Grouping period. By the mid 1920s the SR had rationalised lines in the area to form the Margate–Ramsgate through route, and Ramsgate Harbour was closed.

Holiday local. The Hayling Island branch train near Langston in 1939. A scene which remained unaltered, apart from livery changes and later coaches, until the line closed. The locomotive is Class A1X 'Terrier' No 2635, formerly LBSC No 35 Morden built in 1878. Terriers were the heaviest locomotives permitted over Langston Harbour bridge.

Bournemouth bound from the West Midlands in the 1930s. A train including a GWR six-wheel saloon, three LSWR non-corridors and modern GW corridors, making eleven in all, near Beaulieu Road around 1930. The leading engine is an ex LSWR Drummond L11 class 4-4-0 with an eight wheeled 'water cart' tender piloting a GWR Hall class 4-6-0. Very much typical of the times.

On the West London Extension. An ex LB&SCR B4 class 4-4-0 takes what was probably a holiday period Sunny South Express at Addison Road in the late 1920s. This is another train of very mixed stock indeed epitomising the comfort and discomfort of travelling at holiday time. The first two coaches are modern, the third is a 12 wheel LNWR diner, but the rest are Wolverton LNWR coaches of Victorian vintage. It was a heavy train for one of this class. The picture is dated approximately as No B48 was renumbered 2048 in 1931.

Island Names

The Southern Railway has added greatly to the interest of its locomotives in the Isle of Wight by giving names to them all. The complete list is as follows:

No. W.	Name.	Type.	Immediate former owner.
W1	Medina	0-6-0T	FY&NR
W2	Freshwater	0-6-0T	FY&NR
W3	Carisbrooke	0-6-0T	LB&SC
W4	Bembridge	0-6-0T	LB&SC
W10	Cowes	0-6-0T	IWCR
W11	Newport	0-6-0T	IWCR
W12	Ventnor	0-6-0T	IWCR
W13	Ryde	2-4-0T	IWR
W14	Wroxall	2-4-0T	IWR
W19	Osborne	0-4-4T	LSWR
W20	Shanklin	0-4-4T	LSWR
W21	Sandown	0-4-4T	LSWR
W22	Brading	0-4-4T	LSWR
W23	Totland	0-4-4T	LSWR
W24	Calbourne	0-4-4T	LSWR
W25	Godshill	0-4-4T	LSWR
W26	Whitwell	0-4-4T	LSWR
W27	Merstone	0-4-4T	LSWR
W28	Ashey	0-4-4T	LSWR
W29	Alverstone	0-4-4T	LSWR
W30	Shorwell	0-4-4T	LSWR
W31	Chale	0-4-4T	LSWR
W32	Bonchurch	0-4-4T	LSWR

Number 4 is the most recent addition and was formerly No 678 LBSC. She was built at Brighton Works in June, 1880, and when new was No. 78, and named *Knowle*. – *Meccano Magazine*, February 1930.

went Charing Cross–Folkestone–Dover–Deal (sometimes empty stock for the link) – Ramsgate–Margate–Victoria and a New Romney through service. In 1953 a couple of Folkestone trains were accelerated and named *Man of Kent* and from 1956 the name was extended to another pair. All disappeared with electrification in 1961. The self-contained Hastings route via Battle continued to be the preserve of the Schools introduced in 1931 with, at about the same time, refurbished corridor stock – both of which held sway for over a quarter of a century.

The Central section of the Southern, as the old LBSC became, did see some modern motive power allocated to it before the tide of electrification flooded over Sussex. King Arthurs were introduced to Brighton and Eastbourne services and Schools on the Eastbourne route and the *City Limited* (not a holiday train!) got improved stock. The major improvement came with regular interval services and new and refurbished stock as the tentacles of electric power stretched out to encompass Brighton, Worthing, Eastbourne, Hastings, Littlehampton and Bognor Regis. Most of the variables, plus the light engine workings, of steam traction were eliminated and one could stand at Purley and marvel at the precision with which the trains went through. At times of pressure suburban stock could, and would, be pressed into use to cope with excursionists and five shilling evening trips from East Croydon to Brighton quickly established a following. Some steam-hauled through services remained, such as the *Sunny South Special* from the LMS to Brighton, Eastbourne and Hastings and excursions such as the one that brought a works party from the Midlands into Eastbourne one day, before the inhabitants were awake and shipped them over to France from the pier, returning them about midnight with scarcely any of the denizens of Eastbourne being aware of it.

After the war the alterations were in detail rather than substance except for one charming backwater branch – Hayling Island. Until the summer of 1955 the summer Saturday service had been 17 trains in each direction between Havant and Hayling Island: then it was extended to two dozen each way with a half-hourly service (one fast, one stopper per hour) from 10am to 6pm. Three engines worked the service – Stroudley 'Terriers', all of 75 years old, about the only class allowed on the bridge between mainland and island. The 5 past the hour all stations from

Havant would arrive at Hayling Island at 18 minute past; then the waiting up train would leave at 20 minutes past fast to Havant (arriving at 30 minutes past) where the third engine would back on and work the 35 minutes past the hour fast arriving at Hayling Island at 45 past. That allowed the 47 past all stations (which had been reformed in the bay in the meantime) to proceed to Havant, where the engine released from the 20 minutes past up service, having completed engine duties, backed on to start the cycle all over again. No attempt was made to wait for any main line train, or the whole schedule would be disrupted. It was an enthusiast's and photographer's paradise, as well as a boon to holiday-makers, to have these 'Terriers' charging up and down with their three or four-coach trains, especially when one of the locomotives might be slightly lame and the other two were making up the time dropped.

Another holiday area a little further west had similar delights to offer on summer Saturdays. Portsmouth, although having Southsea as a holiday annexe, saw a large throughput of holidaymakers to the Isle of Wight. During the month of August each year the number of passengers using the Portsmouth–Ryde route soared by tenfold (March 1936: 64,419 – August 1936: 650,265), the major part of this increase being accounted for on four Saturdays and one Monday. Steps had to be taken early in SR days to improve facilities on the island, described in another feature. The O2 class 0-4-4 tanks shouldered the task well, even if the service operated within its own capsule.

Proceeding westward the next large holiday area is Bournemouth. The principal ordinary train was the *Bournemouth Limited* running non-stop to and from Waterloo in just under two hours (8.40am from Bournemouth Central, 4.30pm return) but this was more for business people. For holidays the all-Pullman *Bournemouth Belle* was a more likely candidate – at least in the down direction. The *Limited* title was not perpetuated after 1939 although the service ran with intermediate stops, and, in 1951 Festival year received the title *Royal Wessex*. Even when some two-hour services were introduced in 1957 (today's fastest is incidentally 1 hour 40 minutes), this train was not included.

But the interest in Bournemouth was centred on cross-country business, through trains from Birkenhead and Birmingham GWR, Newcastle, Bradford and a variety of other places well north of Watford,

Royal Arrangements

The Royal Family was no stranger to the Southern Railway, and arrangements for special trains were sophisticated. On 6 May 1939 a 'Royal Special Train' was run from Waterloo to Portsmouth & Southsea (High Level) to convey HM King George VI and Queen Elizabeth, Queen Mary, Members of the Royal Family and Suites. Clearly it was a naval occasion, as the empty stock was then worked forward into the Dockyard, whence it departed after 50 minutes as a 'Private Special' to Waterloo. The train was hauled to Portsmouth by T9 class 4-4-0 No 718, the consist being: Engine, Brake Pullman Car *Lady Dalziel*, Pullman Car *Cecilia* (kitchen leading), Pullman Car *Marjorie* (kitchen trailing), Brake Pullman Car *Montana*, Bogie Van 2348.

Arrangements seem to have been changed at the eleventh hour, for Supplementary Notice No P24/1939 was only issued on the day before to the journeys, cancelling SN No P23/1939. Recipients were commanded to acknowledge on 'the Form sent herewith by next train without fail.'

The Royal left Waterloo No 11 Platform at 12.45, running non-stop via the Portsmouth Direct line to timings very similar to those of the standard 90-minute expresses. The engine carried the usual four white discs as head-code, and the van, two tail lamps. Double block working was in force, and full precautions were specified for the working of trains and shunting on adjoining lines. 'Care must be taken that any Horses, with or without vehicles, which may be within Station *continued overleaf*

continued

Limits are under strict control during the approach and passing of the Royal Train . . .' Level crossings were guarded, and 'at all level crossings which are in the charge of Gatewomen, a competent man must be employed 30 minutes before the Royal Train is due to pass and remain until 10 minutes after . . .' Competent at *what*, one wonders? The tunnels (there were three) were to be inspected 'immediately prior to the running of the Royal Train' to check the condition of the line, while a 'competent' man was to be posted 'at each end an hour ahead so as to prevent any unauthorised person being upon the Railway in or near the Tunnel', while another 'competent' man was to be at each ventilation shaft on top. Station masters were to watch the passage of the train, and the passing times at certain specified stations telephoned to Waterloo.

Inspector Shaw 'must enter in his Report the number of persons (other than Railway Officers) who travel by the Royal Train, and also particulars of any animals that may be conveyed.' Even Royals were not going to be allowed to slip an extra one in free.

'A distinctive chalk mark must be made at the exact spot at which the Footplate of the Engine should be when the Royal Train stops . . . and a man with a Red Hand Signal must stand on the left hand side of the Engine at, or opposite, the chalk mark to ensure the train being stopped dead at the appointed place.' The distance from the centre of the footplate to the centre of the leading door of Pullman Car *Marjorie*, from which the Royal party would alight, was given as 159ft 4in.

Let us hope that it stayed fine.

The Waterloo – West of England Saturday timetable in Summer 1939 showing the five named portions of the Atlantic Coast Express.

indeed even from the Southern's own 'Deal, Dover &c, Margate and Ramsgate, via Guildford', in later years from South Wales via Salisbury and Wimborne, and of course always especially via the Somerset & Dorset from Bath – from Manchester, Liverpool and many other Northern and Midland starting points. The long-standing Brighton–Bournemouth service was steam-hauled to the end amidst the coastal electrics east of Havant. There was little time-interval or any regularity at all about happenings along the congested line through Poole, and Bournemouth West was perpetually like a jig-saw puzzle with surplus pieces.

Summer Saturdays were the only time that a few London–Weymouth services bypassed Bournemouth, taking advantage of the original main line pre-dating it, Castleman's famous Corkscrew, hardly for speed but still quicker than going through the congestion along the coast. Broadstone, where the Corkscrew cut across the Bath–Bournemouth trains and even on summer Saturdays there were a host of locals, was another fascinating place, at any period during the steam age always offering a rich variety in motive power, though seldom passing its passengers with speed.

And then the eleven o'clock from Waterloo to the far west, the most noted non-Pullman train on the system. From 19 July 1926, as part of the Southern's new public relations broom, it became the *Atlantic Coast Express*, later to be nicknamed the *ACE*. The name was chosen in a competition, the winner alas dying as the result of a shunting accident on the Light Railway between Torrington and Halwill. There was no other train quite like it, changing its character amazingly according to time of year and week. In summer half a dozen or more trains might all claim themselves the *Atlantic Coast Express*; it could indeed run in nearly as many separate complete trains at Bank Holiday weekends as it did in 'portions' on winter weekdays. Normally all the portions other than Ilfracombe's consisted of a single composite coach: brake, first-class smoking, first-class non-smoking, third-class smoking, third-class non-smoking. This gave it an odd and not especially pleasing appearance, and of course also meant that passengers going to one of the ultimate destinations had to get in the right compartment, first-class ones usually having no choice.

In 1926 Ilfracombe was reached at 4.24pm, the other portions finishing at Torrington at 4.12 and Plymouth Friary at 4.29. All summer a second train left Waterloo at 11.10 with through carriages for Padstow, Bude, Sidmouth and Exmouth, with of course corresponding up services. Just how popular it could be in summer is demonstrated by the number of seats booked from Waterloo for Friday and Saturday 2 and 3 September: 3,800. Holidaymakers always predominated for the journey to the west, but within Devon and Cornwall many people of course used it for local journeys, a handful of shoppers perhaps returning from Barnstaple on the single-coach Torrington portion maybe hauled by a Drummond 0-4-4 tank built for London suburban traffic in the 1890s but excellently maintained. For many years the Ilfracombe section completed its journey with a through coach from Paddington, the Southern for once showing superiority since its departure from Waterloo was half an hour later and by a longer and harder route.

For Continuation of Saturday Trains, pages 343 and 343a; for Monday to Friday Trains, pages 340 to 341a.

WATERLOO and THE WEST OF ENGLAND.

Saturdays — Down (columns 1–16)

Down.	1	2	3	4	5	6	7	8	9	10	11	12	13	14	15	16
	aft	mrn	mrn	mrn	mrn	mrn	mrn	mrn	mrn	mrn	mrn	mrn	mrn	mrn	mrn	mrn
324 WATERLOO ......dep	10F030	1 30	..	..	..	..	..	..	..	..	..	..	..	..	..	6 0
324 Surbiton ...... "	10F013	..	..	..	..	..	..	..	..	..	..	..	..	..	..	6 15
324 Woking ...... "	11F0 6	..	..	..	..	..	..	..	..	..	..	..	..	..	..	6 41
Basingstoke ......dep.	11F053	..	..	..	..	..	..	..	..	..	..	..	..	..	..	7 34
Oakley		..	..	..	..	..	..	..	..	..	..	..	..	..	..	7 45
Overton		..	..	..	..	..	..	..	..	..	..	..	..	..	..	7 52
Whitchurch A		..	..	..	..	..	..	..	..	..	..	..	..	..	..	7 59
Hurstbourne		..	..	..	..	..	..	..	..	..	..	..	..	..	..	8 4
Andover Junc 376		..	..	..	..	..	..	..	..	..	..	..	..	..	..	8 15
Grateley		..	..	..	..	..	..	..	..	..	..	..	..	..	..	8 27
Porton 338a	mrn	..	..	..	..	..	..	..	..	..	..	..	..	..	..	8 38
SALISBURY, 338a, 376 arr.	2 36	3 0	..	..	..	..	..	..		..	..	..	..	..	..	8 48
dep.	2 48	3 6	..	315	..	..	..	..		..	..	..	..	8 5	..	9 5
Wilton B	..		..	321	..	..	..	..		..	..	..	..	8 11	..	9 11
Dinton	..		..	..	..	..	..	..		..	..	..	..	8 20	..	9 21
Tisbury	..		..	343	..	..	..	..		..	..	..	..	8 28	..	9 30
Semley	..		..	355	..	..	..	..		..	..	..	..	8 38	..	9 41
Gillingham (Dorset)	3 40		..	4 4	..	..	..	..		..	..	..	..	8 47	..	9 50
Templecombe 510, 511	3 53		..	416	..	..	..	..		..	..	7 15	8 41	9b12	..	10 3
Milborne Port	..		..	424	..	..	..	..	..	..	..	7 20	8 47	9 18	..	1011
Sherborne	4 7		..	433	..	..	..	..	..	..	..	7 26	8 54	9 25	..	1019
Yeovil Junction 355 ...arr.	4 19		..	444	..	..	..	..	..	..	..	7 35	9 3	9 33	..	1030
355 Yeovil (Town) arr.	4 32		..	455	..	..	..	..	..	..	..	7 40	9 12	9 47	..	1039
dep.	Stop		..	Stp	..	..	..	..	6 20	..	..	7 45	Stop	9 28	..	1020
Yeovil Junction ......dep.	..		..	..	..	..	..	..	6 26	..	..	7 51	..	9 39	..	1041
Sutton Bingham	..		..	..	..	..	..	..	..	..	..	7 56	..	9 46	..	1048
Crewkerne	..		..	..	..	..	..	..	6 41	..	..	8 7	..	9 58	..	11 0
Chard Junction 355 ...arr.	..		..	..	..	..	..	..	6 56	..	..	8 21	..	1012	..	1114
355 Chard arr.	..		..	..	..	..	..	..	..	..	..	8 37	..	1034	..	1134
dep.	..		..	..	..	..	..	..	..	..	..	8 10	..	9 34	..	11 3
Chard Junction ......dep.	..		..	..	..	..	..	..	6 57	..	..	8 22	..	1015	..	1115
Axminster 355 ......arr.	..		..	..	..	..	..	..	7 5	..	..	8 31	..	1024	..	1122
355 Lyme Regis arr.	..		..	..	..	..	..	..	..	..	..	8 58	..	1147	..	1147
dep.	..		..	..	..	..	..	..	..	..	..	8 4	..	10 5	..	1028
Axminster ......dep.	..	..	..	..	..	..	..	..	7 9	..	..	8 32	..	1028	..	1123
Seaton Junction 355 ...arr.	..	..	..	..	..	..	..	..	7 16	..	..	8 39	..	1034	..	1130
355 Seaton arr.	..	..	..	..	..	..	..	..	..	..	..	8 55	..	11 5	..	1145
dep.	..	..	..	..	..	..	..	..	..	..	..	8 22	..	1023	..	..
Seaton Junction ......dep.	..	..	..	..	..	..	..	..	7 20	..	..	8 40	..	1038	..	1132
Honiton	..	..	..	..	..	..	..	..	7 35	..	8 19	8 56	..	1054	..	1150
Sidmouth Junc. 356 ..arr.	..	..	..	..	..	..	..	..	7 43	..	8 25	9 4	..	11 2	..	1158
356 Sidmouth ......arr.	..	..	..	..	..	..	..	..	8 28	..	8 52	9 37	..	1141	..	1239
356 Budleigh Salterton "	..	..	..	..	..	..	..	..	9 0	..	9 0	1021	..	1157	..	1 2
356 Exmouth ...... "	..	..	..	..	..	..	..	..	9 12	..	9 12	1036	mrn	12 9	..	1 17
356 Sidmouth ......dep.	..	..	..	..	..	..	..	..	7 20	..	..	8 35	9 45	..	..	11 9
Sidmouth Junction ...dep.	..	..	..	..	..	..	..	..	7 45	..	8 26	9 5	1012	11 3	..	1159
Whimple	..	..	..	..	..	..	..	..	7 52	..	8 32	9 12	1020	1110	..	12 5
Broad Clyst	..	..	..	..	..	..	..	..	7 59	..	8 38	9 19	1027	..	..	..
Pinhoe	..	..	..	..	..	..	..	..	8 4	..	8 43	9 24	1032	..	..	..
EXETER Central 357 arr.	..	4 39	..	..	..	..	..	..	8 12	..	8 50	9 32	1040	1124	..	1218
357 Exmouth arr.	..	6 24	..	..	..	..	..	..	8 41	..	9 39	1014	1111	1211	..	1 13
dep.	..	..	..	..	..	..	..	6 45	7 45	8 15	Stop	9 15	Stop	1045	1045	..
EXETER Central ......dep.	..	4 40	4 50	..	..	..	..	7 35	8 18	8 46	..	9 42	..	1137	1146	..
Exeter (St. David's)	..	4 45	5 0	..	..	..	..	7 41	8 26	8 51	..	9 47	..	1143	1151	..
Newton St. Cyres	..	..	..	..	..	..	..	7 51	8 36	9 1	..	..	..	1153	12 1	..
Crediton	..	..	5 17	..	..	..	..	7 57	8 42	9 7	..	9 59	..	1159	12 9	..
Yeoford ......arr.	..	..	5 25	..	..	..	..	8 5	8 50	9 14	..	10 7	..	12 7	1217	..

Saturdays — Down (columns 17–32)

Down.	17	18	19	20	21	22	23	24	25	26	27	28	29	30	31	32
	mrn	mrn	mrn	mrn	aft	mrn	mrn	mrn	mrn	mrn	mrn	mrn	mrn	aft	aft	aft
324 WATERLOO ......dep	7 24	8 35	8 45		..	9 0	..	..	1024	1035	1040	1054	11 0	..	..	..
324 Surbiton ...... "	7 33	8 56	8 56		..	9 19	..	..	..	..	..	..	..	..	..	..
324 Woking ...... "	7 57	9 14	9 20		..	9 37	..	..	..	..	..	..	..	..	..	..
Basingstoke ......dep.	9 15	..	9 52		..	10 9	1024	..	..	..	..	..	..	..	..	..
Oakley	9 24	..	..		..	..	1035	..	..	..	..	..	..	..	..	..
Overton	9 30	..	..		..	..	1041	..	..	..	..	..	..	..	..	..
Whitchurch A	9 36	..	..		..	..	1047	..	..	..	..	..	..	..	..	..
Hurstbourne	9 41	..	..		..	..	1052	..	..	..	..	..	..	..	..	..
Andover Junc 376	9 52	..	..		..	1035	11 1	..	..	..	..	..	..	..	..	..
Grateley	10 3	..	..		..	..	1111	..	..	..	..	..	..	..	..	..
Porton 338a	1012	..	..		..	..	1120	..	..	..	..	..	..	..	..	..
SALISBURY, 338a, 376 arr.	1022	1028	1030		..	1058	1130	..	1152	12 1	1210	1223	1232	..	..	..
dep.	Stop	1032	1042	1052	..	11 2	Stop	1110	1155	12 4	1214	1226	1235	1247	..	..
Wilton B	..	..	..	..	..	..	..	1116		..			..	..	..	..
Dinton	..	..	..	..	..	..	..	1125		..			..	1 1	..	..
Tisbury	..	..	..	..	..	..	..	1133		..			..	1 10	..	..
Semley	..	..	..	..	..	..	..	1143		..			..	1 20	..	..
Gillingham (Dorset)	..	..	..	..	..	..	mrn	1152		..			..	1 27	..	..
Templecombe 510, 511	..	..	1120	1131	..	1140	1152	12 6		..			..	1 38	..	..
Milborne Port	..	..	..	..	..	..	..	1214		..			..	1 45	..	..
Sherborne	..	..	1132	..	..	1153	12 3	1221		..			..	1 52	..	..
Yeovil Junction 355 ...arr.	..	1120	..	1148	..	12 2	1212	1232		..			..	2 0	..	..
355 Yeovil (Town) arr.	..	1132	..	1214	..	1214	..	1243		..			..	2 9	..	..
dep.	..	1112	..	1130	..	1155	1155	..		..			..	Stop	..	..
Yeovil Junction ......dep.	..	1122		1149		12 3	1213	..		..			..	..	..	..
Sutton Bingham	..			..		..	1218	..		..			..	..	..	..
Crewkerne	..			..		..	1229	..		..			..	..	..	..
Chard Junction 355 ...arr.	..			..		..	1243	..		..			..	..	..	..
355 Chard arr.	..			..		..	1 2	..						..	..	..
dep.	..			..		..	1220	..						..	..	..
Chard Junction ......dep.	..			..		..	1244	..						..	..	..
Axminster 355 ......arr.	..			1218		1232	1251	..						..	..	..
355 Lyme Regis arr.	..			1 7		1 7	..	..						..	..	..
dep.	..			1153		1153	..	..						..	..	..
Axminster ......dep.	..			1219		1234	1252	..						..	..	..
Seaton Junction 355 ...arr.	..			1226		1242	1258	..						..	..	..
355 Seaton arr.	..		..	1 4	..	1 4	1 46	..						..	..	..
dep.	..		..	1215	..	1215	Stop	..						..	..	1 50
Seaton Junction ......dep.	..	..	..	1227	..	1244	..	..						..	..	2 5
Honiton	..	..	..	..	1252	1 2	..	..						..	..	2 21
Sidmouth Junc. 356 ..arr.	..	1210	1225	1249	1257	1 10	..	..						..	..	2 29
356 Sidmouth ......arr.	..	1239	1 39	1 39	..	1 39	..	..						..	..	3 35
356 Budleigh Salterton "	..	1 2	1 2	2 48	..	2 48	..	..						..	..	3a29
356 Exmouth ...... "	..	1 17	1 17	3 13	..	3 13	..	..						..	..	3a46
356 Sidmouth ......dep.	..	1146	..	..	..		..	..						..	..	..
Sidmouth Junction ...dep.	..	1212	1227	1250	1258		..	..						..	..	2 31
Whimple	..	..	..	..	1 5		..	..						..	..	2 38
Broad Clyst	..	..	..	..	1 11		..	..						..	..	2 45
Pinhoe	..	..	..	..	1 16		..	..		..			..	..	..	2 49
EXETER Central 357 arr.	..	1229	1244	1 6	1 25		..	..	1 33	1 41	1 54	2 6	2 15	..	..	2 57
357 Exmouth arr.	..	1 13	1 43	1 43	2 42		..	..	2 42	2 42	2 42	2 42	3 12	aft	..	4 11
dep.	..	1145	1215	1215	..		..	..	1215	1 15	1 15	1 15	1 15	1 45	2 15	2 45
EXETER Central ......dep.	..	1233	1249	1 13	..		..	..	1 36	1 45	1 57	2 9	2 18	2 28	2 55	3 22
Exeter (St. David's)	..	1240	1255	1 20	..		..	..	1 42	1 52	2 4	2 16	2 26	2 34	2 59	3 27
Newton St. Cyres	..	..	..	1 30	..		..	..	..	..	..	..	..	..	3 8	3 37
Crediton	..	..	..	1 35	..		..	..	..	..	..	..	..	..	3 13	3 42
Yeoford ......arr.	..	..	1 12	..	..		..	..	..	..	..	..	..	2 51	3 21	3 50

- 1: Via Eastleigh.
- 2: Passengers by this Train must reserve seats in advance
- 9: Calls Lion's Holt Halt 8 10 mrn.
- 18: Restaurant Car, London to Sidmouth.
- 19: Restaurant Car, London to Exmouth.
- 20: Through Train from Portsmouth, page 380
- 21: Calls Lion's Holt Halt 1 22 aft.
- 22: Restaurant Car, London to Sidmouth Junc.
- 25: Atlantic Coast Express, Restaurant Car, London to Ilfracombe. Not after 2nd September.
- 26: Atlantic Coast Express. Restaurant Car, London to Ilfracombe.
- 27: Atlantic Coast Express, Restaurant Car, London to Padstow. Not after 2nd September.
- 28: Restaurant Car, London to Exeter, until 2nd Sept., to Padstow thereafter. Atlantic Coast Express.
- 29: Atlantic Coast Express. Restaurant Car, London to Exeter.

Saturdays — Down, continued (columns 1–16)

Down.	1	2	3	4	5	6	7	8	9	10	11	12	13	14	15	16
Yeoford ......dep.	..	..	..	..	..	..	..	8 6	..	9 15	..	..		12 8	..	..
Bow	..	..	..	..	..	..	..	8 16	..	9 24	..	..		1218	..	..
North Tawton	..	..	..	..	..	..	..	8 23	..	9 31	..	..		1225	..	..
Sampford Courtenay	..	..	..	..	..		..	8 30	..	9 37	..	..		1232	..	..
Okehampton ......arr.	mrn	..	..	..	..		..	8 39	..	9 46	..	..		1241	..	..
Okehampton ......dep.	4 20	..	..	..	..		..	8 42	..	9 48	..	..		1244	..	..
Bridestowe	..	..	..	..	..		..	8 57	..	10 3	..	..		1 2	..	..
Lydford	..	..	..	..	..		..	9 4	..	1010	..	..		1 10	..	..
Brentor	..	..	..	..	..		..	9 8	..	1014	..	..		1 14	..	..
Tavistock C	6 u 0	..	..	mn	758		8 44	9 18	..	1023	..	..	non	1 25	..	..
Bere Alston 357	6 13	..	..	753	811		8 55	9 30	..	1037	..	..	12 0	1 40	..	..
Bere Ferrers	6 21	..	..	8 0	..		Stop	9 36	..	1043	..	..	12 5	1 47	..	..
Tamerton Foliot	6 26	..	..	8 5	..		..	9 41	..	1048	..	..	1210	1 52	..	..
St. Budeaux, for Saltash	6 31	..	..	810	825	8 55	..	9 46	..	1053	..	..	1215	1 57	..	..
Ford (Devon)	6 35	..	..	817	832	9 0	..	9 50	..	1057	..	..	1223	2 3	..	..
Devonport D ......arr.	6 39	6 7	..	823	836	9 5	..	9 54	..	11 1	..	..	1228	2 7	..	..
PLYMOUTH North Rd. "	6 43	6 13	..	828	840	9 9	..	9 59	..	11 7	..	..	1232	2 14	..	..
PLYMOUTH Friary "	6 53	6 24	..	841	853	9 21	..	1011	..	1117	..	..	1243	2 24	..	..
Yeoford ......dep.	..	..	5 30	Stp	Stp	Stop	..	Stop	8 51	Stop	..	10 8	Stop	..	1221	..
Copplestone	..	..	5 38	..	..	..	..	..	8 57	..	..	1014	..	..	1229	..
Morchard Road	..	..	5 42	..	..	..	..	..	9 1	..	..	..	..	..	1232	..
Lapford	..	..	5 46	..	..	..	..	mrn	9 6	..	..	1023	..	..	1237	..
Eggesford F	..	..	5 53	..	..	..	..	8 22	9 15	..	..	1033	..	..	1244	..
South Molton Road G	..	..	5 59	..	..	..	..	8 28	9 22	..	..	1040	..	..	1253	..
Portsmouth Arms	..	..	6 6	..	..	..	..	8 33	9 28	..	..	1046	..	..	1258	..
Umberleigh	..	..	6 12	..	..	..	..	8 40	9 35	..	..	1053	..	..	1 5	..
Chapelton	..	..	..	..	..	..	..	8 45	9 40	..	..	1058	..	..	1 10	..
Barnstaple J. H 354 arr.	..	..	6 22	mn	mn	mrn	mrn	8 52	9 47	..	..	11 5	aft	..	1 18	..
dep.	..	..	6 33	648	725	7 45	8 10	..	9 59	..	..	1111	1230	..	1 24	..
Barnstaple Tn. J	..	..	6 38	710	728	7 50	8 13	..	10 4	..	..	1116	1233	..	1 29	..
Wrafton	..	..	..	7 4	736	..	8 21	..	1012	..	..	1124	1241	..	1 37	..
Braunton K	..	..	6 48	..	739	8 1	8 24	..	1016	..	..	1128	1245	..	1 40	..
Morthoe L	..	..	7 6	734	757	8 21	8 42	..	1035	..	..	1146	1 3	..	1 59	..
ILFRACOMBE ....arr.	..	..	7 15	743	8 6	8 30	8 51	..	1044	..	mrn	1155	1 12	..	2 8	..
Barnstaple Junc. dep.	..	..	6 40	..	..	..	8 18	9 0	10 5	..	11 0	1115	..	..	1 25	..
Fremington	..	..	6 45	..	..	..	8 23	9 5	1010	..	11 5	1120	..	..	1 33	..
Instow	..	..	6 53	..	..	..	8 30	9 15	1017	..	1112	1127	..	..	1 40	..
Bideford N	..	..	7 5	..	..	..	8 39	9 24	1023	..	1118	1133	..	..	1 46	..
Torrington 358 .arr.	..	..	7 [illegible]	..	..	..	8 50	Stop	1047	mrn	..	1144	..	..	1 57	..
Okehampton ......dep.	..	..	..	..	..	..	Stop	..	..	10 0	..	..	..	1 0	..	..
Maddaford Moor Halt P	..	..	..	..	..	..	..	..	..	1012	..	..	..	1 13	..	..
Ashbury, for North Lew	..	..	..	..	..	..	..	..	..	1020	..	..	..	1 21	..	..
Halwill Q 358 ......arr.	..	..	..	..	..	..	..	mrn	..	1029	..	..	..	1 28	..	..
Halwill ......dep.	..	..	..	..	..	..	..	8 15	..	1037	..	..	..	1 36	..	..
Dunsland Cross	..	..	..	..	..	..	..	8 21	..	1045	..	..	..	1 44	..	..
Holsworthy	..	..	..	..	..	..	..	8 30	..	1055	..	..	..	1 54	..	..
Whitstone and Bridgerule	..	..	..	..	..	..	..	8 40	..	11 7	..	..	..	2 6	..	..
Bude ......arr.	..	..	..	..	..	..	..	8 50	..	1117	..	..	..	2 16	..	..
Halwill ......dep.	..	..	..	..	..	..	..	..	..	1030	..	..	..	1 30	..	..
Ashwater	..	..	..	..	..	..	..	..	..	1040	..	..	..	1 39	..	..
Tower Hill	..	..	..	..	..	..	mrn	..	..	1047	..	..	..	1 46	..	..
Launceston	..	..	..	..	..	..	7 44	..	..	1055	..	..	..	1 55	..	..
Egloskerry	..	..	..	..	..	..	7 52	..	..	11 4	..	..	..	2 6	..	..
Tresmeer	..	..	..	..	..	..	8 1	..	..	1112	..	..	..	2 14	..	..
Otterham U	..	..	..	..	..	..	8 11	..	..	1124	..	..	..	2 25	..	..
Camelford V	..	..	..	..	..	..	8 20	..	..	1136	..	..	..	2 32	..	..
Delabole	..	..	..	..	..	..	8 27	..	..	1142	..	..	..	2 39	..	..
Port Isaac Road	..	..	..	..	..	..	8 35	..	..	1149	..	..	..	2 47	..	..
St. Kew Highway	..	..	..	..	..	..	8 40	..	..	1153	..	..	..	2 53	..	..
Wadebridge 358 ......arr.	..	..	..	..	..	..	8 48	..	..	12 0	..	..	..	3 1	..	..
358 Bodmin ......arr.	..	..	..	..	..	..	10 0	..	..	1 19	..	..	..	3 37	..	..
Padstow ......arr.	..	..	..	..	..	..	9 3	..	..	1211	..	..	..	3 36	..	..

Saturdays — Down, continued (columns 17–32)

Down.	17	18	19	20	21	22	23	24	25	26	27	28	29	30	31	32
Yeoford ......dep.	..	..	..	..	..	..	..	..			..		..	..	3 23	..
Bow	..	..	..	1 51	..	..	..	..			..		..	..	3 34	..
North Tawton	..	..	..	1 58	..	..	..	..			..		..	..	3 41	..
Sampford Courtenay	..	..	..	..	..	..	..	..			..		..	..	3 48	..
Okehampton ......arr.	..	1 20	..	2 11	..	..	..	..			..		3 5	..	3 57	..
Okehampton ......dep.	..	1 21	..	2 13	..	..	..	..					3 7	..	3 59	..
Bridestowe	..	..	..	..	..	..	..	..					..	..	4 14	..
Lydford	..	..	..	..	..	..	..	..					..	..	4 21	..
Brentor	..	..	..	..	..	..	aft	..					..	..	4 25	..
Tavistock C	..	1 48	..	2 39	..	..	3 0	..					3 34	..	4 34	..
Bere Alston 357	..	1 59	..	..	..	..	3 11	..					..	..	4 46	..
Bere Ferrers	..	..	..	..	..	..	3 17	..					..	..	4 52	..
Tamerton Foliot	..	..	..	..	..	..	3 21	..					..	..	4 57	..
St. Budeaux, for Saltash	..	..	..	..	..	..	3 26	..					..	..	5 2	..
Ford (Devon)	..	..	..	..	..	..	3 32	..					..	..	5 6	..
Devonport D ......arr.	..	2 17	..	3 8	..	..	3 38	..					4 1	..	5 10	..
PLYMOUTH North Rd. "	..	2 23	..	3 13	..	..	3 42	..					4 10	..	5 14	..
PLYMOUTH Friary "	..	2 34	..	3 23	..	..	3 53	..					4 22	..	5 23	..
Yeoford ......dep.	..	Stop	1 13	..	..	..		..					..	2 52	Stop	3 51
Copplestone	..	..	1 19	..	..	..		..					..	..	..	3 58
Morchard Road	..	..	1 22	..	..	..		..					..	..	..	4 1
Lapford	..	..	1 27	..	..	..		..					..	..	..	4 6
Eggesford F	..	..	1 33	..	..	..		..					..	..	..	4 15
South Molton Road G	..	..	1 40	..	..	..		..					..	..	..	4 27
Portsmouth Arms	..	..	1 47	..	..	..		..					..	Dd	..	4 32
Umberleigh	..	..	1 56	..	..	..		..					..	..	..	4 38
Chapelton	..	..	2 1	..	..	..		..					..	..	..	4 43
Barnstaple J. H 354 arr.	aft	aft	2 9	..	..	..		..	2 38	2 49			..	3 40	aft	4 50
dep.	1 43	2 1	2 13	..	..	..	..	..	2 40	2 51				3v48	4 25	..
Barnstaple Tn. J	1 48	2 6	2 19	..	..	..	..	..	..	2 56				3v53	4 30	..
Wrafton	1 56	..	2 27	..	..	..	..	..	..	..				..	..	..
Braunton K	2 0	2 17	2 32	..	..	..	..	..	2 55	3 10				4v3	4 40	..
Morthoe L	2 18	2 36	2 51	..	..	..	..	..	3 15	3 30				4v22	5 0	..
ILFRACOMBE ....arr.	2 28	2 45	3 0	..	..	..	..	..	3 25	3 40				4v31	5 10	..
Barnstaple Junc. dep.	..		2 22	..	..	..	..	..	..	..				3 45		4 55
Fremington	..		2 29	..	..	..	..	..	..	..				3 50		5 2
Instow	..		2 36	..	..	..	..	..	..	..				3 57		5 12
Bideford N	..		2 45	..	..	..	..	..	..	..				4 3		5 18
Torrington 358 .arr.	..		2 56	..	..	..	..	..	..	..				4 15		5 29
Okehampton ......dep.	..	..		..	..	..	..	..		..			3 30	..		..
Maddaford Moor Halt P	..	..		..	..	..	..	..		..			3 42	..		..
Ashbury, for North Lew	..	..		..	..	..	..	..		..		..	3 50	..		..
Halwill Q 358 ......arr.	..	..		..	..	..	..	..		..		3B16	3 57	..		..
Halwill ......dep.	..	..		..	..	..	..	..		..		..	4 20	..		..
Dunsland Cross	..	..		..	..	..	..	..		..		..	4 26	..		..
Holsworthy	..	..		..	..	..	..	..		..		3 27	4 35	..		..
Whitstone and Bridgerule	..	..		..	..	..	..	..		..		..	4 44	..		..
Bude ......arr.	..	..		..	..	..	..	..		..		3 46	4 54	..		..
Halwill ......dep.	..	..		..	..	..	..	..	..	..	..	3B18	3 59	..	..	..
Ashwater	..	..		..	..	..	..	..	..	..	..	..	4 7	..	..	..
Tower Hill	..	..		..	..	..	..	..	..	..	..	..	4 14	..	..	..
Launceston	..	..	..	..	..	..	..	..	..	..	3 23	3B40	4 22	..	..	..
Egloskerry	..	..	..	..	..	..	..	..	..	..	..	..	4 32	..	..	..
Tresmeer	..	..	..	..	..	..	..	..	..	..	..	..	4 40	..	..	..
Otterham U	..	..	..	..	..	..	..	..	..	..	3 49	4B 6	4 50	..	..	..
Camelford V	..	..	..	..	..	..	..	..	..	..	3 59	4B16	4 58	..	..	..
Delabole	..	..	..	..	..	..	..	..	..	..	4 7	4B24	5 4	..	..	..
Port Isaac Road	..	..	..	..	..	..	..	..	..	..	4 16	4B33	5 11	..	..	..
St. Kew Highway	..	..	..	..	..	..	..	..	..	..	..	..	5 16	..	..	..
Wadebridge 358 ......arr.	..	..	..	..	..	..	..	..	..	..	4 30	4B47	5 23	..	..	..
358 Bodmin ......arr.	..	..	..	..	..	..	..	..	..	..	5 30	5B30	6 30	..	..	..
Padstow ......arr.	..	..	..	..	..	..	..	..	..	..	4 43	5B 0	5 36	..	..	..

- 6: 3rd class only
- 13: 3rd class only.
- 18: Not after 2nd September.
- 23: 3rd class only
- 25: Restaurant Car, London to Ilfracombe. Not after 2nd September. Atlantic Coast Express.
- 26: Atlantic Coast Express. Restaurant Car, London to Ilfracombe.
- 27: Atlantic Coast Express. Restaurant Car, London to Padstow. Not after 2nd September.
- 28: Restaurant Car, London to Exeter until 2nd September, to Padstow thereafter. Atlantic Coast Express.
- 29: Atlantic Coast Express.
- 31: Not after 9th September.

For Sunday Trains and Notes, pages 344 and 345.

By Brighton to Bournemouth. A Waterloo–Bournemouth express passes Battledown flyover near Worting Junction where the West of England main line curves away under the bridge to head for Salisbury. The locomotive is Class N15X 4-6-0 No 2331 Beattie, *one of the seven former LBSCR 4-6-4Ts of the Remembrance class rebuilt by Maunsell in 1934 as tender engines after they were made redundant by electrification of the Brighton line. Except for the last member of the class named* Remembrance, *all were named by the SR after locomotive engineers.*

Pre-1942 the King Arthurs monopolised the working of the train east of Exeter although Lord Nelsons did eventually oust them between London and Salisbury; west of Exeter 2-6-0s and T9 class 4-4-0s were the principal classes with M7 0-4-4 tanks on the branches. The timetable was gradually tightened up until Exeter Central was reached in 3hr 7min, Ilfracombe in five hours and Padstow in 5 hours 49 minutes.

With the war the train lost its name but functioned to slower timings with longer formations but on 6 October 1947 the title reappeared. Timings were slow, especially in the up direction, despite the fact there was now Pacific-haulage right through with changes of engines at Salisbury and Exeter. Substantial accelerations were introduced in the summer of 1952, including the first mile-a-minute schedule on the Southern, when 83 minutes were allowed to Salisbury, Exeter Central was reached in 3hr 5min, Ilfracombe 5hr 10min and Plymouth Friary in 5½ hours. A choice of 65 destinations without change was offered to the traveller from Waterloo in a typical (1955–6) winter service. September 1961 witnessed the final significant acceleration of the *ACE*: two minutes under the three hours to Exeter Central, five minutes under the five hours to Ilfracombe and 6hr 22min to Padstow. Eventually in summer the Ilfracombe time was pared to 4hr 51min and Padstow six hours.

In the sixties the down train became a legend for speed exploits with the modified 'Merchant Navy' engines and it was something of a disappointment if one could not record 90 with the 11 or 12 coach load going down to Exeter; the coveted three figures was recorded several times on the service, even to a maximum of 104mph. The harder work for the locomotives was on the up service, not so productive of high speeds. All this disappeared in September 1964 with down-grading of the route. Its counterpart today is the eight-coach diesel-hauled 11.10 which fizzles out at Exeter St David's at 14.32. Ichabod indeed!

Gateway to an Island. A panoramic view of Ryde Pier Head in 1964 on a summer Saturday. On the left is the queue of passengers waiting to board the Portsmouth ferry, then the double track pier tramway operated by the SR with petrol driven trams as two independent single lines, and on the right the four track Pier Head station, with Class O2 0-4-4T No 22 Brading *leaving for Shanklin. In the right background is one of the ferries, PS* Ryde.

An Island Railway

It could be said there were two Southern Railways, the mainland one, which however varied was at least the subject of considerable integration, and that entirely self-contained on the Isle of Wight. In some ways it would be a claim that would not stand up. Like that of most islands, the attraction of the Isle of Wight's railways lay partly in the longevity of its motive power and rolling stock, but this was of course left over material from the mainland. Much signalling and other apparatus eventually came to be the same as on any other part of the Southern . . . certainly the products of Exmouth Junction concrete works were here as elsewhere.

But in other ways the island's railways were quite different. Indeed, it is better to talk of the island's railway, for though (as we will note in a moment) the history was extremely complex, the whole system – six termini, five junctions – came to run as a single close-knit unit, incidentally at the peak of its prosperity with a surprising variety of through services. The very individual character it developed owed as much to the loyal service of several generations of indigenous railwaymen as to the antiquated equipment and the viciously sharp traffic peaks. The frequency and length of trains, numbers of passengers, smart stopping and starting and junction connections, specials for Passenger Luggage in Advance, a section double track in summer and two separate single lines in winter, substantial coal and other freight . . . it could not fail to interest anyone with a railway inkling from across the mainland.

Though the island is just 23 miles east to west, thirteen north to south, five separate railways were involved before the 1923 Grouping. Three were locally-based concerns: the Isle of Wight Railway, from Ryde St John's Road to Ventnor and the branch to Bembridge; the Isle of Wight Central, from Ryde St John's Road to Newport and Cowes, also the cross-country route from Newport to Sandown and the branch from Merstone to Ventnor Town (later West); and the grandly named Freshwater, Yarmouth & Newport, linking just those places. Though operated by the IoWR and the IoWCR, the key section between Ryde St John's Road and Ryde Pier Head, was owned jointly by the LBSC and LSWR.

Much of the island's motive power and rolling stock had of course been purchased second hand by the local companies so in 1923 the Southern inherited a veritable collection of antiques, including all of the IWR Beyer Peacock 2-4-0Ts, built new for the line, some as far back as the opening in 1864. Though ultimate control was now exercised from Waterloo, the Southern wisely based senior managers on the island. At first there was a traffic superintendent based at Newport, and a representative of the chief mechanical engineer's department to look after locomotives and rolling stock. From the beginning of 1930 the two posts were combined and the mechanical assistant for the Isle of Wight, at that time A. B. MacLeod, who had been there from 1928, took over the traffic and commercial functions as well, and virtually became Pooh Bah, the Lord High Everything Else of the Island system representing all the various departments. Of course he had to report to all top departmental officers at the all-Southern HQ. In practice this meant considerable day-by-day freedom. Just as Parliament had controlled King Charles by regulating the money supply, so Waterloo knew its power. Macleod has told how with his operating hat on he had had representations from drivers that an additional water column would save delays in taking water at Ryde Pier Head. A memorandum was sent to the Locomotive Running Department at Waterloo asking for the new water column to be approved. This involved the outdoor machinery engineer who sent a request for the island assistant to examine the proposal to see whether a new water column was feasible and to report back. Naturally MacLeod, with his mechanical engineering hat on, reported back to the outdoor machinery engineer that the proposal had been examined and was feasible. In this case approval was duly sent, and water column provided.

When it came to replacement locomotives and rolling stock this was a major top level decision based on the first reports from the island manager to the new owners immediately after the grouping and a directors' inspection. Given the vastly great priorities for new works on the London suburban electrification schemes and im-

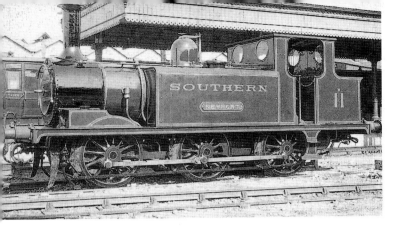

Island Terrier. A class which had a long history on the Isle of Wight was the LBSCR A1X 0-6-0T, being bought secondhand by Island companies and with others sent to the Island by the SR. Although used on lighter trains they had enlarged bunkers to increase coal capacity. This is No 11 Newport *fresh from the paintshop – the chalk marks for the lettering are still visible. It still exists, preserved at the Isle of Wight Steam centre at Havenstreet.*

provements to main-line long distance services it was surprising how much was done to improve train services on the Isle of Wight during the early grouping period. Replacement locomotives and coaches all had to be ferried over the water, mostly by the mid 1920s on the Southampton Docks floating crane. Much of the track was relaid, particularly sections of old light flat bottomed rail. Additional passing loops were provided and the double single lines south from Ryde St John's Road to the divergence of the Cowes line about a mile away was converted for summertime conventional double line with a new scissors crossover and signalbox at Smallbrook Junction. In winter the box switched out and the two lines ran independently from Ryde St John's Road again. St John's itself was given a 'new' box . . . well, it came from Waterloo Junction, made redundant by the re-signalling of the Charing Cross – London Bridge area. A new locomotive running shed at St John's Road replaced

Southern standardisation. What might be termed the standard class on the Isle of Wight in Southern days was the former LSWR O2 0-4-4T, of which there were 23 examples. All differed from those remaining on the mainland by having enlarged bunkers designed by the Island manager A. B. MacLeod in the early 1930s, Westinghouse air brakes, and names. This is an unusual photograph showing No 23 Totland *in wartime black livery. It was transferred to the Island in 1925 and was withdrawn 30 years later.*

the original corrugated iron 'barn' as MacLeod described it. And more up to date machinery was installed in Ryde Works, on the down side of St John's Road station. These works took over all repairs and maintenance of locomotives and wagons. The old locomotive workshops at Newport were refitted to look after the coaches.

Gradually former LSWR Class O2 0-4-4Ts were sent to the island to replace the older types. They were supplemented by additional ex-LBSC Terrier 0-6-0Ts for lighter duties to accompany those of the same type already taken over from the Central and Freshwater lines. Finally in the early 1930s four of the larger exLBSC Class E1 0-6-0Ts went to the Island for freight work, based on the extensive Medina Wharf built by the Newport & Cowes in 1877. Once all the island's heavy goods came in here.

As the summer Saturday traffic grew heavier, needing more trains, particularly on the Ventnor line, the Island O2s were given larger bunkers, which were extended back from near the bottom and doubled the coal capacity to 3 tons and saved light running from Ryde Pier to St John's Road shed for coal in the middle of intensive duties. The 'MacLeod bunker', as it was known, gave the Island O2s a distinctive modern appearance compared with their mainland sisters, which quite belied their late 1880s design. Further coaches, mostly old London, Chatham & Dover bogies were sent over to supplement the LCDR and LBSC four-wheelers, but gradually bogie stock worked the majority of the 'best services'. All were fitted with the Westinghouse compressed air brake which was standard on the Isle of Wight right up to the end of steam in 1966. It was a much more powerful brake than the vacuum and island drivers proverbially stopped on a sixpence, entering platforms quite rapidly – just like their electric counterparts on London suburban services.

While there was just about enough traffic for all year services, inevitably the summer saw peak use of island trains as more people went there for holidays from the 1930s. With changeover day on Saturdays, as one week's holidaymakers made their way home in the morning and new arrivals started arriving in their thousands (indeed more than 35,000 passengers were carried on a single day at the height of the peak) from mid morning on, the island Summer Saturday train service, with its extensive single line network, had to run like clockwork if things were not to go badly wrong. And indeed the new timetable for 1930 was tried out on the island manager's O-gauge clockwork model railway to see whether it would work!

By 1933 traffic had again increased and an even more frequent Saturday service was needed with four trains an hour on the Ventnor line (three to Ventnor and one to Sandown) and one an hour to Newport and Cowes. The latter had increased to half hourly by 1938. This meant that Smallbrook Junction was handling twelve trains an hour, six each way with the two down Cowes trains crossing the paths of the four up Ventnor line trains over the scissors crossover, and all needing delivery or collection of the electric staff for the sections from Smallbrook to Brading and Smallbrook to Haven Street.

The slightest delay perhaps in despatching a train from Ryde Pier or a badly steaming engine, which took a couple of minutes over schedule to Brading, could upset the rest of the day's working. Trains from Pier Head could not wait for specific boats from Portsmouth on Saturdays. Moreover with most passengers in family groups with children and mountains of luggage it was not like handling the London commuter peak services. Families could not be rushed, and if one train was missed there would soon be another.

Luggage itself was becoming a massive problem by the early 1930s and the Southern Railway in conjunction with the other mainland companies stressed the advantage of sending luggage in advance from home stations and delivered to the passenger's boarding house or hotel, hopefully to arrive before the owners did. PLA, initials that meant a lot to everyone in the islands catering trade, arrived mainly on Fridays and was sent back to the mainland late on Saturdays (it was barred before 4pm) and on Sundays. In the 1930s much of the luggage was carried in four-wheel luggage vans marshalled at the Pier Head end of trains to speed transfer to and from the ferries. The luggage was containerised in that the suitcases and trunks were loaded into wheeled caged trollies (precursors of BRUTES) at each station which were pushed up timber ramps into the luggage vans. At Ryde the trollies would be taken out of the vans and coupled to be hauled by petrol tractors to the quayside where cranes lifted the trollies one by one into the ferries. A similar procedure was adopted at Portsmouth but here the luggage was unloaded into individual items for the various trains to London, Birmingham, Cardiff or wherever. In post war years when more coaches were sent to the Island to replace the ageing LCDR stock, much rebuilding took place to provide luggage space in the brake thirds at the Pier Head end of trains, the displaced compartment pieces being used to add passenger accommodation to other former brake coaches marshalled further down the trains, and several luggage-only trains were scheduled.

Even though the Isle of Wight section was part of the forward looking Southern Railway, the island staff, and particularly those in Ryde Works, which in later years took over coaches as well, had to make do and mend to a much greater extent than at the mainland workshops. It was not a case of telephoning Eastleigh to get some out-of-stock item put on the next train. Much ingenuity was used at Ryde Works in making, repairing, and finding new uses for different items. Parts for the workshop heating system for example were converted from old Westinghouse brake air reservoirs, and a small four-wheel hand driven trolley, *Midget*, was built from scrap materials for use in shunting coaches and wagons around the works yard to save a steam locomotive duty.

The Southern's Isle of Wight section continued in much the same way not only until the end of the SR but well into BR days until the end of steam in 1966. Certainly the six years in which A. B. MacLeod was in charge from 1928 to 1934 set a firm foundation, and it was only the accountants' questioning of the island railway economics in the early 1950s that heralded

Remote branch. The Isle of Wight might have had intensive services in the north at Ryde but in the far south it was a total contrast on the former Isle of Wight Central branch from Merstone to Ventnor West. Terrier 0-6-0T No W8 Freshwater hauls a single coach which was more than enough for the handful of passengers that used the line. It was the Island's earliest casualty, being closed in 1952. No W8 was luckier; originally on the Island as the Freshwater company's No 2, it returned to the mainland in 1949 soon after this picture was taken but was later preserved and returned to the Island and is now at the Isle of Wight steam centre at Havenstreet.

change. The Freshwater, Ventnor West, Brading and Newport–Sandown lines were closed. More closure proposals followed in the Beeching years, and, although Shanklin–Ventnor and Smallbrook–Cowes lines were shut, the Ryde–Shanklin section survived to be modernised. Third rail electrification came to the island. Naturally the trains were not new, but 40 years old, from London Transport. The island's loading gauge precluded original Southern electric stock. And they are still there, twenty years later, after a predicted life of less than ten years, for again the Ryde maintenance staff have used all their skills in keeping their now unique electric trains running, and still handling peak summer Saturday traffic, although not quite so intensive as it was in steam days.

Not all of the Cowes line disappeared, for a section between Havenstreet (the later rendering as one word) and Wootton survives as a preserved steam railway, and moreover with talk of linking it back to Smallbrook Junction to connect with the island electric trains, now part of Network SouthEast, in a joint promotional venture with BR. Island railway initiative dies hard.

For every passenger, a suitcase. Summer Saturday at Ryde Pier Head with passengers who did not take advantage of 'luggage in advance' arrangements struggling down the platform to find a place for themselves, their families and their luggage in the Island's compartment coaches.

9
SHIPS AND DOCKS

The Southern's fleet for short sea crossings was second to none. It included some of the most beautiful cross-Channel vessels ever constructed, and the exceptional looks did not belie their performance.

Years ahead of its time, the marine department was responsible for the introduction of many innovations: the first purpose-built cross-Channel car ferry, the *Autocarrier*; the first passenger-train ferry link with the Continent, the *Twickenham Ferry* and her sisters, also allowing cars to be driven on and off by special side-loading link-spans at Dover and Dunkirk; the first Denny-Brown fin stabilizer, fitted to the *Isle of Sark*; the first double-ended car ferry, the *Fishbourne*, for use on the Isle of Wight services; and one of the earliest UK ships fitted with the Voith-Schneider method of propulsion, the *Lymington*.

This tremendous record partly resulted from the Southern's close association with the famous Dumbarton shipyard of Wm Denny & Bros Ltd. Denny's first cross-Channel steamers were constructed for the Belgian Government's Ostend–Dover service in 1888; such was their success that other forward-looking marine departments quickly revised their plans. Although the actual railway of the London Chatham & Dover became something of a music hall joke, its shipping operations were excellent. In 1896, Denny's provided them with a trio of paddle steamers for the Dover–Calais link.

Following the 1899 working union, the South Eastern & Chatham introduced the world's first cross-channel turbine steamer, *The Queen*, and in the years leading up to the formation of the Southern Railway, Denny of Dumbarton produced eight more outstanding examples.

The London Brighton & South Coast also quickly adopted turbine steamers for the Newhaven to Dieppe route; the *Brighton* of 1903 was another Denny product. The longer crossing required faster ships and this remained so until the introduction of the car ferries in 1964.

The South Western Railway's fleet was also mainly Scottish in origin but John Brown of Clydebank and Fairfield of Govan provided most of the newer units. Although engaged on the longest of Channel crossings to Le Havre, the Channel Islands and to Saint Malo, the ships remained small and their designs basic, traditional open promenades offering sitting passengers little in comfort in anything more than a breeze. But a high proportion of travellers booked cabins. After 1923, the Southern soon plated in the open promenades on many of the older ships for the benefit of less wealthy passengers.

What was essential for a successful cross-Channel ship design? These steamers were often likened to 'Atlantic liners in miniature'. Space had to be provided for perhaps over one thousand passengers, their luggage (which was in those days vast), the Royal Mail. There had to be

passenger lounges, bars, smoke rooms, restaurants, cabins – and everything in duplicate for the two classes of passenger. The ships were in essence the proverbial quart in a pint pot, and Denny of Dumbarton succeeded simply because they were masters of their trade.

Although the South Western was the strongest of the three major companies at the grouping of 1923, and the combined fleets all adopted its funnel colour of buff (with the addition of a black top), its ships were the oldest and its routes felt the pinch of competition from the Great Western at Weymouth.

The Southern years were remarkably stable so far as fashion and demand are concerned. True, motor cars became frequent sights on board, and far fewer people travelled first class, many more – including families – went on Continental holidays of around a fortnight, and there was indeed embryo air competition at the top end of the market by 1939. But most people travelling across the Channel took it for granted they would walk on and off ships with traditional facilities. Changes were generally to the technical specification, the wider use of turbines especially helping performance. Diesel power was not adopted for any major vessel. The pressures must certainly have been present as the Belgian's Dover–Ostend fleet introduced high-speed diesels in 1934. That enabled the Belgians to claim a third world record: the fastest paddle steamer, turbine passenger steamer and now the fastest motor passenger ship. The Southern certainly watched the magnificent performance of the Ostend ships, but it believed that diesels were not only too costly but would take up too much space. Perhaps they would be cheaper to operate, but coal was still inexpensive and the vibration which diesels caused would inconvenience the passengers, especially on overnight sailings. It was indeed not until 1967 that British Rail

A reproduction from the Southern Railway publicity booklet entitled A Souvenir of Southampton Docks. *The photographed page is captioned 'Liners at Home – Ships in Dock'. The LSWR took over the docks in 1892 opening the Ocean Dock in 1912. The floating dock was the largest in the world.*

131

Heady Southampton

After a record 1935 (18,000,000 tons gross entering) the Port of Southampton looked forward to a calendar of red letter days at the start of 1936; it also being announced that the *Normandie* would in future make her east-bound calls here instead of Plymouth:

13 January. Official opening of the Baltimore Mail Line's sailings from Southampton to Baltimore and Norfolk.

31 January. *Stirling Castle* (Union Castle Line), due at the Docks from the builders' yard.

7 February. *Stirling Castle* begins her maiden voyage to the Cape.

26 March. *Queen Mary* (Cunard White Star Line) due at Southampton from the builders' yard.

15 May. *Athlone Castle* (sister ship of the *Stirling Castle*) expected to make her first appearance at Southampton.

22 May. *Athlone Castle* begins her maiden voyage.

27 May. *Queen Mary* makes her maiden voyage to New York.

introduced its first cross-channel diesel car ferry. Dover received its first such railway-owned vessel two years later.

It is difficult to believe in this day of jumbo-sized roll-on roll-off ships that things were ever so different. It is the freight industry which has demanded the radical rethink of the traditional cross-channel ship design. Higher vehicle decks, tighter schedules with minimum turn-round times of 75 minutes, 24 hour operation for 50 weeks of the year: the demands are so great that the average life-span of a modern ship will frequently not exceed twenty years.

Compared to this, some of the Southern's ships had remarkable careers. The *Hantonia* (1911–52) and *Biarritz* (1915–49) lasted throughout its happy reign. The basic design changed little: the ships of the Southern provided that essential sea-link between railway trains on both sides of the Channel and were a part of that great European network. They had to sail on time and have a reserve of power available to make-up lost time if necessary.

With such easy workloads by today's standard, Southern ships were always immaculately maintained. The fact that each ship had only one crew ensured that there was pride and purpose. It was not until the introduction of the Dover–Dunkirk train ferry in 1936 that all this began to change, for these ships worked around the clock and crew workings subsequently brought about a gradual decline in on-board standards. The word, 'Ferry' was adopted, the word used today to describe virtually all short-sea traders with their constant comings and goings.

The Southern's magnificent short-sea passenger turbine steamers were definitely not ferries in ethics or practical terms. Each had its own distinctive atmosphere, and from the commercial point of view the restaurants, bars, shops and other on-board facilities were possibly more important than the takings in fares. They were indeed so great as to encourage conservatism, a danger identified by some operators on the railway side who rated speed and productivity more highly than comfort.

The formation of the Southern saw all overhaul and refit services based on Southampton; without dry-docks of their own, the SE&C and LBSC had normally used the multiplicity of services then offered on the Thames.

The South Western had already started expanding Southampton and in 1920 had attracted the Cunard Line. With ever greater liners now using the Hampshire port, a huge floating dock, capable of lifting ships

Channel packet TSS Canterbury *was built in 1929 by Wm. Denny & Bros Ltd as a first class only vessel for the* Golden Arrow *service from London to Paris. In 1931/2 she was converted to a two class ship. After World War II* Canterbury *reintroduced the* Golden Arrow *service on 16 April and continued until relieved by* Invicta *in October 1946. She was then used principally on the Folkestone–Boulogne service until September 1964 being sold for scrap in July of the following year.*

of up to 60,000 tons, was built by Armstrong Whitworth & Co and commissioned in 1924. The P&O Steam Navigation Company returned in 1925, and three years later North German Lloyd brought their *Bremen* and *Europa* in on all homeward calls from New York in addition to their existing west-bound visits. With the great increase in traffic, the Southern embarked on its most ambitious and expensive scheme – the massive £8m Southampton Docks extension.

Southampton lies on a flat peninsula between the rivers Itchen and Test with the original docks being constructed in the soft silts of the former. The plan meant reclaiming vast areas of tidal salting and marshland along the eastern bank of the Test and building a two-mile-long quay to enclose it. Once the in-filling had been completed, sheds, warehouses, cranes, railway lines and a network of roads were constructed. At the far end of the New Docks, the world's largest dry dock was built. Work started in June 1931 and took two years, massive excavations being needed. The dock is 1200ft long, 165ft wide with a height of 59ft from floor to lip. When full it holds 58 million gallons of water. With a liner inside the water can be pumped out in just four hours.

At the end of July 1933, King George V and Queen Mary sailed up Southampton Water in the Royal Yacht *Victoria and Albert* and the King named the new dock, The King George V Graving Dock. It was later to accommodate the giant Cunarders *Queen Mary* and *Queen Elizabeth*.

Sir Herbert Walker called Southampton Docks, 'The jewel in the

Dover. This aerial view shows the foot of Dover's Admiralty Pier (left) and the stern of the car carrier Autocarrier *in berth 1. In the centre the Dunkirk train ferry* Twickenham Ferry *sits in the specially constructed dock with both sets of lock gates closed in order to bring the ship's train deck up to the same level as the rail link-span ashore. After many problems, the Dunkirk ferry finally opened in October 1936. The old Lord Warden Hotel can be seen in the centre, top.*

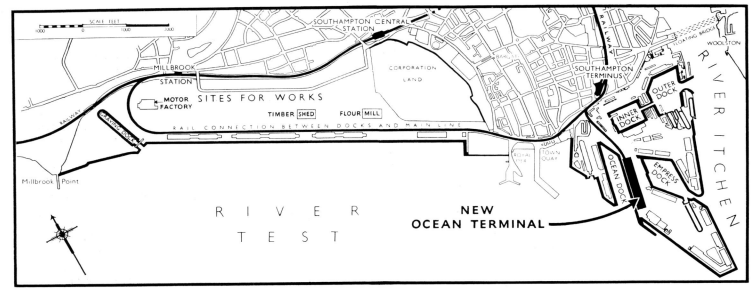

Plan of the new Ocean Terminal evolved by the Southern Railway and completed by British Railways. It was formally opened by Prime Minister Clement Attlee on 31 July 1950.

Publicity

How John Elliot joined the Southern to improve its publicity image has been told in earlier pages.

A few days after he took up his post an advertisement appeared in the daily papers carrying a message explaining what was being done to overcome difficulties, summarising points made by Walker to a meeting of mayors from the region served.

Soon Elliot could move to the offensive. Hitherto planning electrification projects was kept secret. Now it formed the basis for publicity.

Elliot found a capable assistant in F. V. Milton, a long serving railwayman. Between them Southern poster art was highly developed. Maybe their work lacked the ultimate artistic flair of the LPTB and LMS, but they were second to none from the viewpoint of selling. The main thrust was of course the creation and advertising of the 'Southern Electric' image, taking advantage of the outward flood of commuters in the inter-war years. 'Live in Kent and be content' or *continued opposite*

Crown of the Southern Railway'. Apart from the vast amounts of traffic using it from all over the world, the Southern's own steamers continued to be kept extremely busy sailing from their base in the old Outer Dock.

During the thirties the former South Western twins *Normannia* and *Hantonia* (1911) were the mainstay of the Le Havre route while the *Dinard* and *St Briac* (1924) operated to Saint Malo. The latter of these twins also operated cruises and was the only vessel of her type to be fitted with a swimming pool. The Channel Islands run was worked by the sisters *Isle of Jersey* and *Isle of Guernsey* (1930) along with their newer near-sister *Isle of Sark* (1932), while the *Brittany* (1933) was the mainstay of the Channel Islands – Saint Malo link. Meanwhile the *Lorina* (1918, named after Sir Herbert Walker's second wife) enjoyed a peripatetic career, and the converted Royal Navy sloop *Ardena* operated to Cherbourg and then to Caen until her withdrawal in 1931.

The Southern also had a fleet of nine similar cargo vessels, all built on the Clyde by D&W Henderson between 1924–28. The *Haslemere*, *Fratton* and *Ringwood* maintained the Southampton-based services. However, during the height of the Channel Islands produce season, extra tonnage was brought in from Dover, the sister ships *Deal*, *Hythe*, *Tonbridge*, *Whitstable* and *Minster* all helping at one time or another. The *Minster* was allocated permanently after being made redundant at Dover in the wake of the introduction of the train ferry service in 1936. The ninth sister, *Maidstone* appears never to have been used at Southampton.

The Newhaven to Dieppe route was, in many ways, the odd man out as following an agreement with the Western Railway of France in 1867, its ships were jointly owned, a two-thirds share being taken by the French and the minor share held by the Brighton and its successors. The agreement was not finally abandoned until 1985 when Sealink finally left the historic route under total French control.

In Southern days, the French operated the *Newhaven* (1911), *Rouen* (1912) and *Versailles* (1921) while the three British ships were the *Paris* (1913), *Worthing* (1928) and the *Brighton* (1933). The latter were magnificent specimens embodying all the latest passenger comforts. Their enclosed promenade decks and fine lines very much followed those of earlier ships built for the Southern at Dover. Their builders were, of course, Denny. Cargo vessels were operated by the French and consisted of the *Bordeaux* (1912), *Brest* (1900) and the *Rennes* (1925).

It was not until 1926 that the Southern absorbed the Newhaven Harbour Company, an independent operation which had existed under that name since 1878 but which was able to trace its origins back to 1730.

Folkestone Harbour remained very much the same throughout Southern days although in 1931 a disastrous attempt was made to enable the powerful Z class tank engines to work the branch line from Folkestone Junction. A new, stronger, swing bridge was constructed to allow access to the Harbour station but it was a costly failure and the Stirling R1's continued their reign.

Dover has always been the busiest of cross Channel ports but the Southern's relationships with the owner, the Dover Harbour Board, were always poor. All services were from the Admiralty Pier at the west end of the harbour on which the SECR had built its superb Marine station. Not only did the Southern's services to Calais, and briefly in the 'twenties to Boulogne, operate from here, but the Belgian Marine's Ostend link too.

In the summer of 1928, Captain Stuart Townsend, unhappy about the high rates the Southern charged for the carriage of motor cars, had chartered the coaster *Artificer* and began operating his own service from the Eastern Docks to Calais. Once the Southern had brought down its rates then Townsend planned to withdraw, but such was his success that the famous Townsend name continued its associations with the port until swallowed up by P&O Ferries in 1987.

In response to Townsend's service, the Southern chartered the coaster *Abington* on the Calais link while its own *Whitstable* carried motor cars on the Folkestone–Boulogne route. In March 1931, the *Autocarrier*, originally intended to be the tenth of Henderson's series of cargo boat for the Southern, commenced working as the first purpose-built car ferry – although cars were still lifted on and off in the time-honoured fashion. She was replaced in July 1947 when the converted *Dinard* moved up Channel from Southampton to open a new seasonal service from Dover Admiralty Pier to Boulogne (Bassin Loubet).

continued
'Live in Surrey free from worry' were common suggestions. Other posters stressed the frequency and reliability of Southern Electric services. 'Why not live on the live line?' some asked; and there was the man in process of being stood up at Brighton and musing 'She's late, but of course I'll wait for at least six more trains' (ie an hour).

The Southern got publicity from other directions, the big speculative builders such as New Ideal Homesteads invariably stressed the proximity to their estates of a Southern Electric station and its frequent services in so many minutes to London, while brochures such as 'Southern Homes in Surrey and Hampshire', published by the Southern, were available free. First class commuters received a quarterly *Over the Points* (Written by E. P. Leigh Bennet and illustrated by 'Fougasse').

The second thrust was the promotion of holiday traffic. This was spearheaded by the creation of 'Sunny South Sam', the cheerful and caring guard ably backed up by that classic poster of a King Arthur heading a West of England express at Waterloo and under the admiring gaze of a small boy off on his holidays – one of the most evocative railway posters of all time.

The first car ferry. The SS Autocarrier, *built by D & W Henderson of Glasgow, was intended to be another cargo vessel similar to the* Haslemere *but was altered before completion to carry cars and passengers. She was the SR's reply to Townsend Bros and was the first UK railway owned cross-Channel car ferry.* Autocarrier *was never equipped with drive-on facilities and a car is shown here being loaded by crane. She was withdrawn in 1954.*

There were, during the Southern era, two foreign companies operating steamer services from Folkestone. The Dutch, Zeeland Steamship Company (SMZ) had switched its Flushing service from Queenborough (Isle of Sheppey) to Folkestone in 1911 but in 1927 it switched yet again to the LNER's Harwich. Secondly, there was the ALA company (a joint venture between the LMS and the French) which switched its overnight service from Tilbury–Dunkirk, to Folkestone in May 1932 and continued to operate it for four more years with the Southern as the new British partners. The link's sudden decline lay in the introduction of the train ferry service from Dover which, after many delays, finally commenced in October 1936 before which time the lead ship of the three train ferries, the *Twickenham Ferry*, had been sold to ALA for £150,000.

The French contribution to the Dover–Calais service had been the two huge paddle steamers *Le Nord* and *Pas de Calais* but in 1923 the Southern had transferred its turbines *Invicta* (1905) and *Empress* (1907) to French ownership, these two vessels being far more of a complement to its own service which was soon to receive the *Isle of Thanet* and *Maid of Kent* (1925). The transfer was not to last long however as in 1930 and 1932 SAGA introduced its *Côte d'Azur* and *Côte d'Argent*, two ships very much based on the lines of the Southern's most prestigious ship, the one and only *Canterbury*.

The *Canterbury* was created for the Dover–Calais passage of the all-

Isle of Wight paddle steamer. PS Sandown *approaches Portsmouth Harbour in the late 1930s. The vessel moored alongside is the* Sandown's *sister ship the PS* Ryde. *Both were built by Wm. Denny & Bros Ltd, the* Sandown *in 1934 and* Ryde *in 1937.* Sandown *was withdrawn at the end of the 1965 summer season and scrapped but* Ryde *lasted until 1969 and survives as a floating night club moored in the River Medina near Cowes.*

Pullman London–Paris through train, the *Golden Arrow*, starting in May 1929. Everything about her was outstanding and until the depression of 1931–2 she carried just 300 passengers in an opulence that the route had not seen before and has certainly not seen since.

So popular had this special service become that in 1939, the Southern went to Denny's for a larger ship. Because of the war, the *Invicta* did not take up the service for which she was built until October 1946. Not only was she the Southern's largest but remained the English Channel's largest cross Channel steamer for another twenty years.

The Isle of Wight services underwent great changes, the remainder of Portsmouth–Ryde's 'Joint-fleet' being replaced by paddle steamers *Shanklin* (1924), sisters *Merstone* and *Portsdown* (1928), *Southsea* and *Whippingham* (1930) and *Sandown* and *Ryde* (1934 and 1937).

The old 'horse boat' traffic between Ryde and the mainland, by which livestock and motor cars were transported in half-barges pulled by tugs, was replaced in July 1927 by the double-ended car ferry *Fishbourne* on the new link between Portsmouth slipway and deep-water Fishbourne, a small settlement to the west of Ryde on Wootton Creek. Sisters *Wootton* and *Hilsea* followed in 1928 and 1930. Motoring holidays were growing in popularity and many people were no longer content to walk on and off ships to the island.

Denny of Dumbarton also built the *Lymington* for the western Solent crossing between Lymington and Yarmouth in 1938. She was driven by Voith Schneider propulsion, allowing her to be thrust in any direction. A tremendous advance on her paddle steamer forebears, she made the navigation of the twisting Lymington River much easier. The vessel still sails today, fifty years on, as Western Ferries' *Sound of Sanda*, a magnificent innings and ample testimony to the Southern.

During World War II the Southern fleet performed magnificently as hospital ships, transports and as landing ships for infantry, while the cargo vessels frequently found themselves in the role of net layers. The car carrier, *Autocarrier* became a NAAFI ship at Scapa Flow while the train ferries made ideal mine-layers. Twelve ships were lost, five major units within the first year of the war.

During the evacuation of Dunkirk, Southampton's *Normannia* and *Lorina* and Newhaven's *Paris* all became victims of dive-bombing attacks as were the *Brighton* and *Maid of Kent*, both caught alongside at Dieppe in the previous month. The *St Briac* was mined off Aberdeen in March 1942 while Dover's other 'Maid', the *Maid of Orleans* hit a mine in June 1944 when returning 'light ship' from the D Day beaches. Two Isle of Wight steamers were lost, both with mainland names. The *Portsdown* was kept on the Ryde route along with her sister *Merstone* and the older *Shanklin*. After heavy overnight raids on Portsmouth towards the end of September 1941, the *Portsdown* struck a mine and was lost off the harbour mouth whilst engaged on her first run of the day. The *Southsea* too had hit a mine that February and although she was beached near the Tyne, became a constructive total loss. Among the cargo ships, the *Tonbridge* was dive-bombed off the north Norfolk coast in August 1941 while the *Minster* and the *Fratton* were mined and torpedoed off the Normandy coast in June and July 1944. The list says nothing about the bravery and skill employed by the Southern's mariners in performing

Hotel Imperial

The hotel Imperial at Hythe was originally built by the South Eastern Railway; and at the same time of course they built the horse tramway from Sandgate to Hythe, which went past the hotel, which then stood rather at some distance from the town, and of course on the sea front rather than the main road.

It is understood that the railway sold the hotel sometime before the grouping; and of course the tramway closed in 1921. One gets the impression that the South Eastern's investment in the Hythe and Sandgate branch, the hotel and the tramway, all went sour at about the same time, with the failure of the scheme to extend the branch to Folkestone Harbour, and the tramway up the hill into Folkestone town – in both cases probably because of the opposition of Lord Radnor, who was the owner of the freehold of practically the whole of the better part of Folkestone, and thought this was the best way to keep it as an up-market seaside resort.

In the long run the policy has been disastrous, Folkestone nowadays lying in ruins to prove it; but the South Eastern Railway, and following them the Southern, had pretty well lost interest in doing anything to develop in the Folkestone and Hythe area by the early 1920s. Hythes Hotel Imperial survives as a prosperous high-grade independent operation.

often dangerous tasks in difficult conditions, especially in the evacuation of Dunkirk. As premier operator on the short-sea crossings, it was assumed by Southern men that the company had a key role to play. Pride of service always came before fear.

Replacement ships came quickly after the war: the cargo *Winchester* (1947), three Isle of Wight passenger ferries (1948), and new passenger steamers for Southampton, *Falaise* (1947) and Folkestone, *Maid of Orleans* (1949). There were even plans for a new train ferry service between Southampton and Le Havre.

Essentially, in what is a railway book, it is hard to give full credit to the various ships, wharves, piers, docks and the minor harbours that the Southern owned, and even to detail the short-lived and seasonal services the ships operated. But perhaps this brief review emphasises that here was no peripheral operation, but one of the world's greatest and certainly most progressive maritime enterprises, an essential and indeed profitable part of the Southern Railway, very much one of the family in peace and in war. Of all the blows struck by nationalisation, none caused more sadness or frustration than the segregation of maritime (and indeed other) from railway activities.

Lost Opportunity

The story of traffic through the Channel Ports between the wars was one of lost opportunity and frustration. The lost opportunity was the seventeen years' wait for the train ferries. The excellent military port at Richborough a mile up the Great Stour from Pegwell Bay, opened in 1916 and the three purpose-built train ferries each with a capacity equal to fifty wagons had moved vast quantities of military stores including locomotives and rail mounted guns to France without hitch or hindrance through the channel over the bar. Yet all of this, which was going for the taking, even as a temporary expedient until the decision about the Channel Tunnel was made, was rejected and the three ferries handed over to the Harwich service involving a sea crossing three times as long with a correspondingly longer turn-round time, thus giving a third of the Dover or Richborough capacity.

Of course to have used Dover then with its 25ft tidal range would have meant building an enclosed dock (which anyway was built seventeen years later) but the cost of this would have been justified by the much quicker turn-round. Harwich has a 12½ft tidal range and Richborough 14ft and neither need an enclosed dock. So why go to Harwich? Is it likely that if the SE&C or the SR had built Richborough they would have so readily abandoned such capital expenditure?

The more probable explanation may well be that the Southern Board and Sir Herbert Walker were at the time so deeply engaged with the vexing problems of amalgamation, electrification and later with the development of Southampton that the extra problem of the train ferries was simply shelved. Perhaps Sir Herbert would have preferred to have privatised the sea link as he did the other non-railway activity – catering. The men who had worked at Richborough wondered why it was so abruptly abandoned.

Late Boat Trains

The frustration stemmed from the walk-on-walk-off ferries and was experienced by London East Division and their customers, not by the Shipping Division. There were the all too frequent late starts to up boat trains 'Waiting Customs'. The twenty-one mile journey from Calais to Dover took nearly three hours with fifty five minutes at each port when movement was suspended. Many times I personally had to report to Sydney Smart that the evening peak working would be upset by the boat trains running up late in forced paths.

On one occasion I ventured to ask him why they could not do the customs examination on the vessel itself. To which he replied: 'You might well ask, Shervington, I have many times; our mariners say it can not be done because the ships are not designed for it, the Customs & Excise would not agree, because they and the passengers might be too sea sick. Its all round objects. What they really mean is that they find they make more out of meals and gifts than out of fares. But get a ticket and go and see for yourself.'

I did just that, then and again thirty years later, and came to the same conclusion as Sydney Smart.

And so they went on building mini Atlantic liners with Palm Courts and restaurants intstead of floating customs sheds with gift shops strategically placed. This could have reduced the journey time between Calais and Dover (with French co-operation) from 21 miles in 3 hours to 21 miles in 1½ hours *saving 1½ hours.* R. Shervington, critical on this point though with many generous things to say about the Southern, when proposing the company's toast.

10
THE SOUTHERN AT WAR

Over ten thousand SR men served with HM Forces and to help fill the gap approximately 8000 women were recruited. Here is one working as a parcel porter probably at a London suburban station. The traffic is obviously part of the war effort as the parcel on the barrow is endorsed 'Shoes Canvas Prs . . .'

Signalmen remaining at their posts even when unexploded bombs were feet away, drivers braking hard or sending up smoke to lessen the chance of the German plane overhead making a direct hit, many a locomotive rolling into a crater, booking clerks and stationmasters dashing from safety to perform some urgent or even routine task when all hell was being let loose around them, five of London's termini out of use simultaneously, and – not least – a third of a million soldiers snatched from death (many by the company's own ships) at Dunkirk landed and safely despatched inland over just a few days. There was drama a-plenty in the Southern's war, great acts of heroism, some of which were much publicised and suitably rewarded.

Yet the great merit about the wartime Southern was its very humdrum matter-of-factness. For by far the majority of time over most routes, passenger trains went about their business at almost peacetime speeds with almost peacetime regularity, and even most of the great extra events – the civilian evacuations, planned like the early ones or unplanned like that under the very bombardment of the V1 'flying bombs', the constant moving of coal, food and military supplies around the system ending of course with the build up to D Day – were very largely taken in stride. There was great pride in doing the job *by routine*, absorbing extra pressures, even remaining courteous. 'The Enquiry Office Staff will gladly give further information of alternative services,' stated a notice listing cancelled trains during one of the evacuations.

Ultimately the whole nation became aware of its debt to the Southern. One of the BBC's most popular wartime documentaries (whose script was published as a bestseller) featured the work of the railway during the Dunkirk evacuation. We heard a railwayman who had been scrutinising train upon train that came to rest for a short refreshment period ultimately discovering his son back safely on British soil. Stories of individual bravery, such as that of engine drivers taking their trains to safety against all odds, and the young man who jumped on a locomotive he thought he could drive to haul a rake of coaches away from an inferno, of comic asides like the RAF pilot who had brought down one of the flying bombs gesticulating to the driver of a goods train to stop, which he did just short of the rubble caused by the bomb's crash, and of misunderstandings like the box to box message about mines coming down by parachute somehow gathering the words 'Germans landing by parachute' – of course they added a little gilt, but railwaymen were impatient of those who exaggerated them out of context. The real joy was the professional pride in the job, the routine way in which even large craters were filled in and rails relaid, the matter-of-factness with which hand signalling had to be resorted to when Waterloo's power box was

War damage at Portsmouth. Portsmouth received more than its fair share of bombing and the Harbour station received a direct hit on 12 August 1940. Four trains in the station were damaged, fire gutted the access to the landing stage and a water main was smashed. This and further damage in January 1941 was so bad that only one platform was repaired. No rebuilding was carried out until the end of the war.

lifeless, the way in which the whole machine seemed veritably designed to be doing what it was. 'If only the Army could operate with as few written instructions as the Southern Railway does,' a general was alleged to have remarked after the Dunkirk dispersal. *The Times* commented that the Southern had 'lavished upon the emergency its great and peculiar experience of the handling of masses'.

In truth the Southern's performance with remarkably high morale during the war was the final proof that Walker had developed an exceedingly well-run railway. There were, of course, a number of special factors. Because the Southern ran few ultra-fast expresses, speeds were reduced less than on the main lines of Britain's other three railways (which had the odd effect of temporarily giving the Southern the nation's fastest start-to-stop timings), and though frequencies were reduced for the most part services remained generous. Many trains were horribly overcrowded. Planning had been done carefully before the war; the only thing that went wrong during the first round of evacuations in 1939 was that consistently too few children showed up, many parents deciding to keep them at home, a pattern repeated in every evacuation. And there were many evacuations, for initially children had been sent to areas that came in the front line of bombardment and invasion threat. Mountains of food and other supplies had to be moved for the same reason. Planning also paid handsomely so far as the wartime HQ at Deepdene at Dorking was concerned. Key staff were housed partly in a former country house hotel and partly in adjoining caves, despatch riders always on hand for emergency messages should other communications fail. The general manager split his time between Deepdene and Waterloo where his office was destroyed.

Next, and importantly, the Southern had avoided over-centralisation, the men on the ground (especially the signalmen) being used to taking their own decisions in the light of circumstances. There was a great

Preventing Explosions

One of the saturation raids on Portsmouth: bombs were falling in clusters almost continuously, and all round houses were blazing. No water: the mains were damaged. Amid all the uproar, a railwayman acting as firewatcher on the highest part of the station roof was ready to try and kick, hit or otherwise dislodge any odd fire bomb which fell but did not penetrate. Whenever there was a momentary lull in the noise this man's voice could just be heard giving a dissertation on mountain goats and how fortunate they were to be able to leap from rock to rock. The station was likely to be hit at any minute, but he did not leave his post. Everybody who could be was in shelter, but duty called the writer to the deserted two-level terminal platforms. Two engines in steam at the buffers; a T9 4-4-0 No 287 and an Adams Jubilee No 620. On both engines, the driver was sitting watching anything there was to watch. Both had sent their fireman to safety in the shelter. 'Someone's got to stay with her,' said the driver of the Jubilee. 'Otherwise she might blow up!' As if everything else around wasn't already!

All Hell

I booked on duty at 11.5pm and left the Loco Depot at 11.30pm to work the 12.53am Cannon Street to Dartford.

On going up to Cannon Street between Surrey Canal Junction and London Bridge, a fire had started over by Surrey Docks and loads of incendiaries were dropped all the way to London Bridge and the City.

We stopped the engine at Borough Market and the fireman put out incendiaries. On arriving at Cannon Street, Platform 6, bombs began to drop, then the aspect signal lights all went out, and then some bombs dropped outside the station, bringing clouds of dust.

A fire then started at the side of the station, and it then rained bombs and there seemed no stopping. The fires were then like huge torches and there were thousands of sparks.

The smoke from the fires blacked out the moon, and fires seemed everywhere, and then the station roof caught alight.

To save the trains catching fire, two engines, coupled together, No 934 and 1541 (Schools Class, *St. Lawrence*, and H Class 0-4-4T), pulled out of Platform 8 on to the bridge. We stopped twenty yards ahead of the other train, and then, after about ten minutes we ducked down on the footplate. We counted three bombs, the last one was terrific, and very close. There was a massive explosion and our engine seemed to roll; at first we thought our train had been hit. The debris flew in all directions – we were very lucky. My fireman said at the time, 'Look out – we are going in the drink, and I said, 'I thought my back week had come'
continued opposite

Fratton locomotive shed building and some locomotives were also damaged but all were repaired and returned to traffic.

tradition of knowing what to do rather than having to be told. All the wisdom of Solomon could be conveyed in conversations between boxes, and masters of vital yards like Feltham developed their individual *esprit de corps*. Control was in fact actively maintained by the chief officers, with praise, encouragement and occasional blame, and in later days Control in the narrower railway sense of which train should take priority was inevitably developed, but the man on the job knew that he counted in a way that was not universally true across Britain. Attention to detail was ever encouraged on Walker's railway and, for example, stores seldom ran out to delay the restoration of locomotives damaged by the blitz.

The Southern's experience in handling great holiday and race crowds obviously helped. Enormous peaks were again almost routine. Finally, thanks to electrification, a high peace-time level of maintenance and even war-time building, the railway was never short of steam power, and with the Brighton works which had been more or less retired back in full production, locomotives were built for the LMS and LNER as well as armaments manufactured, the latter indeed starting even before hostilities were declared.

No railway ever made so great a strategic contribution to Britain's position in the world, or could ever do so again. Most of the very factors that made things like the Dunkirk dispersal work so smoothly have been destroyed: there is no longer such a pool of spare rolling stock (provided by all four main-line companies) and signalling has been so centralised that one shudders to contemplate what chaos a few flying bombs would inflict. But then today's mass movements, except in and out of London,

would be faster accomplished by road. The Southern's wartime exploits have to be seen against the background of the railway still being the prime mover of food as well as other goods, of much of the merchant navy still being coal driven, and that if it were decided to create an American military depot in a quiet Hampshire village that automatically meant the village station had to transform itself from dealing with hundreds to tens of thousands of goods wagons annually.

As international tension heightened at the end of August 1939, the evacuation of schoolchildren from London took place in the off peak hours of 1–3 September – as already mentioned, just the first of many evacuations. A complete blackout was ordered from 2 September. This made travel after dark very troublesome but even worse was its effect on sorting sidings, where not only vital work was slowed down but the danger to yard staff was greatly increased. As soon as was practicable shaded blue lamps were fitted under station canopies and in carriages; at this period all SR carriages were already fitted with blinds. A limited form of lighting was allowed at marshalling yards, extinguished only on receipt of an air raid 'red' warning signifying that hostile aircraft were approaching. The colour light signals were too bright and needed hoods to shield the light, while if an air raid warning was in progress the intensity of the light was reduced. Even before war was declared, steam tender engines had been fitted with rails to carry anti-glare sheets to reduce visibility from the air when the firebox door was open.

The tremendous effort made by the SR in electrifying its suburban lines and several main lines with the resultant improved train services and upsurge in speculative house building encouraged people to live further out and travel to work by train. It had been envisaged that on the outbreak of war an intensive bombing campaign would start, which in the event, so far as the London area was concerned, did not materialise until September 1940. Nevertheless on 11 September an emergency timetable came into force. In effect this was based on a 45 per cent reduction of service allied to an overall line speed of 45mph. The trains remaining became grossly overloaded, travellers were left behind, and a great deal of wrath erupted from season ticket holders. A week later a weekday summer service was restored on Southern electrified lines, pending the issue of a more reasonable timetable which came into force on 16 October, with subsequent revisions. Evening services were reduced to clear the tracks for all-important freight traffic.

Much of the foregoing affected all railways equally, but the first major contribution of the Southern was soon to come. The British Expeditionary Force sailed from SR ports, largely from Southampton Docks, in September 1939. The rapid advance of the German forces, the invasion of Holland and Belgium were totally unforeseen. Any hopes of rapidly reinforcing the Western front were quickly dispelled and the evacuation of our forces became the overwhelming priority. Thus came about one of the great feats of the war – 'Operation Dynamo.' Ships large and small were despatched to the South Coast in an all out effort to rescue our men from the hostile beaches of Dunkirk, constantly under fire from the Luftwaffe. Naturally ships of the Southern fleet were heavily involved and some were lost, but anything that could cross the Channel joined in the rescue work, from harbour tugs to pleasure craft.

continued

[a reference to the method of final payment of wages if a railwayman leaves or dies in service].

We looked round and found that the bomb had made a direct hit on the boiler of No 934, and it had also blasted our train, and turned part of the train over on its side.

My fireman and myself went to see where the driver and the firemen were, and I am pleased to say they had got off the engine in time.

Then looking round, we found our train had caught fire, and the fireman with buckets of water tried to put the same out, but it was impossible as a strong wind was blowing up the Thames, and the fire got the master.

I uncoupled my engine from the train, and drew back about two yards, and secured the engine, then crossed the bridge until dawn – watching the fires. It was just as if Hell had been let loose.

I am pleased to say there was no one injured and we were all lucky to be alive.

Every railwayman at Cannon Street was very cool and calm, and all assisted in every possible way under those trying and unique conditions.

That is my account of the Blitz. – Driver L. Stainer's experience of 10–11 May 1941 as quoted in the Southern Railway's *War on the Line* by Bernard Darwin, 1946.

Naming ceremony brochure of one of the new mixed traffic (!) Bulleid Merchant Navy Pacifics Blue Star, built during World War II.

Nicknames

Railwaymen's nicknames reveal an acute ability to sum up essential features. Here are a few Southern examples:

The 4COR emu units provided for the 1937 Portsmouth electrification were called *Nelsons*. They were the first emus with gangway connections which were the 'nose', while they had only one window on one side of the gangway, the other side, the 'blind' one, had the route indicator, and of course the *Nelsons* were bound for 'Pompey' itself.

The series of emus introduced in 1941 and numbered 4101-10 were called *Queen of Shebas*. They were the first four-car suburban sets, and the first stock on the Southern with six-a-side seating. The origin of the name was obscure, but H. P. White in 1961 quoted from 1 Kings, chapter 10, verse 2: 'and she came to Jerusalem with a very great train'.

In the 1960s the commuters from Haslemere were known as *Flour Graders*. Their uniform of dark suits, bowler hats, and rolled umbrellas recalled the contemporary advert for flour, the product being represented as having every grain graded by a group of cartoon men thus dressed.

Train crews of trains on the Mid-Hants line between Alton and Winchester referred to going *Over the Alps*. This derived from the heavy grades on each side of the gable summit at Medstead & Four Marks.

Between Eridge and Polegate was commonly *The Cuckoo Line*. This came from the tradition the first cuckoo of summer was released on Heathfield (the principal station) Fair day.

continued opposite

Naming Ceremony

OF

BLUE STAR

AT

WATERLOO STATION

Friday, 18th December, 1942

BY

The Rt. Hon. Lord Vestey

Blue Star Line

accompanied by Southern Railway Chairman, Mr. R. Holland Martin,
and General Manager, Mr. E. J. Missenden

Once landed at a South Coast port the troops had to be despatched as quickly as possible to escape the chance of enemy air activity and it was at this point that the Southern's experience in conveying crowds came to the fore. On 21 May the SR superintendent of operation was warned to make provision for the landing of up to 300,000 troops mainly at ports on the South Coast. The following day representatives of the four main line companies, those of the War Office and the Railway Executive Committee met and several important decisions were taken. The discretion of the railwaymen could be counted upon, 186 ten coach trains were to be provided of which the SR share was the largest – fifty five. Trains were to be despatched as soon as possible after disembarkation and as far as possible they were to avoid the London area – in the event less than a fifth of the evacuation specials passed through London. Many sidings in the vicinity were emptied to permit the stabling of the requisitioned carriages in readiness, while the down line between Hothfield on the Maidstone East line and Ashford West was put to similar use, allowing some two miles of closely marshalled trains to stand in readiness. On 27 May a chalked notice appeared at London Bridge and other stations involved: 'Passengers for Coulsdon South, Merstham, Redhill and Reigate change at Coulsdon North and proceed by bus. The train service between Tonbridge, Redhill and Reading is liable to interruption.' Two days later that line's service was suspended altogether for the duration of 'Operation Dynamo' which officially began on 27 May, although in the previous week over 24,000 troops were moved in fifty five special trains, a modest movement compared with what was to take place over the next nine days.

In that concentrated time the Southern's achievement was all part of what has come to be known as the 'Miracle of Dunkirk.' Without knowing when, where or even how many troops were to be landed nearly 300,000 troops were despatched in 567 special trains slotted in to minimise disruption to the ordinary timetable. The most easily reached ports of Margate and Ramsgate were the least equipped to deal with a sudden upsurge of traffic. Instead of peacetime day trippers Margate dealt with 38,000 troops and Ramsgate 43,000, in both cases special omnibuses being required to take them to the stations, which despatched seventy five and eighty two trains respectively. A further 35,000 troops and 9,000 refugees were landed at Folkestone Harbour, whence sixty four special trains had to climb the steep grade to Folkestone Junction, where reversal was necessary, after which they were fitted in between trains from Dover, which bore the brunt of the traffic.

Dover despatched 181,000 troops in 327 trains and on the last day of evacuation there were no fewer than sixty vessels in the harbour. Locomotives took water at Ashford, Tonbridge or Faversham and special coal trains were run to Redhill, where the engine shed was at times so busy that light engines were sent to Three Bridges for attention. At the end it was found that over three hundred tons of ash had accumulated at Redhill. The exhausted, hungry and often ill clothed troops were fed and given clothes where needed by means of alternate trains on the main line stopping at Headcorn or Paddock Wood, both four track stations. At each there were forty RASC soldiers assisted by at least as many ladies from the locality. They served many thousands of sandwiches, sausages, meat pies and hard boiled eggs washed down with as much tea or coffee as possible in stops not exceeding fifteen minutes.

No sooner had this massive exercise been carried out than it was considered prudent to evacuate all non-essential civilians from the Kent Coast area in case refugees should hinder military operations in the event of invasion. As it happened there was another good reason since as soon as the Germans had their heavy guns in position on the French Coast by August 1940, for four long years the Kent Coast was under bombardment over a wide area. Of over 3,000 shells fired in that time some 2,200 fell on Dover. The threat of invasion and possible parachutists dropping brought about the removal of all sign posts, painting out of station names, construction of anti-tank traps and formation of the Home Guard, which included nearly 20,000 Southern railwaymen. Others were involved in Civil Defence or First Aid and their training was soon to be put to the test.

Hostile air attack started in a rather desultory fashion, usually with hit

continued
The name 'Bluebell' for the Horsted Keynes–Sheffield Park–Lewes line was certainly not in common use until possibly the protracted closure row. It was not widely adopted until re-opening as a preserved line. In LBSC days trains between London and Brighton via East Grinstead and Haywards Heath used *The Inner Circle* and via Eridge and Uckfield *The Outer Circle*.

The Southampton & Dorchester was built through Wimborne as Bournemouth was then non-existent and one of its promotors, A. L. Castleman, practised as a solicitor at Wimborne. It was known as *Castleman's Corkscrew* (and sometimes The Watersnake) in view of its circuitous route.

With their light traffic and infrequent services, the Southern lines west of Exeter were widely known (at least in the London area) as The Southern's *Withered Arm*.

145

Trains running hours late were far less common on the Southern than other lines – even the long West of England route – during the war's most difficult days and the equally tough immediate postwar period. But the steam services were not immune from poor coal and poor maintenance. A Schools 4-4-0 made especially heavy work with an overloaded Dover–Charing Cross express one brilliant Sunday evening during the first days of peace.

Short rushes down the hills of the switchback route were followed by painful crawls up to the next summit, giving newcomers to the route ample time to take in the lush countryside with its fruit farms, hopfields and oast houses, and thrice the procession halted to give the fireman a chance to increase the steam pressure.

The last of these stops was by a semaphore signal, showing all clear, just short of a tunnel entrance, the summit of course being inside the tunnel and the driver fearful that he lacked sufficient power to make it.

Eventually pressure was up, the safety valve lifting. 'Its blowing up,' announced one passenger, meaning to be encouraging. 'My God,' the general reaction.

and run raids not far from the coast. The first bomb on SR property fell on Redbridge sleeper works, near Southampton, in June 1940. Three months later the concentrated blitz on Greater London started and when attention was diverted elsewhere in May 1941 there had been a period of constant bombing for 252 days, during which adverse weather grounded the bombers on only two nights.

During this period all London termini and their approach lines were damaged. Where bridges or viaducts were involved the army was often called in to assist and some remarkable feats of repair work were carried out quite expeditiously. On the first day of the blitz the lines on viaduct between Vauxhall and Waterloo received a direct hit putting eight tracks out of action. Two tracks were restored the following day, three more within ten days, two more a week later and full normal running was resumed by 1 October. In that month Durnsford Road Power station at Wimbledon was damaged severely reducing its generating capacity by half. This was a serious incident and took four months to repair. In a later raid a German aircraft was shot down and fell on Victoria station near to the platform used by visiting Heads of State. The subsequent report concluded 'Many important foreign missions have arrived at Victoria, but never before in this manner.' At the end of December there was the notorious fire bomb raid when St Paul's Cathedral was surrounded by fires but survived. Waterloo, Charing Cross, Cannon Street and Holborn Viaduct all suffered severe damage; in less than a week normal working was restored.

In March 1941 a porter walking across Hungerford Bridge to report for duty advised the stationmaster that in the darkness he had tripped over a landmine quite close to the signalbox. The signalman was warned of the danger, but with one platform already ablaze and more fire bombs falling he felt it advisable to keep watch from his prominent position. Eventually as the fire grew nearer the signalbox an inspector insisted that he should come down. First the signalman extinguished two incendiaries on the bridge and on his return was intrigued to find that the intense heat had welded the landmine to the track. Fortunately the fire brigade arrived in time to save the signalbox and a Naval officer defused the landmine. On the same night a direct hit on Southwark Street bridge destroyed means of direct access to Blackfriars and Holborn Viaduct.

In April 1941 bombs and incendiaries put five terminal stations out of action, Waterloo, Victoria, Charing Cross, London Bridge and Holborn Viaduct. A month later a very severe raid took place, as it happened the last for some time. Again five terminals were out of action but this time it was Cannon Street's turn and Holborn Viaduct escaped attention. A Bricklayers Arms driver running light to Cannon Street to work the 12.53am to Dartford, a train for Fleet Street's press men and printers, stopped at Borough Market Junction to extinguish incendiaries on the track. On resuming his journey he found bombs falling on the station. Another engine was present, No 934 *St Lawrence*, and it was decided that both engines should haul eight coaches out of the station for their protection. This having been done the crews took shelter below their engines and soon after heard three bombs falling, one of which hit one of the engines although mercifully the four men escaped injury. The light engine driver concluded his report on that night's events with a masterly

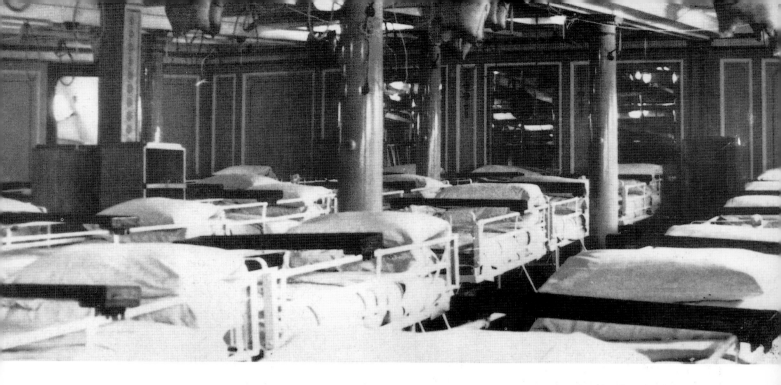

piece of understatement. 'In my opinion', he wrote, 'this was a proper nightmare.'

The London suburbs suffered equally badly as did the outlying areas, notably those near the coast. In August 1940 Portsmouth Harbour station was bombed and set on fire. The remains of the gutted coaches in the station were not recovered until six years later. Gosport also received regular attention. The engine shed was destroyed in December 1940, ironically by an unexploded bomb previously pronounced 'safe.' William Tite's 1842 station sustained serious damage in March 1941. To the west both Exeter and Plymouth suffered, while to the east, Brighton suffered some daytime hit and run raids. The engine shed was raked by cannon fire in October 1942, but worse was to come in May 1943 when five bombs fell within minutes on railway property from six aircraft retreating low over the sea. Two bombs fell on the goods yard, one on Lovers Walk carriage sidings, one on Preston Park Pullman Car Co works, while the worst knocked two arches out of the London Road viaduct, cutting off access to East Sussex other than via Haywards Heath. It had been the practice to steam haul main line electric stock to shelter in the mile long tunnel on the Kemp Town branch, but this was no longer possible until the viaduct was repaired. Inevitably a number of locomotives were damaged by enemy action. Most London engine sheds were bombed but Nine Elms suffered worst with four heavy raids between 1940 and 1944. The only engine withdrawn beyond repair was rebuilt Drummond 4-6-0 No 458 damaged in 1940. The 1941 raid caused greater havoc including a direct hit on cab and firebox of Lord Nelson Class 4-6-0 No 852 *Sir Walter Raleigh*, which nevertheless returned to service two months later. Near Portsmouth, Fratton shed received an intense attack in 1941 when twenty engines were damaged in its roundhouse. Worst affected was Class T9 4-4-0 No 118 which had a bomb pass through the firebox and explode on impact with the pit. The report noted that 'the engine was suspended over a bomb crater on its

Wartime conversion. Many of the Southern's ships were turned over to war service, three being lost during the evacuation of Dunkerque. The Isle of Thanet was converted into a hospital ship with her first class restaurant converted into a ward for the wounded.

leading bogie and the trailing bogie of the tender'. But the forty two year old engine was repaired and survived another ten years.

Luftwaffe pilots showed a marked partiality for the Schools class, most of which worked on the hard hit lines between London and the Kent Coast. On 7 September 1940, first day of the London blitz, No 900 *Eton* was the first victim at North Kent East Junction close to the main docklands target. In October Nos 912 *Downside* and 936 *Cranleigh* were victims, the latter falling into a bomb crater outside London Bridge. No 927 *Clifton* was standing adjacent to No 852 at Nine Elms. Worse was a direct hit on the cab and firebox of No 934 *St Lawrence* on Cannon Street bridge, repair taking four months. Trains were regularly attacked near the Kent Coast and in 1942 No 917 *Ardingly* stopped at Deal with a Charing Cross train when three bombs fell causing widespread damage. Later two more Charing Cross trains were shot up, with No 922 *Marlborough* at Westenhanger and No 912 *Downside* at Deal. By this time the Works could cope with such incidents and Ashford had both engines back in traffic two days later.

Shooting up trains was not confined to the Kent Coast. A pull and push train was attacked near Newhaven as early as July 1940. In August Lord Nelson Class No 860 *Lord Hawke* on a down Bournemouth express was derailed at Swaythling as an enemy bomber dropped three bombs in its path, a similar fate befalling T9 4-4-0 No 115 at Fareham a fortnight later. A rural line to suffer a severe attack with many casualties was that between Horsham and Guildford with a pull and push train raked from end to end near Bramley. There was one small victory when a Focke Wulf 190 flew so low over a train near Lydd that its wing tips hit the boiler, which burst bringing the aircraft down and killing the pilot. The engine crew escaped!

The main workshops were all deeply involved in work for the war effort but escaped relatively lightly. Eastleigh was undamaged, Lancing and Brighton sustained minor damage. But Ashford was the worst affected, being only a few minutes' flying time from occupied French airfields. Its first damage was in July 1940 and subsequently it was estimated that local spotters gave some 2,000 warnings of enemy aircraft approaching. The locomotive works escaped damage until 1943 but most locomotives damaged were back at work within a month, the worst affected, Class E 4-4-0 No 1515 taking eight months to repair. The 'flying bomb' period caused little damage to locomotives with one unlucky exception. A Spitfire shot down a V1 flying bomb which exploded on a bridge near Rainham, Kent, as a down Ramsgate express was approaching. There was no time to stop and King Arthur Class 4-6-0 No 806 *Sir Galleron* plunged into the crater with many casualties.

With the build up of troops and military materials in readiness for the invasion of Europe air attacks on London recommenced in the early months of 1944. To assist in providing the vital links for the supplies new sidings were laid down at Micheldever and Brockenhurst to ease the burden on Feltham and Eastleigh. Although the whole of the South Coast was declared a militarised zone, the lion's share of men and materials was concentrated in an area within easy reach of Southampton Docks. Here the construction of parts of the Mulberry prefabricated harbour units was carried out, which after D Day were towed out and

Top right. Southern preserved. Schools class 4-4-0 No 928 Stowe, *preserved in SR Maunsell livery, seen here on the Bluebell Railway in August 1981 working the 12.23 Sheffield Park – Horsted Keynes train at Three Arches cutting.*

Right. Island vintage train. Ex LSWR O2 class 0-4-4 tank No 29 Alverstone *approaching Ventnor station Isle of Wight around 1959. All Island engines were named by the Southern including the O2s, 0-6-0 Terrier tanks and the 0-6-0 Class E1 tanks used for freight. In the early days of BR ownership these engines were kept in malachite green with the full British Railways lettering on their side tanks. Steam finished on 31 December 1966 leaving nothing but a truncated electrified line from Ryde Pier to Shanklin worked by ex London Underground stock. Sic transit . . .*

'Ramblers at Rowfant'. Southern Railway Class E4 0-6-2T No 2490 runs into Rowfant station with a local train from Three Bridges to East Grinstead in the 1930s. A party of ramblers are waiting for the train after their long walk through the Surrey countryside. In the surge of interest in healthy outdoor pursuits in the 1930s the branch line trains were very popular for gaining access to remote areas. From a painting by Don Breckon.

GOLDEN ARROW
JIG-SAW PUZZLE

40 Pieces Interlocking.

SOUTHERN
853

The GOLDEN ARROW LIMITED
(London — Paris de Luxe service)
NELSON CLASS ENGINE

assembled at Arromanches for the landings of troops, vehicles and vast amounts of stores. D Day came on 6 June 1944 and the landing craft, some built at Eastleigh works, set sail from many points on the coast.

As soon as the main landings had taken place and the enemy was driven back, ships, troops and stores literally poured out of Southampton Docks and by this time the Luftwaffe was sufficiently weakened and demoralised to be unable to prevent it. From 12–22 June sailings were at their peak, storms in the Channel caused a few days' setback and after that until mid September there was little let up. By VE Day over 3,500,000 Allied troops had sailed from Southampton and the military stores tonnage dealt with in the seventeen weeks after D Day equalled the Docks combined imports and exports tonnage for the year 1938. As soon as the port of Cherbourg was taken American Forces restored its port facilities so that the three Southern train ferries could sail to and fro loaded with British and American locomotives, ambulance trains, covered wagons and petrol tank wagons in prodigious numbers. The first through train was seen in Normandy heading east on 5 September, a USA 2-8-0, many of which had been prepared for traffic at Eastleigh, hauling an ambulance train of LNER Gresley coaches. After four long years, peace in Europe was only months away.

It was only a week after D Day that the first V1 flying bomb fell on a bridge in East London and the long suffering residents of London, Kent and surrounding counties were again under attack from the air. Although only twenty six fell on SR property they exploded on impact causing blast damage over a wide area, so that railway property suffered from several hundred that fell near the tracks. Worst damage in Central London occurred on 18 June when one scored a direct hit on the east side of Charing Cross bridge over the Thames. Although trains started running on the west side the next day, it was three months before normal service could be resumed. In November the first V2 rocket bombs fell,

Here we go – Newhaven Harbour soon after D Day (6 June 1944) showing British troops embarking on landing craft.

Top left. Admiral and Premier. Southern Railway Lord Nelson as new alongside the ex LB&SCR Gladstone before the latter's move to York for preservation in the LNER's museum there. This colour print was reproduced in the Journal of the Stephenson Locomotive Society which sponsored the preservation of Gladstone.

Left. Pocket jigsaw. An excellent piece of Southern Railway publicity available to passengers on the 'Golden Arrow' and purchased aboard ships crossing the Channel. Made up of 40 interlocking wooden pieces and manufactured by the Chad Valley company of Harborne, Birmingham (which also made the GWR jigsaws) this shows No E853 Sir Richard Grenville at the head of a 12 coach train, nine of them Pullmans. The legend bottom left reads 'The Golden Arrow Limited' (London–Paris de Luxe service) 'Nelson' class engine.

Caution!

The time came, in the 1930s, when it was decided to replace the very old LSWR distant signal at Daggons Road with a more modern fixed distant. The original idea was simply to remove the connecting wires and put a new fixed signal with only the yellow lamp glass in place of the old workable one. Sad in a way. But everyone was a little shaken when, the wire connecting the signal to the signal box having been cut, the entire distant fell over. It was all that was holding the post upright!

but although sixteen fell on the SR in general they caused less disruption and by this time the civil engineers had had four years experience of rapidly filling bomb craters and restoring broken communications. The last bomb to cause damage to the railway fell at Chislehurst in March 1945, after which Allied forces had overrun the last of the rocket launching sites.

Of the 1,819 locomotives in stock at the outbreak of war 189 had been damaged and one destroyed. However the SR was in a strong position having at a stroke lost all its holiday traffic and it was able to loan locomotives to the GWR, LMS, LNER and War Department. During the war it built sixty five steam and one electric locomotive for its own use as well as 130 Stanier Class 8F 2-8-0s for the northern companies. 153 carriages were damaged beyond repair and over four thousand less seriously damaged. About a thousand wagons were destroyed but Ashford Works turned out 11,935 new wagons for the four main line companies, of which over seven thousand were for SR use. In addition a further two thousand were built for the Government mainly for use overseas.

Compared with the 1939 figure the staff at the end of the war remained constant, but some seven thousand women had been recruited on a temporary basis to replace staff on active service. 170 railwaymen were killed by enemy action while on duty. Management and staff had every reason to be proud of their effort.

Years of Conflict at Borough Market Junction

Take a small signalbox with a 35 miniature-lever electro-mechanical frame controlling a four-track main line from a six-track station in one direction, with the four-track line continuing in the other direction but with an equally important double-track line branching off from all four tracks, handling 100 trains an hour at peak times and more than 1,000 trains every 24 hours and you have a basic picture of Borough Market Junction, situated until the 1976 resignalling about 200yd west of London Bridge station on the busy commuter routes to Cannon Street and Charing Cross.

There is little doubt that for its size and number of tracks Borough Market Junction signalbox, perched on the edge of the complex of bridges, brick arches and steel girders carrying the railway over the maze of streets and the market just south of the River Thames, handled the most concentrated amount of traffic of any signalbox on BR. Clapham Junction might have its 2,400 trains a day but it had, and indeed still has, twelve principal through running lines to Victoria and Waterloo, but none of them conflict with each other, and some of the additional running lines – connecting with other routes to the south east and the north west – have underpasses to keep conflicts even between trains on these to a minimum. There is no real comparison with Borough Market. London Bridge signalbox certainly had to handle all the trains that passed Borough Market Junction and more, but it, too, had more tracks on which to spread them and, although there were numerous flat crossings causing many conflicts between up and down trains, there was

room for manoeuvre between them.

The junction at Borough Market went back into the mists of time but the effect was that although on the London side of New Cross, towards North Kent East Junction, the tracks were paired by use – down, up, down, up, down, up, with the first pair on the north side serving the Greenwich branch and local trains through New Cross to Lewisham, and the last pair on the south side carrying main line long distance trains to Sevenoaks and beyond – by the time London Bridge station was reached all had been shuffled through flat crossings to have the three down lines on the north side and three up lines (after a two up track bottleneck) on the south side of the through high level station at London Bridge.

West of London Bridge the six tracks had become four on the viaduct – down, down, up, up, and it was Borough Market Junction's job to split them for the four tracks into Cannon Street, and the pair for Charing Cross, which at Metropolitan Junction just 300yd to the west, open out again to four tracks. Thus all up trains for Cannon Street had to cross all down trains from Charing Cross. It was not always like this for in South Eastern & Chatham days most trains to and from Charing Cross also served Cannon Street. This meant that such trains reversed in the Cannon Street terminus and ran round the west side of the triangle to Metropolitan Junction and there was not so much confliction at Borough Market.

But with the new suburban electrification in the mid 1920s and the resignalling of lines between Charing Cross, Cannon Street and London Bridge with continuous track circuiting and mostly four-aspect colour-

Borough Market battleground. Top left, where the action was, inside Borough Market Junction box which controlled the junction for roundly 50 years from the 1920s resignalling by the Southern Railway to the next resignalling when the confliction was removed and the lines came under the control of London Bridge signalling centre in 1976. Top right, four at once, two down trains and two up, outside Borough Market box. Bottom left, close working with little more than 15yd between a down Charing Cross service and an up Cannon Street crossing in front of it. Bottom right, three together as up and down Charing Cross services pass, and one on the right comes round from Cannon Street. Sometimes all four Cannon Street tracks would be occupied at the same time.

light signals (several of them in clusters rather than vertical), trains for Charing Cross no longer worked via Cannon Street, although some empty trains for Charing Cross departures worked from Cannon Street. As further electrification was carried out in the south eastern and southern suburbs so the frequency of electric trains increased. By 1939 with electrification of the Maidstone and Gillingham lines the only steam services left at Cannon Street and Charing Cross were those to Hastings, former SER main line services via Sevenoaks and Tonbridge to Ashford, and those running via the SER's North Kent route via Gravesend and Strood to the Chatham route to Ramsgate. In the last summer before World War II in the Monday to Friday peak hour 40 trains were handled at Borough Market Junction in each direction, 19 electric and one steam from Charing Cross and 13 electric and seven steam from Cannon Street.

By the completion of the Kent Coast electrification in 1961, with diesel-electric trains to Hastings, steam had been eliminated which allowed extra paths to take the peak hour total to almost 100 trains. Moreover by then many of the suburban services were running as ten car formations and the long distance main line trains as 12 cars, which took about 12–15 seconds longer to cross the

junction than the eight-car trains of pre-war days at the 15mph–20mph which was usually the speed of most trains through the junction with its absolute limit of 20mph imposed by the severe curvature. Thus seconds counted.

Because of the low speeds and the unique layout, overlaps beyond signals were short, much less than the quarter mile for acceptance purposes at most semaphore home signals in mechanically-signalled areas, and the 200yd usual for four-aspect colour-light signals on open line. At Borough Market Junction the up inner home signals had 50yd at the most, while the down home signal from Charing Cross had no more than 15yd to the conflict of the up local line to Cannon Street crossing ahead of it. And it was used, every day, with down trains from Charing Cross coming to a stand at the home signal with up Cannon Street services just those few yards in front of them.

As far as possible trains were scheduled in groups to make best use of parallel working, with up to four trains on the Cannon Street tracks together, two up and two down, or one each way to Charing Cross. But since there was heavy commuter traffic at Charing Cross, clearly that could not be the only way of working, since it would have

155

given Charing Cross only half the Cannon Street service. In fact, just as many trains were scheduled to and from Charing Cross in the main 5– 6pm peak hour as Cannon Street.

Certainly an up Charing Cross service could use the up local line at the same time as an up Cannon Street on the up through line, but the problem lay with the down Charing Cross services which could not avoid crossing the up Cannon Street trains to the down through line even if a down Cannon Street could run parallel on the down local line.

Borough Market Junction signalbox also controlled the west end of London Bridge station through tracks, including the up platform starting signals and the down signals controlling entry to London Bridge platforms 1, 2 and 3. 'Train ready to start' plungers were provided on the up platforms 4, 6 and 7 (line 5, between platform 4 and 6 tracks had disappeared by the 1950s) to Borough Market Junction. The maxim of the Borough Market Junction signalmen (normally two on the two daytime shifts, one for up trains and one for down) was never to clear a signal before they could see the whites of the drivers eyes! It was not in the local regulations, indeed it was probably never written down at all, but the effect was the same. The working was so tight and speeds generally so low, that the holding of a signal at danger until a train was actually approaching it, and then clearing it, did not really cause delay.

London Bridge starting signals were cleared for up trains, if the line was clear to Borough Market Junction home signals, as soon as the platform staff operated the train ready to start plunger, but the Borough Market home signals were not cleared in anticipation of a train leaving London Bridge. The platform staff might have pressed the ready to start plunger for an up Cannon Street train, the platform starting signal might have changed to single yellow, but that did not mean that the train was actually going to leave. Just as the guard was about to wave his flag, a few more passengers ran up the subway from the booking hall below and one left a door open after he got in. Valuable seconds were lost while a porter had to run forward to close it and then go back to see the guard to give him the right away and relay it to the driver. Time enough perhaps for the Borough Market signalman who had a closely-approaching down train from Charing Cross to pass it over the junction and clear of the points before the up Cannon Street was even in sight round the sharp curve alongside the high bridge girders.

Because of the close spacing with Metropolitan Junction, the latter box had a slot control on Borough Market Junction's up home signals towards Charing Cross to protect moves round the west side of the triangle, but in later years these were few. Unusually in colour-light areas for working in fog, fogsignalmen were employed at the home signals, and block working was instituted with Metropolitan Junction to hold down Charing Cross trains there if an up Cannon Street was crossing the junction. It was deemed too risky to rely on the 15yd overlap of the down home signal.

A visitor to Borough Market Junction signalbox during the evening peak would find the two signalmen quietly concentrating on their own ends of the frame conferring more by telepathy than speech. The down man worked levers 1 to 14 and the up man 16 to 35, each watching partly the track diagram for the red lights showing the train positions as they occupied and cleared track circuits, the train describers (originally the SE&C Walker rotary pattern, rather like a clock face with a hand pointing at a coded description, but later the SR pattern with a vertical list of descriptions indicated by lights alongside), and occasionally glancing out of the box windows to confirm what the track diagram indications told them. They needed to know just that bit more – exactly where a train was, for an up Cannon Street closely approaching the up home signal would probably just get its tail over the junction before a down Charing Cross train just passing Metropolitan Junction box would need to stop at the home signal.

Behind the levers were signal repeaters which showed the full aspect of the signals, unlike modern installations which show only red or proceed. Point indicators showed a letter N for normal or R for reverse, but the signalmen gave them but the merest glance to check that the equipment had responded to the lever. And so it would go on, day in day out, levers pulled, more than two for some trains, for it was one lever – one function, one for the points, one for the signal. Train proceeds, levers restored, other levers pulled, trains pass, sometimes one, perhaps two, even three, and occasionally four at a time, every few minutes.

It all lasted until 1976, when as part of the London Bridge resignalling, which covered several miles of both South Eastern and Central Division routes well out into the suburbs, the track layout between New Cross and Borough Market was completely rationalised, the sorting of up trains for Cannon Street and Charing Cross largely being done in the New Cross area. As a result the three tracks on the north side of London Bridge became down/ reversible/up Cannon Street and the three on the south side, plus an extra squeezed in on the site of a redundant parcels platform, were for Charing Cross. At Borough Market the northern pair formed the down and up Cannon Street, and the southern pair the down and up Charing Cross, with an emergency crossover from the up Charing Cross to Cannon Street, and all controlled from London Bridge panel signalbox. The years of conflict were over.

11
RUNNING SHEDS AND WORKSHOPS

It is a warm July Saturday afternoon in 1938. In Ashford Works, the clangour of riveting hammers in the erecting shop is stilled, the sputter and ghostly flashes of the electric welders over for the weekend. The unnatural quiet allows the electrician and his mate, overhauling the contactor gear of one of the overhead cranes, to hear the passing trains outside, the accelerating three-cylinder beat of a Schools getting away with a Dover express. Below them, caught in the shafts of sunlight through the glass roof, locomotives stand inert and wheel-less, in varying degrees of *deshabillé*, some of them such skeletons as to defy identification. Nothing stirs.

Twenty five miles away, things are very different. Traffic is building up in a rehearsal for the busiest weekend of the year in Thanet. On top of the weekday service, there are over 25 regular Saturdays-only trains coming in, with a number of excursions from the Greater London area on top of that. The engines all finish up on the modern Ramsgate shed for servicing, some arriving in pairs or threes from Margate to keep line occupation down. The ashpits are choc-a-bloc and with engines queuing; Arthurs, D1s and E1s, 2-6-0s, an L, even an 0-4-4 tank. Fortunately the turnover is fairly rapid, for they have not come more than 80 miles or so and fires are not heavily clinkered. The coaling plant seldom has to dispense more than a couple of tons on to any tender, but the coalman is earning his money keeping the bunker fed. The back shift (late turn) foreman is organising the incoming engines on to the various shed roads so that they can be retrieved in time order for their return workings; for the trains starting from Margate he will assemble them in

South Eastern suburban depot. Purley shed (ex SE&CR) in 1926 is home to H class 0-4-4 tank No A512 and other Ashford products. Note the extensive coal stacking operation in progress. Built in 1898, it closed following electrification of the Caterham and Tattenham Corner branches.

South Western shed. Passengers on the platform at Guildford could while away the time with a grandstand view of engines being coaled and watered and having fires and smokeboxes cleaned before their very eyes. No 390, an ex LSWR K10 is in wartime black livery in 1945.

threes or fours to slip through the passenger service. The warm sea air is enriched by a lacing of Betteshanger coal smoke. The sharp hiss of steam from open cylinder cocks mixes with flange squeal, the hollow rumble of coal falling into tenders and the metallic clang of shovels on fireholes and rakes in ashpans. To the casual onlooker it appears to be chaotic; in fact it is highly organised chaos.

Not every Southern engine shed was up to Ramsgate's standard. Some of them could only be described as dreadful places in which to service locomotives. Almost all were straight dead-end sheds, for the round-house had never really caught on south of the Thames. There was never much money about for improvement of running sheds on *any* railway, and maybe it was scarcer still on the Southern, with electrification for ever casting doubt on the long-term future of the sheds. Not only that, but as the third rail spread, some of the outer depots such as Purley and Coulsdon closed down or became mere signing-on points for motormen; the residual steam locomotives were allotted to other depots, increasing their inadequacy. There were a few sheds that were very sound – Eastbourne, for example – but the only really modern depot taken over in 1923 was at Feltham, opened in the previous year to serve the new hump marshalling yard there. It was a straight six-road shed with the luxury of a full-length 50-ton engine-hoist and wagon-hoist type coaling plant. Within the next twelve years six more new depots were built, in each case on new sites chosen for their adequacy and their proximity to the traffic sources. They usually brought into the fold the staff and

158

locomotives from other small local depots which then closed. Ramsgate, for instance, opened in 1930, took on the work of Margate, Ramsgate Harbour and Deal. Amazingly, perhaps, not all of them were provided with mechanical coaling and ash-handling plants; a new elevated hand coaling stage was built at the new Hither Green shed in 1933!

Along with these new sheds, plenty of the awkward ones survived, and there was never any question of a sustained shed yard modernisation programme in the 1930s as practiced by the northern companies. Bournemouth was on a cramped site; there had been ideas about moving the depot to Branksome, but they came to naught. Brighton was tightly wedged in the main line fork. New Cross Gate was a collection of ancient sheds, one of which was so constricted that if an engine stood in the entrance pedestrians could not squeeze past, a situation of some potential danger. The new depot at Norwood took over much of its work. Salisbury was very congested, and much of the fire-cleaning had to be done before engines managed to even get on to the ashpits! Tonbridge was another such. Yeovil did not even have a turntable, and engines had perforce to be turned at Yeovil Junction, 1½ miles away.

And yet, despite all these physical handicaps, the footplate, yard and maintenance staff did a remarkably good job. Apart from random running repairs, there was a schedule of maintenance examinations which bore a striking resemblance (even if it was not quite as comprehensive in its coverage) to the LMS system later adopted by BR. There was a philosophy of 'leaving well alone', a feeling that as many casualties were probably caused by components which had been dismantled for examination as by those left untouched. Applied with discretion this was remarkably successful. At the same time, depots with King Arthurs, which could get distinctly rough with early coupled axlebox wear, were not averse to reconditioning a full set, even when it meant lifting the engine by old hand-operated hoist or sheerlegs.

The bigger depots made a strong point of self-help in keeping engines in good condition, with the active support of the locomotive running superintendent at Waterloo. Stewarts Lane had taken over the Longhedge Works erecting shop after its closure in 1911, which, while limited by being of the 'traverser-and-short-pit' type, enabled shed staff to do quite comprehensive work on engines up to 4-4-0 size. A mile or two

Busy Saturday in Thanet. The train – a 'long set' of non-corridor coaches for Saturday extras or excursions – from the London area, does not warrant three engines, but the first two were hooked on at Margate to save line occupation by light engines heading for Ramsgate shed.

Eastleigh shed. This 1939 photograph shows a Urie S15 still carrying its stove pipe chimney and headcode for a Bournemouth line train alongside Maunsell Q class 0-6-0 (his final design) built in July of the previous year. The letters 'A' and 'B' on the footplate valences perpetuate an LSWR power classification scheme.

away, Bricklayers Arms was provided with a brand new repair shop in 1934, complete with 50-ton overhead cranes, drop pit, machine and fitting shop, wheel lathes and smithy. The thinking behind its building was to avoid light engine mileage to Eastleigh works, but there must also have been confidence that engines requiring what would later be classed as a Light Intermediate Repair could be back in service quicker if tackled on the doorstep rather than (as, for example, on the LMS)

Somerset Ostrich. The little Southern shed at Templecombe was a haven of peace, not quite big enough to house its sole occupant, ex LSWR K10 4-4-0 No 145.

waiting to be called into a main works. Perhaps this could be regarded as a fore-runner of the new BR concept of Cost Effective Maintenance. And could the works have coped with this additional load anyway?

World War II did nothing to improve Southern depots, particularly in the London area. The 'Brick', New Cross Gate, Nine Elms and Stewarts Lane received more than their fair share of the London blitz, and Fratton, too, suffered seriously. They were patched up in due course; brick walls and slate roofs gave way to acres of corrugated asbestos. Even then they remained very unattractive workplaces by comparison with most industry in the south. The ashpits and their surroundings were often buried under mountains of ash and clinker, making further fire-cleaning perilous in the extreme. But the march of the third rail was steadily closing depots in Kent; only on the Western Division did steam remain pre-eminent to keep active such sheds as Nine Elms, Eastleigh and Bournemouth.

By 1967 it was all over. Some sheds were quickly demolished to make way for new developments, a few adapted for diesel use. Some linger on, silent and weedgrown, to this day. But no more do men pick their way about their lawful occasions in sooty gloom; gone is the cheerful banter round the vast cast iron messroom kettle on the range, the grubby locker room with its discarded Weekly Notices, the clink of tool-bucket on zinc-covered stores counter, the cosy warmth of the sand house. An era of industrial heritage has gone for ever.

The Southern's workshops have fared rather better, with two surviving to this day though adapted to new workloads. They started as an unusual bunch, for there were not a lot of such shops in rural areas. Indeed, the very ethos of a 19th century heavy engineering works, which most railway workshops were, demanded that it be surrounded by other works interspersed with cobbled streets of rather mean terraced houses for its workforce. So why should the Southern be so favoured that three of its four main works areas should look out, if sometimes a little tenuously, on green fields, trees and cows? Even in some cases the sea?

It had not always been so. Some of the early radial lines out of London had set up works in the London area, and despite increasing inadequacy some had lingered on, Nine Elms until 1909 and Longhedge until 1911. But sheer necessity had driven them out to green field sites in the far-flung parts of their empires; the LSWR had plumped for Eastleigh (Bishopstoke as it was then known), opening its new carriage and wagon works there in 1891 and following with the locomotive works in 1910. The South Eastern had selected the market town of Ashford, in the 'Garden of England', as early as 1849 for its locomotive, carriage and wagon building and repair activities, to replace Bricklayers Arms. In both cases extensive company housing estates had been built for a transplanted workforce. Only the LBSC had resisted the blandishments of full development in South London and had built locomotive and carriage and wagon establishments in Brighton in 1852; would that they had picked their sites better to deal with future developments, for by 1912 they were forced to build a new carriage works on a green field site at Lancing, outside Worthing.

So the works which gravitated to the new Southern Railway were a very mixed bunch indeed. At the bottom of the scale was, without

Basingstoke in under 42 minutes
Green (ML) go, whistle, flag. Like the start of a horse-race. A hiss, close the cylinder cocks, needles on the red line, the safety-valves show a white feather. No blowing off, we're underway. Full regulator and slowly wind her in to 50 per cent cut-off as we pass Vauxhall, slowly gathering speed before the check for Clapham Junction. Just past Nine Elms the safety-valves lift as the engine's eased for the compulsory slack through the station at Clapham; before the engine clears the road-bridge the regulator's back in the roof and we're climbing towards Earlsfield. I've got the injectors on and shovelling hard. 17.30 Bournemouth, first stop, Basingstoke 48 miles away and up hill much of the way. Having fun as we roar through Wimbledon, hanging on the whistle. The fire's burning well, water bobbing in the top of the glass, and the needle reads 240lb. Eric Saunders, my mate and driver, grins like a loon. We'll beat 'Madman' Hooper – Basingstoke in under 42 minutes! A rattle as Raynes Park Junction disappears behind, speed into the seventies, and the coal crackles as it leaves the end of the shovel.

The game was on, to the passengers it was just the journey home from the city. We knew different – we had been waiting for our rota to bring us round to this turn ever since Gordon Hooper challenged anyone to beat his Waterloo–Basingstoke in 42 minutes. Before they put the final nail in steam's coffin, we who loved the railways decided to make the best of what was the swan song. I was eighteen, and lived and breathed railways, and this was my schoolboy, romantic notion of what railways were about. The famous railway races to the North, the locomotive exchanges, testing your skill against the machines . . .

When you are flying along into the eighties, the fire shivers like blancmange, coal is virtually

continued overleaf

continued

sucked from the end of the shovel, the small pieces and dust being ignited before they touch the fire-bed, whisked through the tubes and straight out the chimney top, Sooty, that was Eric's nickname, gave the bankers of Surbiton a blast – I shovelled. Merchant Navies were a fireman's engine, some said they would steam on a candle. What many people forget, when talking of fast and furious runs being done, was if the fire-boy did not get his act right nobody went anywhere! The fire-boy is the unsung hero of the piece – it is his sweat and skill that keeps them on the boil.

When you whistle through Woking it is all in front of you, the climb to Milepost 31, the steepest grade, but the work was all laid on as you sped through Hersham to go at Brookwood. You needed a full glass and 240lb/sq in and the way you did it was head-down and bottoms-up shovelling – and by Weybridge and Byfleet the only break in shovelling was to catch a distant signal that came up first on the fireman's side. As we began to climb I urged Sooty to let her out to see if, instead of losing speed on this piece of ground, we could either hold our speed or accelerate on this, the steepest grade. We broke even! Past MP 31 the road eased toward Fleet, and a drop of tea to wet the whistle.

These runs were recorded by many an enthusiast, and have been much discussed. It was hard work but fun, and not a few surprises. One night we had the area station manager on the train: he climbed on the tender where I was pulling coal down just to shake my hand. Another night an American railroad engineer came and begged a footplate ride to Winchester. He was most impressed as were, no doubt, the passengers who arrived ten minutes early instead of late.

It was good to be there. – Carl David Wilson.

question, Brighton locomotive works. It was built on several different levels on a hillside between the station approach tracks and a low level goods yard. Stroudley had purchased additional land in 1870 to provide space to bring in carriage and wagon work so that the carriage works site in the fork of the London and Hove lines could be adapted as the locomotive running shed. But it proved yet another attempt to squeeze a growing terrier into a small rathole. The erecting shop was a good one, but the rest of the works was no great shakes and internal transport between shops was particularly difficult. However, one function it *could* perform well was the riveting up of new boiler shells, and while Ashford continued to build new boilers they were sent to Brighton in 'knocked-down' condition to be assembled. If any works was going to be expendable this one was, and under the depression conditions of the 1930s, with available capital steered towards electrification, so it proved. Under Southern auspices it continued to rebuild LBSC classes and built a smidgen of new locomotives up to 1929. By 1934 it was on a 'care and maintenance' footing, the Brighton line engines going to Eastleigh or Ashford for overhaul along with most of the machine tools, and it was used only for limited running repairs.

At the other end of the scale was Eastleigh. Drummond had started with a clean piece of paper to lay out a 92 acre site for his new locomotive works and transferred staff, machine tools and work there from Nine Elms in a meticulously phased operation. The main building contained erecting and machine shops, boiler and wheel shops, paint shop and smithy. The 'hot and dusty' work – foundries, forge, etc – were in a separate building alongside. But the legacy of Nine Elms lived on in ageing machinery and systems of work, and little changed until the 1930s.

The third locomotive establishment, at Ashford, fell between the other two in usefulness. It suffered somewhat from having grown, Topsy-like, in piecemeal fashion; there had been considerable extension and modernisation in the first decade of this century, including a new erecting shop with longitudinal pits in place of the old shop with single pits served by a traverser, yet the Ashford running shed was not elbowed out to an independent site until 1931. It suffered from its South Eastern Railway origins; the railway had persisted as a small-engine line, and the works was geared to them. Even with the new erecting shop the biggest engine it handled was the LMS Class 8F 2-8-0 during World War II until the main line diesels were built there. Maunsell had found on his arrival in 1913 that Ashford was not fully on top of its workload, and with new construction taking second place to repair work it often took three or four years from authority until new locomotives appeared. An extreme example of its limitations, at a time when CMEs were loth to sub-contract, showed itself in the inability of the iron foundry to produce a monobloc cylinder casting for the 3-cylinder 2-6-0s; it proved necessary to adopt the unusual course of using two castings, one incorporating the left hand and middle cylinders, the other the right hand one.

Weighing up his works in 1923, Maunsell soon realised that under unified management a degree of rationalisation had to be the name of the game, using the inherent strengths of the best works to take over the load of poorly laid out or equipped ones. Ashford's carriage works left a great

London shed. Handling coal in large quantities called for mechanical plants. Rebuilt Bulleid Pacific No 34100 *Appledore* is about to collect perhaps five tons from the Nine Elms plant. The concrete stumps are the remains of a previous installation.

Eastleigh erecting shop in early BR days. There are 14 engines visible in varying states of overhaul, including six unrebuilt Bulleid Pacifics, a Nelson, a Schools and King Arthurs. There are two Pacific crank axles on the middle road: the sprocket for the chain driven valve gear is clearly visible.

deal to be desired, part being only able to handle four and six-wheeled coaches. First it lost its new carriage building work, and then carriage overhaul. By contrast, Eastleigh and Lancing both had spacious assembly shops capable of flow-line production. Eastleigh was equipped to undertake all new carriage construction, including at a later stage Bulleid's all-steel stock. Lancing became the centre for all carriage overhauls, achieving a throughput of up to 2,500 vehicles a year. In practice the distinct roles of these two works tended to become blurred, Lancing producing most of the underframes and bogies on to which Eastleigh either built new bodies or transferred second-hand ones.

At both Eastleigh and Ashford the erecting shops changed over in the 1930s from the traditional arrangement of one gang carrying out the complete mechanical overhaul of an engine to one of specialist gangs with the engine being moved progressively down the shop to them. This brought a substantial reduction in the time taken for repairs. At Eastleigh, for instance, a general repair to a King Arthur, which previously had taken three months (including the best part of a month in the paint shop) came down to nineteen days in the shop (with painting done while the fitters were still working on the engine) plus one or two days at the running shed for ancillary preparation work. In this period, too, Eastleigh became the sole supplier of iron and non-ferrous castings following the installation of a continuous casting plant. Ashford was selected as the works to build any diesel locomotives, and the first, a small batch of shunters, came out in 1937.

The near-demise of Brighton has already been touched on. The works was not disposed of, however; it would have been difficult in the thirties to find a candidate for its takeover. But war intervened. In 1940 it reopened, extensively re-equipped, to maintain a repair capacity in the

LBSCR works. Brighton built many of the light Bulleid Pacifics, and 21C128 begins to take shape after the boiler has been lowered into the frames. The engine has been wheeled at an early stage to enable the oil bath to be put in position before the boiler is fitted.

event of war damage to the other works, and to contribute to war production. Two years later it started building new locomotives again with material contributions from other works, notably 93 LMS Class 8F 2-8-0s which latterly were appearing at a very creditable rate of one a week. This new construction continued in the post-war period until 1957 – it was the main centre for building Bulleid's light Pacifics and undertook much work on the smaller BR standard classes – but with the impending rundown of steam Brighton works could not be sustained and closure came in 1958. The site is now a car park.

Any works tends to become self-satisfied while independent, but any search of cupboards by strangers quickly reveals the skeletons within. So it proved when Brighton engines migrated to Eastleigh and Ashford for overhaul. The laxity of much LBSC repair practice was such that parts were being made 'to sample' without drawings, while the erecting shop chargehands seemed to have carte blanche to specify how parts were to be reconditioned and repairs carried out. The frames of the Brighton individually-sprung bogies were ever a source of weakness – the LNER had similar problems – but instead of getting to the bottom of it and redesigning, these frames were being indiscriminately patched, even in some cases being given full-length flitch plates, with gay abandon.

Eastleigh had a reputation for sound workmanship. It was also noted by the *cogniscenti* in the late 1930s for its small but growing museum. Two old locomotives formed the nucleus, and interesting artefacts of the previous century were being steadily added. Alas, in 1940 it succumbed, save for a few small items, to the wartime scrap drive.

After another World War and nationalisation in 1948, it was apparent that major upheavals would come; it was merely a matter of time. The locomotive repair workload began to be eroded in the late 1950s as the first fruits of the Modernisation Plan appeared in the shape of main line diesels, and electrification took in, first the Kent main lines and, in 1967, the Bournemouth line. The scrapping of redundant steam locomotives, both pre- and post-amalgamation, became a cataract. Ashford repaired its last steam locomotive in 1962, and was then re-equipped to become a mass-production wagon works. 16 ton mineral and freightliner wagons took over the erecting shop from Maunsell 2-6-0s, and up to 50 a week were churned out. But in the early 1970s its future began to look anything but secure. There was a hope that its position would make it a prime candidate for the building and maintenance of Channel Tunnel rolling stock, particularly the enormous car-carrying shuttle vehicles, but the cancellation of the 1970s tunnel project in 1975 made this impracticable. With the serious loss of freight traffic and the consequent drying-up of wagon orders, Ashford ran out of work and closed completely at the end of 1981.

Lancing continued to overhaul coaches until 1965, when it was closed and sold off; the site is now an industrial estate. Eastleigh locomotive works was run down in the 1960s, and having got rid of steam it was re-equipped to overhaul coaches, EMUs, diesel and electric locomotives, the old carriage shops being modified to become an EMU/DEMU servicing facility. By 1987 the works had been reduced in status to a light maintenance depot retrieved from British Rail Engineering Ltd. Dugald Drummond must be turning in his grave!

Coal Trial

In 1948 'Merchant Navy' Pacific No 35005 was fitted with a mechanical stoker in order to explore the possibility of burning grades of coal inferior in both quality and size (and thus by implication, cheaper); it was a time of particular difficulty in obtaining adequate supplies of good quality large coal. After some familiarisation running, dynamometer car trials using the ex-LMS No 1 car were conducted between Waterloo and Exeter over a period of a week. Each day a lower-grade fuel was fired than the day before. The load was about 12 coaches, empty stock.

On the Thursday the tender was filled with some Derbyshire slack of which a substantial percentage was little better than dust, the sort of stuff that you see being put to stack at any modern power station. All the way to Salisbury a cloud of coal dust blew off the tender, and all attempts to damp it down were unavailing. The fireman was struggling, and there was a continuous trail of dirty smoke from the chimney. Somewhere on the way an unidentified flying object broke one of the large end observation windows of the dynamometer car, and within minutes there was a layer of fine coal over floor, seats, everything. When you walked about it crunched under your feet. Even the paper recording roll was getting steadily grubbier.

The word from the footplate was that steaming was very poor, and by Basingstoke we were in real trouble. We staggered over Grateley summit and coasted the ten downhill miles into Salisbury. When we climbed on to the footplate the pressure was only about 100 pounds and the fire was for all practical purposes OUT. The trial was terminated there and then; there was no alternative. – A. J. Powell.

12
THE SOUTHERN IN THE WEST

Three Minute Piece

In the late thirties the *Atlantic Coast Express* would sweep fast and splendidly into the wide, curved down main platform at Salisbury. The moment the train stopped, the fireman leapt down between tender and train and simultaneously the driver, spinning the reversing wheel, set back. Vacuum broken, coupling unhitched and let fall against the tender with a clang. Quick blow up of the brake with the reversing wheel spun again as the fireman got out from under and the 'King Arthur' was already moving forward as he rejoined it. Instantly, the regulator was opened wide and in full fore gear the engine absolutely tore off down the main line as if going non-stop to Exeter. About 600yd away it braked sharply and swung left into Salisbury Loco.

Before that, the moment the engine was clear of the crossover at the platform end, the replacement 'Arthur', often with a Drummond water cart eight-wheel tender, would move back on the adjoining road, over the crossover and gently set back on the train. Coupled at once, the new engine blew up the train brake – thirteen coaches, which took rather longer! And then right away to Sidmouth Junction, Exeter, Ilfracombe, Torrington, Bude, Padstow and Plymouth! And this operation from stop to re-start was allowed exactly four minutes. Once it was seen done in a little over three.

Gradients, tunnels and junctions are the first images that come to mind when asked about the Southern west of Salisbury. And of these the most powerful are junctions. An endless variety of them sharing just two things in common: periods of intense activity between long siestas, and the attaching and detaching of coaches to trains from and to Waterloo.

Attaching and detaching was indeed a way of life on the Southern in the West, one of the few characteristics equally strong east and west of Exeter. In most ways, of course, Exeter marked a sharp dividing point: between one of the nation's railway raceways and the often painfully slow Withered Arm, between a main line throwing off short branches and a system that was almost all branches, a railway that gathered together bulk loads from the rich countryside it served and from the further west, and that struggling to earn its keep from a mainly harsh upland territory.

Attaching and detaching, it seemed, almost everywhere, but especially at the junctions. The East Devon branches had their daily all-the-year-round through coach from Waterloo, as sometimes did also Yeovil Town and sometimes Lyme Regis. The through coaches for Sidmouth and Exmouth, having left the main train at Sidmouth Junction, finally separated at Tipton St John's, where throughout the day there was continual attaching and detaching of locomotives, that of the Exmouth train running round it in the yard clear of the running tracks. But about a dozen other places on the main line and branches were terminal points for trains, mainly from Exeter, some of them running at times that changed little over decades. Apart from the two hourly express departures from Waterloo, there was absolutely nothing standard about the timetable.

Exeter Central was a cathedral of attaching and detaching. On ordinary days virtually all Waterloo expresses to the far west lost their restaurant car and powerful locomotive here and were then split in two for the descent to St David's. Usually the Plymouth section left first, for throughout its life, like the South Western before it and the Southern Region afterwards, it was in keen competition with Paddington for traffic to South West England's premier city. North Devon was only given priority with the *Atlantic Coast Express* and the overnight train which also carried the newspapers.

Passengers bound for the far end of the system at Padstow had two further rounds of attaching and detaching: at Okehampton, where naturally the Plymouth portion was again given priority, and at Halwill Junction, where the Padstow and Bude trains could be despatched more rapidly one after the other, but Padstow enjoyed priority. From 1925, when priorities were reversed, Ilfracombe trains were despatched ahead of Torrington ones at Barnstaple Junction, another mecca of attaching

and detaching, some all-within-Devon services still having separate Ilfracombe and Torrington coaches, local trains terminating, and milk, parcels and other tail-end traffic for ever being added, especially to evening trains going south east. Such was the pressure of shunting and other movements at Barnstaple Junction that after World War II it was seen as a great step forward when some trainsets ran through from the Western at Taunton on to Torrington.

As to the west of Exeter, there was an annoying number of stations on the Withered Arm where trains started and terminated. Bideford was traditional starting point of a Sunday morning train to Waterloo, and Launceston of a Sunday afternoon service to Okehampton while the rest of the North Cornwall line kept Sabbath peace. An early morning weekday local for Barnstaple started at South Molton Road (later King's Nympton), children and workers crowded in the third class compartments of the single composite coach as its progress resounded in the Taw Valley on a crisp winter's morning. An evening workers' train from Plymouth, including ex steam railcars with cast-iron gates to keep passengers safe, reversed at Bere Alston and terminated at Gunnislake, several daily trains went from Plymouth to Tavistock, and for many years a late afternoon one made Brentor its terminus. At times even Holsworthy had its 'short' train from Bude. On the Torrington–Halwill Light Railway for many years an evening train for clay workers was advertised as starting from Dunsbear Halt, while on Tuesdays the Petrockstowe–Torrington morning train started back at Hatherleigh.

Gateway to the west. Exeter Central, formerly Queen Street in LSWR days, was the Southern's point of entry to the far south west. It was the end of the express part of the journey from London, where long distance trains, other than those for East Devon resorts, were broken down into separate portions for Plymouth, North Devon and North Cornwall. Here in August 1954 Class M7 0-4-4T No 30676 leaves the up side bay for Exmouth with a mixed rake of LSW stock. On the middle through track a Bulleid Pacific stands with restaurant car and two ordinary coaches waiting to attach them to a Waterloo service.

West Country meeting place. Down the road from Central is Exeter St David's where the Southern met the Great Western on the latter's territory. By a quirk of geography Southern trains from London to Plymouth passed in the opposite direction those of the GWR also running from London to Plymouth. Because of its superiority the Great Western demanded that all LSW/ Southern trains should stop in St David's and not gain a time advantage by running non stop, particularly hard on the Southern's London bound trains which faced nearly ¾ mile of 1 in 37 between the two Exeter stations, entailing double and sometimes triple heading as here with a Drummond 700 class 0-6-0 No 30317, N 2-6-0 No 31610, and Bulleid Pacific No 34060 with the 11.35am Plymouth Friary to Waterloo on 9 August 1958.

All the attaching and detaching was done expeditiously throughout the system, for the Southern in the West was a well run railway. Much of it was not well built, Brunel's desire to go straight through obstacles not being shared by the Waterloo men seeking the completion of the routes to the Atlantic. The up-round-and-avoid-it principle was indeed adopted even for the only continuously double track route beyond Exeter, sweeping round the north of Dartmoor (and up and down some of its foothills) to Tavistock and Plymouth. But if cheaply built, it was magnificiently maintained – in the spirit that the Southern greatly upgraded the narrow-gauge Lynton & Barnstaple immediately after acquiring it. And it was run as well as it was maintained, with a distinct *esprit de corps*, not quite as rich as the Great Western's but proud in its matter-of-factness.

The nature of the pride was naturally different east and west of Exeter. The railwaymen between Salisbury and Exeter saw their trunk route as one of the nation's best. Had not the Salisbury & Yeovil (mainly because it built itself as a trunk, ignoring towns like Shaftesbury a few miles off its ideal path and refused to build any real branch) made more money for itself than virtually any other British line? Even the absence of water troughs gave no inferiority feeling, because with all the experience of attaching and detaching they could change the locomotive of the *Devon Belle* of later Southern days in a jiff at the unadvertised Wilton stop.

West of Exeter it was harder to take pride in speed and much antiquated procedure had to be followed, such as hand-clipping points at crossing stations between Exeter and Barnstaple, so that the tails of trains too long to be accommodated in the loops could be set back in refuge sidings. But the territory served by the Withered Arm depended on its railway to an enormous extent. Milk that otherwise would have to have been turned into cheese at a lower price was rushed daily to London. Cattle were transported economically. Lime and fertilisers needed to tame the great plateauland north and west of Dartmoor came by train. All the Atlantic resorts depended on the summer weekend expresses for their livelihood. Even many of those who toured North Devon by car came by train and temporarily bought a used motor. Hundreds went to work and shop daily in Barnstaple, Okehampton, Wadebridge and Plymouth by train. Fish from Padstow, clay from Petrockstowe and Meeth on the Torrington–Halwill Junction line, strawberries and flowers from the Tamar Valley, rabbits from most country stations, especially in the war years, military specials at Okehampton – the Withered Arm may have been seriously underused but it was not without its substantial businesses. Only one traffic was notably absent: coal. During Southern days most coal came by sea, to a series of ports on both coasts. Yet it is the coal trade that perhaps best emphasises how important the railway was, for the port of Fremington on the Bideford line was developed and for decades largely served the railway's own substantial fuel needs at Barnstaple.

There is also one other aspect about pride in the job on a rambling system of glorified and actual branch lines west of Exeter. Wage rates in this territory were traditionally poor, below those of South Devon and South and West Cornwall, reached by Brunel's broad gauge earlier in railway history, and serving more non-agrarian industries. Standardised

railway pay was welcome and occasionally seemed princely, especially where between periods of real activity men had time to tend their gardens, or pay a leisurely visit to the pub.

The nickname Withered Arm might suggest ridicule, but it was no laughing stock. Station work was accomplished and trains despatched with alacrity unfamiliar on neighbouring Great Western branches. Heavy seasonal traffics were taken in stride with excellent planning. It was basically efficient even when time had seemed perpetually to have stood still, an impression vividly given by most of the trains themselves. This indeed is true both to east and west of Exeter. Stations might suddenly sport some piece of noveau concrete art produced by Exmouth Junction's famous concrete works which began pushing its wares with enthusiasm even in South Western days, and stations were also ever adorned with posters proclaiming progress. The spread of upper quadrant signals, some on concrete posts, suggested the Southern might indeed be leaving the Great Western behind. But the trains! Many inherited in 1923 were passed on in 1948 with little thought of replacement meantime. All the numerous tank engines used in the west were of pre-1914 vintage until well into BR days. And well after nationalisation the traveller could still spread himself in what was probably the largest third class seat produced on any scale, that between the window and door into the lavatory on a standard South Western non-corridor coach. Of course not all compartments enjoyed access to a lavatory; you had to choose your seat according to your bladder habit.

In East Devon the Southern had almost a network of branches to the South coast – Lyme Regis, Seaton, Sidmouth and Exmouth, each with its own character. The Axminster – Lyme Regis branch was lightly constructed which restricted locomotive types which could work it. Thus it was home to two vintage Adams 4-4-2Ts (three in post war SR days after one was bought back from the East Kent Railway); No 30584 is seen arriving at Axminster on 29 October 1948.

171

Milk for the capital. Seaton Junction was one of the Southern's milk collecting points. Class S15 4-6-0 No 30823 leaves Seaton Junction on 11 June 1962 with a milk train bound for Vauxhall.

The Other View

Down in the West Country, the difference between the lines served by Paddington and Waterloo was almost that between church and chapel, between establishment and upstart. From the year that the first route through Cornwall was planned, friendships and even marriages were made and broken as the two railways battled it out.

From the Great Western perspective (and even in the 1940s there were thousands who had taken an almost religious vow of allegiance to Paddington) the Southern and its predecessor had been cunning in keeping the rightful railway off the coast all the way from Minehead to *continued opposite*

Every detail of these vehicles, but especially the heavy decor, was dated. So was the whole ambience of the lengthy strings of non-corridor stock used on the busy Exmouth branch. But then even the *Atlantic Coast Express* was no marvel, consisting largely of single coach sections, composite first, third and brake, though at least these were post 1923. Riding was rougher than on the Great Western, seating infinitely inferior to the LMS, picture windows slow to appear, woodwork rougher hewn. And always that distinct Southern polish-cum-disinfectant smell that somehow reassured that while the thing may have been rattling around since grandfather's day, at least there was no danger of catching something nasty.

Going to South Coast resorts the better-to-do would of course have gone by Pullman. Only the West Country had to rely on the Southern's own hospitality, though throughout the West the Southern franchised its parcel delivery service. That seemed most strange to the Great Western enthusiast who saw Paddington exploiting every commercial opportunity itself. Only after World War II and the introduction of the ill-fated *Devon Belle* did luxury come to the Southern in the West. The train, along with the Merchant Navy class locomotive now used to haul expresses to Exeter and the light Pacific West Country class beyond, gave the Southern a quite different profile just before nationalisation. 'First in the Field' proclaimed the posters portraying Bulleid's machines. All of a sudden the Southern seemed avant-garde. The *Devon Belle*, introduced in 1947, was not a commercial success and even before its early death was down to an Ilfracombe-only express on summer

172

weekends – the very time the railway had an increasing surfeit of traffic, the *Atlantic Coast Express* running in several sections with restaurant cars through to Ilfracombe and Padstow, and a car-carrying train introduced from Surbiton to Okehampton.

As on the Great Western, summer Saturdays became increasingly important. A separate Plymouth–Portsmouth train ran to supplement the Plymouth–Brighton, ordinarily the only one with restaurant car west of Exeter; separate Padstow, Bude, Plymouth and Ilfracombe sections all proclaimed themselves the *Atlantic Coast Express*; an Exmouth–Cleethorpes through service ran via the Somerset & Dorset at Templecombe. These and many more taxed the system as at other times it was under-utilised. Pressure at the junctions did not increase proportionally since more whole trains meant less dividing and joining. Now Wadebridge shed's only West Country showed its superiority over older machines by taking a whole train to Exeter. Upon how many passengers it brought back would depend the livelihood of a string of small resorts along the North Cornwall coast. (It is interesting to reflect that a report on the West Country's economy published in the 1950s called for just one additional section of railway, from Wadebridge to Newquay; what then of the North Cornwall line?)

But gradients. Always a nuisance, they now became the rationer of what the railway could achieve. Queuing for the down section up Honiton Bank and through the tunnel could stretch back to Sherborne, and it was a very good summer Saturday that did not see many westbound trains checked at Axminster. The country's steepest main line, between Exeter St David's and Central, was a dramatic obstacle to efficiency. Not merely did Southern up trains impede Western down ones before they were tucked into their own platform 3, but having attached banking engines (often plural) the whole cortege had to cross the down Western as it struggled up the foot of the incline. The Ilfracombe lines' gradients were another nightmare with double heading and banking often needed in both directions, the Great Western's through trains via Taunton of course adding to the burden. An engine failure or just shortage of steam could and did keep Ilfracombe's taxi drivers and waiters working well into the night.

There were gradients everywhere: a fierce one immediately out of Tipton St John's restricting the weight of Sidmouth trains; a cruel climb with switchback characteristics up from Coleford Junction on the Barnstaple line up through North Tawton to Okehampton (what memories of an overloaded all-stations train taking an eternity as it struggled up slippery rails on a misty summer Saturday), and gradients and curves on the grand scale on the Light Railway from Bere Alston to Callington, possibly the Southern's most exotic route of all. And even where there were not especially challenging gradients, except when running beside estuaries and rivers, the Southern in the West was always up or down as well as usually round, with extremely hard locomotive work, as from Tavistock to Okehampton, locomotives left in low gear to slog it out. But there were locomotives and locomotives. To the end of their days, well beyond nationalisation, Drummond's 4-4-0 T9 'Greyhounds' lived up to their name, lifting lightweight trains over summits at 40 to 50mph and often reaching 70mph on undulating sections, as

continued
Newquay but had paid the price in seeing the Withered Arm's territory suffer far more from depression than the rest of the South West.

True GW men relished the stop always inflicted on the 'foreign' trains running through Exeter St David's, and many a knowing glance was given when one of the new-fangled Bulleid 'West Country' Pacifics – dismissed as 'Southern Capers', shades of the atmospheric – that so dramatically reduced the average age of Exmouth Junction's locomotive fleet in the late 1940s slipped on its feet. Clang, clang, clang; most un-Churchward. At least one GW stalwart positively refused to travel behind one of the Capers forming the tea-time train from Teignmouth to Exeter though it had about the longest gaps in the whole day's service on either side of it. 'Rather be seen dead.' The Southern provided machine and men for one daily train each way between Exeter and Plymouth for route knowledge. 'The damn thing does not even have ATC.'

Some credence was added to these extreme views when reports about maintenance difficulties with the Light Pacifics and the heat the firemen had to endure on the footplate (one did actually faint in Devon) – and especially when, shortly after one machine woke a sizeable slice of North Devon travelling all the way to Ilfracombe with its whistle stuck open, the streamline casing of a larger version of the Caper caught that of a passing train en route from Waterloo to Exeter, seriously scratching most of an *ACE*.

Little realising how efficiently the Southern actually served its difficult territory, the GW extremists lost no opportunity to pour scorn on it. Why, its loading gauge prohibited the emergency passage via Okehampton of the *Cornish Riviera*, though this could happily be accommodated on the Teign Valley; and Bulleid's tavern cars, mock brick outside, claustrophobia in!

Through coaches from Waterloo. What on a weekday would probably have been one or two coaches detached from a Waterloo – Plymouth service blossomed out on peak summer Saturdays into a complete train with restaurant cars from Waterloo to Exmouth, seen here in August 1963 after reversal at Sidmouth Junction where its main line locomotive was detached and now in the charge of Ivatt LMS designed 2-6-2T No 41307 and BR standard 2-6-4T No 80042, to run via Tipton St John's.

North Devon terminus. Ilfracombe station from the wooded hills of the Slade Valley with a Bulleid West Country or Battle of Britain Pacific leaving the long platform with this section of the Atlantic Coast Express. *During the week Ilfracombe slumbered but on busy summer Saturdays the lengthy platforms could be tested to their limit – as was the motive power which needed piloting or banking up the steep grades between here and the Barnstaple. At busy times all manner of engines were used as pilots – even Great Western 45XX 2-6-2 tanks from that company's Barnstaple shed.*

between Halwill and Launceston, over track perfectly maintained for such speeds.

An enthusiasts' special taking a 'Greyhound' to Padstow for the last time and seeing its gracious body turned in the evening sunlight beside the Camel is one of the writer's many vivid memories of the post-nationalisation Southern in the West. Others are of an evening rush hour at Wadebridge with three trains ready to leave eastward and one the other way to Padstow; a wartime Summer Saturday when Ilfracombe's shunting engine was so short of steam that it took three attempts to haul an empty train out of the siding up the start of the incline to clear the points to set back to the platform; splendid afternoon teas on exhilarating non-stop runs from Yeovil Junction (reached by autocar from Town) to Exeter; Barnstaple Junction with everything packed to capacity in the war, a complete girls' school returning up country from evacuation compressed into three extra coaches added by the station pilot; the procession of mainly antiquated trains out of Plymouth Friary and through North Road during the evening rush hour, their passenger complement declining rapidly after nationalisation; a double-headed passenger train tailed by fifteen vans of strawberries that blasted its way up from Calstock Viaduct to Bere Alston, while the main line train was delayed a quarter of an hour waiting for connecting passengers; passengers disgorging from Exmouth's neat red-brick four-platform station at the end of two single-line branches, almost Liverpool Street-like; and the everlasting exchange of whistle codes as passenger, freight and Meldon Quarry stone trains prepared to tackle the gradient up from Exeter St David's to Central. St David's may have been GWR and the GWR insisted on stopping every Southern wheel in it; but audibly it was pure Southern.

All the great scenic points in the West were GW, yet the Southern had

Furthest west. Padstow was as far as you could go in a Southern train on its own metals, 260 miles from Waterloo, and a world away from the busy Southern electric network. It was the preserve of T9s, N class Moguls, O2s, and the veteran Beattie well tanks shunted here. Just a handful of trains a day to Okehampton or Exeter, some going through to Waterloo picking up more coaches from Plymouth, Bude or Ilfracombe on the way. T9 4-4-0 No 30709 waits to work the 3.13pm to Exeter on 22 May 1961.

The Station For . . .

The Southern gladly carried on the South Western's West Country tradition of stations advertising themselves as being for somewhere else, and even those that honestly proclaimed themselves 'Roads' did not have their distances from the towns or villages concerned stated in the timetable. Thus South Molton Road proclaimed it was 2½ miles from Chumleigh (Eggesford boasted it was 3) but overlooked the fact that it was nine miles from the town it purported to serve. Because of complaints, after nationalisation it was renamed *continued opposite*

greater variety. Great Western branch lines were always Great Western branch lines. There was nothing in common beyond the smell of the interior of the carriages between the Lyme Regis train hauled by an Adams tank and the mixed train on the grandly-named but little used North Devon & North Cornwall Junction Light Railway. Ilfracombe and the Plymouth suburban station of Turnchapel might have been on different planets. There was a certain unity if only from the railway point of view along the double track all the way from Reading to Penzance, but it was hard to reconcile the *Atlantic Coast Express* that had roared through the lush scenery of South Dorset and East Devon, with one fleeting view of the English Channel, was on the same railway at all going past Delabole slate quarry and ending where the Camel meets the Atlantic. Yet, ironically, the station architecture from Salisbury all the way west *was* (and what remains still is) substantially the same, because the South Western built a gable-ended house every time it extended the line over the half a century it took to link up with its early purchase, the Bodmin & Wadebridge.

Undoubtedly the landscape strongly influenced the Southern mood, with strong contrast between the south coast ambience east of Exeter and the moor and plateau to the west. But strictly railway factors added to the contrasts and diversity. The system was built over an enormous time span, from the days of ease in raising railway capital to those of hoping ends would meet. It included several oddities such as the Light Railways, the last of which – Torrington–Halwill, 1925 – was done so badly that most things like signals needed replacing within years. Then, many stations including important ones like Barnstaple Junction remained virtually untouched Victoriana, while Exeter Central, Okehampton and Ilfracombe boasted various degrees of modernity, as did Exmouth Junction shed and the extremely successful Meldon stone quarry (still very active despite requiring many miles of hilly railway especially to serve it). Signalboxes were mainly extremely ancient or modern. And at the end ancient, inherited locomotives were often on exchangeable rotas with the 'first in the field' Bulleid Pacifics, while 2-6-0 Moguls of intermediate age would be seen shunting at Bere Alston or Holsworthy.

It was thus ever an interesting railway, each piece of exploration throwing out some new surprise, such as the mountain route to Callington, perhaps surpassing the GW's Princetown branch, the modern sea-level stations at Exmouth and Seaton, with Sidmouth's traditional station a mile inland because that resort wished to discourage the tripper trade, the extensive fish quays and facilities at Padstow, Fremington's booming railway-owned harbour, with its three steam cranes importing coal and exporting clay that never went anywhere near a main line. But then Bodmin North, though it once had a through coach from Waterloo, did not seem to have much to do with Exeter and beyond, and as for Wenford Bridge, for the young reporter allowed to ride with the driver before pilgrimages there became popular, here was a rail heaven on earth where it seemed perfectly natural to be delayed while acorn-eating pigs were cleared off the line and to take water by gravity from a stream by the engine built in the year of the collapse of Gladstone's first government. With hindsight perhaps GWR buffs disparaged the Southern in the West, and especially the Withered Arm, because it worked on a shoe string. The Southern could not afford the ubiquitous pannier tank of more recent vintage, or new two-car non-corridor branch set. It actually built no new non-corridor coaches for steam trains in its entire history. As was pointed out in the Introduction, it was always short of money – and (except with government help as with the Padstow fish quay) the further west the more so. Yet with what it had it ran a reliable and often outstanding service that was the backbone of much of the West's agriculture and tourism.

It always played second fiddle to the GWR in the greater West Country. It held its head high at Exeter but gave Plymouth a much slower service, and then, as already stated, at the cost of relegating North Devon. After the GWR started modernising its Barnstaple branch, introducing automatic token exchanging to allow 40mph running through station loops by non-stopping trains, there was an evil pact between the two railways that neither would invest further in North Devon. So the railways there became fossilised, and even at the peak of the holiday trade in the 1950s and 1960s that meant that Waterloo–Ilfracombe trains, too long for the crossing loops at stations such as South Molton Road, had to set back their tails into the refuge sidings over points locked by hand. (With so much running around to do when the system was used to full capacity on summer Saturdays, the signalmen at certain stations were exonerated from having to enter times in the train register.) How slow the general standard was even on ordinary days is epitomised by the fact that the *Atlantic Coast Express* reached Ilfracombe only twenty minutes after the Waterloo departure of two hours earlier. Ultimately, in BR days, the earlier train terminated at Barnstaple since to have continued it to Ilfracombe would have delayed the *ACE*.

Apart from the negative North Devon pact of the thirties, there were few strategic discussions between the rivals; just everlasting tensions. Southern men implied you were consorting with the devil if you left

continued

King's Nympton, still for Chumleigh but now forgetting all about South Molton as earlier it had of course ignored King's Nympton, itself hardly nearby. Many a passenger wished he had gone by the Great Western instead; it was only a mile or so away. Near Plymouth, 'St Budeaux for Saltash' neatly ignored the fact that the GW actually crossed the Tamar in these pre road-bridge days.

Braunton was for Saunton Sands, recognised when a 'West Country' Pacific was named after it. Most ambitious was Bideford claiming to be the station for Hartland, thirteen miles away. Mortehoe for Woolacombe later became an amalgamation of the two, and then forgot it was also for Lee (Devon).

The honours for sheer numbers in this respect fall to the North Cornwall line, whose first station, small and remote Maddaford Moor Halt was for Thorndon Cross; the complete legend made the nameboard almost as long as the halt itself. Ashbury was for North Lew, but grandest of all was 'Halwill for Beaworthy, Junction for Bude, North Cornwall and Torrington Lines', to quote the station nameboard, giving an impression of a rural Clapham Junction set in the Devon fields. At Dunsland Cross the nameboard informed one to 'alight here for Shebbear College'.

On the North Cornish moors, Otterham sounded far busier than it was advertising itself for Wilsey Down and Davidstow (2½ miles) and Crackington Haven (5 miles). Camelford was more obviously the station for Boscastle and Tintagel. Naturally neither Port Isaac Road nor St Kew Highway hinted how near, or far, they were from their namesakes.

After World War II, the ultimate prize was perhaps taken by Wrafton. A sign provided by a short-lived airline but happily displayed by the Southern invited you to change for the flight to Lundy.

Nine Hour Turn

Ilfracombe's turntable, high above the town, was noted for its exposure to Atlantic gales. Once they were turning a Maunsell N 2-6-0 in an especially strong wind. No refinements then like vacuum hoses to power the thing. It had to be pushed laboriously round by hand by driver and fireman.

Suddenly, half way round, the full force of the gale caught the engine side on. From being heavy to move it suddenly became very easy indeed. When they could not slow it, one of them shot the locking bolt in an attempt to stop the rot. The bolt instantly broke off and that was that. The mogul stayed there turning briskly for nearly nine hours before the gale abated.

Mixed train. The Southern was mostly a passenger railway and not much given to mixed trains on branch lines though the practice was certainly not unknown. One line where this was the norm rather than the exception was the North Devon and Cornwall Junction Railway joining Torrington with Halwill Junction and worked by the E1R rebuilds of LB&SCR 0-6-0 tanks. E1R 0-6-2 tank No 32095 leaves Torrington on 17 May 1950 with the 1.05pm mixed up to the clay pits at Peters Marland climbing the 1 in 66 gradient from the River Torridge.

Ilfracombe on a summer through train to Paddington, though this would save over twenty miles and before the war Taunton was reached with creditable speed. Barnstaple GW was bypassed (signalboxes were open in summer at all three ends of a triangular junction) and a restaurant car added at South Molton. But during the war, when every freight train leaving Barnstaple for up country was made up to its maximum load (allowing for vehicles that had to be added en route to Exeter or Taunton), great were the arguments and tricks between Southern and Western men to have loads sent the other way. 'Everybody knows that the Taunton route is for South Wales, the Midlands, the North of England and Scotland, and NOT for London,' pontificated the Southern's stationmaster.

Boundary disputes became more animated (and wasteful) after nationalisation. When a summer Saturday train for Manchester was started at Exmouth for operational reasons, the Western Region refused to allow the Southern to advertise it as a through service lest Exeter people bought their tickets at Central instead of St David's station. For a long time Western trains still did not call at the halts between Bodmin and Wadebridge because the Western only enjoyed non-stop running powers. Wasteful duplication of facilities continued at Plymouth, Barnstaple, Launceston and Bodmin. When an upstart journalist suggested some rationalisation, such as closure of the Southern between Halwill Junction and Launceston, routing traffic via Lydford, the Southern's divisional manager at Exeter cancelled his engagements and had himself chauffeur-driven to tell the staff at the two intermediate stations that their jobs would never be in jeopardy. Though the two railways had saved some money at Lydford (and Launceston) by sharing a signalbox, or rather combining two separate boxes with their independent frames and instruments under one roof, it was only because of the threat of bomb damage that a wartime physical connection was provided. A similar emergency link was built at St Budeaux where the two routes ran in parallel, but not until 1964 was the sensible economy made of running Southern trains into Plymouth over it, saving the cost of a separate route through Devonport.

The surprise to railwaymen of the age would be that *we* should be surprised by such attitudes and happenings. The railway was a way of life, and never more so than on the Southern in the West of England. History was writ deep in the character of that way of life. The standard

Amazing survivor. One of the three Wadebridge based 0298 class 2-4-0 well tanks of Beattie's design No 0314 shunts clay wagons on the Wenford Bridge branch. The Southern in the west retained a number of elderly classes, the Adams 4-4-2 tanks at Lyme Regis, M7 0-4-4 tanks on push pull services and O2 0-4-4 tanks again at Wadebridge – all into the 1960s.

gauge had been robbed of the premier role in the South West, and had had to fight its way through tough geography ultimately to reach the Atlantic. Paddington and Waterloo were as different as church and chapel in a part of Britain not known for elasticity of mind. Wherever the two systems met, they observed their separate rituals, in some cases – as at Yeovil Town – with separate houses for separate stationmasters. When men of the two systems met, they observed each other, but usually from a distance. 'We didn't have a need to talk, but I often wondered how it was possible to put twenty shovelfuls of coal on at a time and then sit down,' said a Western fireman of his Southern equivalent on a West Country Pacific.

It was a locomotive of another Bulleid class, a Merchant Navy, that reached Exeter early on the much-publicised inaugural run of an accelerated *Atlantic Coast Express* in September 1961. It was the very day that the Western 'rationalised' its West of England services out of Paddington, one of the then new Warship-class diesels being unable to maintain the relaxed schedule. The Waterloo–Exeter route enjoyed a rich Indian Summer of steam, as Southern men prepared for bitterness they knew they would experience when ultimately everything Southern west of Exeter went Western. There were a number of earlier boundary changes, at one time commercial and operating coming under different

Southern help. Although the Barnstaple–Ilfracombe line was owned by the LSWR and after the Grouping was purely Southern, the Great Western had running powers for its services from the Taunton line. However the ferocious gradients over the hills in North Devon – six miles of mostly 1 in 40 between Braunton and Mortehoe and nearly four miles at 1 in 36 down to Ilfracombe – meant double heading even on relatively light trains, like this four-coach train forming the 6.37pm from Ilfracombe to Taunton with GW 2-6-0 No 6327 piloted by SR Class N 2-6-0 No 31856 on 27 July 1963.

jurisdictions, but the old order lingered on far longer than seemed likely and was then brought to a cruel end.

The creation of a Plymouth Division incorporating all routes in the West coincided not only with dieselisation but the Beeching era of closures – following the loss of huge amounts of traffic. Drastic surgery was obviously unavoidable, equally among branch lines in East Devon and to the West of Exeter. But there was great anger among Southern men at the way the Waterloo–Exeter trunk was downgraded and substantially singled west of Salisbury. Earlier the arguments had seemed to support the development of the Southern's slightly shorter route. It was forecast that all daytime passenger trains would go their way, electrification being extended from Basingstoke to Salisbury, Yeovil and even Exeter, while night and goods trains would run via Bristol, allowing the closure of much of the Castle Cary route between Reading and Taunton. That was, however, before the dramatic growth of stone traffic in the Westbury area.

To be sure, the Western got it wrong. Though much traffic was driven away by a slower and far less reliable service, Waterloo–Exeter refused to die and in the mid-1980s ranked as the eighth most important InterCity route. Everyone admits that singling was a mistake. Several stations have been reopened and extra trains run, while the Exmouth branch also once more enjoys a frequent service throughout the day and even Barnstaple has more trains. But that is about all that is left of the Southern in the west: Salisbury–Exeter–Barnstaple (though no trains run right through), the Exmouth branch, a branch from Crediton through a totally-closed Okehampton (except for occasional charter specials) to Meldon for quarry traffic only, and a self-contained St Budeaux–Gunnislake local line with reversal at the former main-line station of Bere Alston. Waterloo had been cunning, persistent and clever in keeping the Great Western off the Atlantic seaboard between Minehead and Newquay, but because it reached resorts along that coast late in railway history, after the main course of development had been set, there was inadequate business to support it in the motor age. Those who felt it monstrous that

Joint line to Bournemouth. The LSWR and Midland Railway became partners in the once disreputable Somerset & Dorset Railway, passing this ownership on to their successors the Southern, then the LMS. In 1930 the locomotive stock was assimilated by the LMS and the coaches by the Southern. Under BR, regional boundary changes brought greater Southern and later Western involvement in locomotive work. The Southern light Pacifics took a share in the more important workings from the mid 1950s but LM power was still prominent and often SR and LM locomotives double-headed the heavier trains as here with 2P 4-4-0 No 40503 piloting West Country Pacific No 34044 Woolacombe *as they climb out of Bath with the* Pines Express. *In 1962 the WR diverted S&D through services via Reading and Basingstoke and in 1966 the S&D closed.*

an important resort like Ilfracombe should lack a railway had to contend with the fact that by 1960, except in high summer, trains reached the end of the line with an average of less than ten passengers.

Yet Ilfracombe, Bude and Padstow would not have reached even their present sizes but for the railway's support, and agriculture, horticulture and the clay industries were all totally dependent on rails until well after World War II. The Ilfracombe Goods once had their own locomotive class; nearly a century later, the Bude goods remained the most important trading institution at the market town of Holsworthy, and the daily shunt by a 2-6-0 Mogul was equally important at Bideford, Tavistock, Budleigh Salterton. The shedmaster at Wadebridge, in charge of a particularly motley assortment from the single West Country Pacific to the Beattie tanks (for the Wenford Bridge clay traffic), ranked with the headmaster in the social hierarchy. Those in charge of Fremington Quay and Meldon Quarry well knew they were running the most important commercial undertakings for miles around. Exmouth Junction was among the great railway meccas of Britain; Central held its head high and owed nothing to St David's. Even the stationmaster at Plymouth Friary, close to the city centre but only reached by a most tortuous passage in and around the city, was someone for a young journalist to respect.

Memories are of a richly diverse system, but always an orderly one. Of the rapidity with which the daily through coach from London was tucked in the bay platform and cleaned at small resort stations. Of the impeccable timing of commuter trains from Plymouth up the Tamar Valley. Of the clockwork precision of Barnstaple Junction, always a noisy place with locomotives whistling and blowing off, neatly viewed from a bridge at the down end where Ilfracombe trains screeched over complicated, curved pointwork of exactly the kind engineers hate today, and the signalman timed his walk out on the balcony to exchange tokens to the exact second. And inevitably of the smart attaching and detaching throughout the system that was not so much a ritual but as matter of fact as breathing.

Sore Business

In those leisurely days before World War II, the summer Saturday Padstow portion of the *Atlantic Coast Express* ran non-stop from Exeter to Launceston – yes, not stopping at Okehampton nor even at Halwill Junction. The engine was often an L11 4-4-0, one of Drummond's 'Hoppers' with small wheels, and, as the road was heavy, it had to go hard where it could. Most of the time trains stopped to change the single-line tablets but this one did not and a favourite sadistic trick with a newcomer on the engine was to show him how to pick up the tablet from the signalmen holding it out. Dead easy – you simply put your fist through the large loop. Quite all right if a little sore at 20mph. But at 35 or even 40 one's upper arm and shoulder was one vast red welt at the end of the run! The penalty of missing was severe: brakes on hard, train stop, alight and run back along the track for it in total disgrace.

13
SOUTHERN FREIGHT

An up goods train comes over the Battledown flyover to join the line from Salisbury. Behind an S15 4-6-0 are about thirty box wagons with early potatoes and tomatoes from the Channel Islands, the first six wagons fitted with vacuum brakes. In afternoon sunshine an ex-LBSC 0-6-2T trundles a dozen wagons, mainly private owners' coal wagons, up the North Downs valley towards Woldingham on its leisurely way to Tunbridge Wells West. In the foggy gloom of a November night the 21.10 from Angerstein Wharf headed by a W Class 2-6-4T clatters through Charlton station at the start of its roundabout journey to Norwood Yard via Maidstone West, Tonbridge and Redhill, rails from the permanent way depot and coke from the gas works conspicious down its long length.

Extending this list of random examples of Southern freight trains would underline the disparate nature of the company's traffic. There were no heavy flows of traffic such as the continual progress of Garratt-hauled coal trains up the Midland line of the LMS from Toton to Cricklewood. The comparative unimportance of freight was underlined by the prohibition ('embargo' was the official term) of goods trains on running lines in the London suburban area during the morning and evening peak passenger periods.

The Southern's constituent companies were among the few whose receipts from passenger traffic exceeded those from freight, and it followed the Southern was the only one of the Big Four to be in this position. In 1933 goods receipts accounted for only 24 per cent of the total. In general the system served suburbia, coastal resorts and inland market towns, which even in the 1920s were sending more and more agricultural traffic by road. In 1928 the chairman complained bitterly of this 'increased diversion', and there were ever appeals to the staff to be vigilant in protecting what was seen as the railway's natural traffic.

Important sources of originating traffic, other than London itself, were few. Though not without mineral traffic the Kent coalfield and the Devon and Cornwall china clay pits were limited in their output, and transits normally short. The ports, especially Southampton, of course produced traffic, but the main source was the growing industries of Thames-side. Much traffic came southward across London from the other railways, as we shall see.

With the exception of the nightly express goods trains from Nine Elms to Plymouth Friary, Exmouth Junction and Weymouth respectively, and the one from Exmouth Junction up to Nine Elms, which conveyed meat traffic from Devon and Cornwall, there were few long distance through trains. In 1937 the 01.50, 02.05, 02.40 and 02.55 departures from Hither Green to Dover Priory, Westerham, Sevenoaks and

Maidstone East respectively were more representative. In the late 1940s a train set out from Tonbridge on Saturday evening with two or three wagons behind an O1 class 0-6-0 for Hildenborough and Sevenoaks Bat and Ball.

For these reasons there was comparatively limited investment in freight as opposed to passenger facilities. The Southern maintained the fleet of ageing locomotives inherited from the constituent companies, especially 0-6-0s, ex-LSWR 700 'Black Motors', ex-LBSC 'Vulcans' and the ubiquitous ex-SEC Wainwright class C. The Southern added the S15 4-6-0s, Maunsell modifications of the Urie H15s, but the main additions were the various series of mixed-traffic 2-6-0s, which bore the brunt of the freight haulage as well as summer weekend extra passenger trains. The Z class 0-8-0T, a rare example of an eight-coupled build, was for shunting only. The WD2-8-0s, drafted in to handle the enormous wartime traffic were of an unprecedented size and power. As with through passenger and van trains, all freight trains remained steam hauled even after electrification had reached beyond the suburbs to the South Coast. It was not until 1946 the two mixed traffic electric locomotives, CC1 and CC2, began to haul freight trains between Norwood and Horsham. The third locomotive No20003 was built by BR.

There was also some investment in new terminals. One of the best examples was at Margate, on which freight handling in the Thanet area was concentrated. Another was at Fratton (Portsmouth). On the other hand there were only marginal improvements to the London terminals. The introduction of insulated containers to handle imported meat traffic from Southampton was aimed at winning back traffic lost to the road, and the 1934 introduction of a fully-fitted overnight goods train from

Trip working. A cross-London transfer freight from the London Midland Region to the Southern leaving Willesden in 1950 (or slightly earlier) and heading for Old Oak Junction. The lines on the right are the electric Broad Street – Richmond tracks and the girder bridge crosses the Grand Union Canal. The locomotive is a Maunsell class S15 class 4-6-0 No 840 and is still in wartime black livery.

Night Goods

Possibly the most exciting oper-ation on the Southern was at Nine Elms goods station, now no more. There was stiff competition with the GWR for West of England traffic and special attention was always given to the express goods, vacuum fitted, at 10.20pm to vir-tually all points west of Salisbury. A certain amount of marshalling had to be done at the last moment; and the staff used to keep the vans – old four-wheeled vans with vacuum pipes but often ordinary link couplings without screws – in the shed roads until the very end so that last-minute consignments could catch the train, almost like commuters.

By 10.10 there would be an Adams G6 0-6-0 tank at the front of each rake of vans – about fourteen to eighteen as a rule on each shed platform. Then a whistle blew, cries of 'Shut her up', the van doors were slammed and sealed, and the shunters (about five of them) would signal the rake away. A shunter clung precariously to a wagon at the point where the rake was to be divided, his shunting pole over the buffer stocks and under the coupling. The little tank engine would be opened right up – a thrilling sight indeed – and with its blast shouting to high heaven and with an astonishing, almost solid, galaxy of sparks from the chimney it would come lurching wildly out of the shed and across the appalling track up the yard, everything depending on whether it could attain a high enough speed for the shunt.

When the facing points were approaching, the engine would whistle sharply, jam on its brakes
continued opposite

Elderly survivor. An ex LSWR Drummond L11 class 4-4-0 carrying a BR number - 30173 but with 'Southern' still adorning its tender, takes a long up freight out of Southampton on 13 January 1951.

Nine Elms to Exmouth Junction was aimed at retaining general goods traffic. Loaded to 49 wagons and a brake, it was timed over the 82 miles to Salisbury, where engines were changed, in 106 minutes, an average of 46.5mph – the top speed was 60mph – and became the pride of the line second only to the *Atlantic Coast Express*.

Goods working was centered on marshalling yards, large and small. Local pick-up services brought in from and distributed traffic to the numerous goods depots and private sidings, a few heavier, faster trains connected the yards. It was no doubt fearsomely expensive. The locomotives might be Victorian, their capital value nil, but mileages were inevitably low, waiting times long, though since the earliest days of electrification, if not earlier, there was a keen tradition of moving freight briskly along an open road so as to clear the section for the following passenger train. Indeed even in the deepest West Country, once rolling Southern freight wheels tended to revolve faster than on comparable GW lines.

What is regarded as the first marshalling yard dated from 1862. It was Herne Hill Sorting Sidings, located immediately north of the station on the 'City Line' to Holborn Viaduct. The site at Blackfriars goods was so limited that space for sidings to sort wagons was lacking.

The Southern had three main yards in London, a not unexpected number in view of its organisation, freight as well as passenger, into the three sections, Western, Central, and Eastern. All the yards were inherited from the constituent Companies. The largest and most modern was at Feltham, completed only in 1922. The others were Norwood and Hither Green, laid out by the LBSC and the SE&CR respectively. A locomotive shed for freight motive power was provided at Feltham and the Southern later built sheds at Norwood and Hither Green.

These yards were the destination of numerous transfer freights from the London yards of the other companies. They came via the North & South Western Junction and Kew Bridge; the West London through

Kensington; the Widened Lines and Snow Hill; and a few over the East London Line. The Southern locomotives shared haulage over the first two routes. But the 'foreign' locomotives were also common. This meant the approaches to Hither Green were one of the very few locations where engines of all four Grouping companies could be seen.

In the late 1930s about forty trains a day came from Cricklewood (LMS) and Ferme Park (LNER) over the Thames by Blackfriars Bridge. To ease congestion at London Bridge, in 1929 the Hither Green transfers were diverted via Elephant and Nunhead and over the new spurs at Lewisham. The 1938 West London working timetable reveals 41 trains passing onto the Southern on an ordinary weekday, 16 Southern hauled, 14 LMS and 11 GW. Two or three daily trips came from the LNER over the East London line.

Not all these transfer workings were bound for the Southern's yards, for the 'foreign' companies owned a number of goods and coal depots in South London. The largest was the GWR's at South Lambeth; among others were Falcon Lane (Clapham Junction) (LMS), Brockley Lane (near Nunhead) (LNER) and Knight's Hill (near Tulse Hill) (LMS).

Outside London there were connections with the GW at Reading, Basingstoke and Salisbury. Freight for Dover arrived at the former and for Southampton at the two latter. Prior to 1914, when ships were coalfired, steam coal from South Wales reached Southampton via Salisbury, but after 1920 merchant fleets began turning to oil.

There were also exchange points where the three north-south cross-country lines met the Southern; the Didcot, Newbury & Southampton at Winchester; the Midland & South Western Junction at Andover Junction; and the Somerset & Dorset at Broadstone. But these, as well as other common points such as Exeter, were comparatively unimportant in Southern days – until, that is, World War II, when they suddenly more than justified their existence and were saturated with traffic, delays being inevitable on the long and often steeply-graded single-line sections.

There were a number of important provincial marshalling yards, some of them very well equipped. Exmouth Junction (Exeter) was the point on which traffic to and from the 'Withered Arm' was concentrated. Northam/Bevois Park (Southampton) was the point of concentration of the port and local traffic, while Hoo Junction (east of Gravesend) dealt with the ever growing North Kent traffic. One of the later yards was Tonbridge West Yard, always popularly known as Jubilee yard as it opened in 1935, King George V's Silver Jubilee.

The Southern had two major London Goods Depots. Nine Elms was inherited from the LSWR. It dealt with large quantities of perishables from the West Country and Southampton. The LBSC and South Eastern depots were adjacent, located on the Bricklayers Arms Branch. Willow Walk (LBSC) was amalgamated with Bricklayers Arms in 1932. All these had a heavy outward general goods traffic brought in by railway collection vehicles from railway-owned receiving depots and from warehouse and industrial premises in central London. Even in 1946 one would see notices hung up 'SE&C Carman please call'.

Blackfriars was the ex-LCD depot. In Southern Days it specialised in 'market traffic', vegetables and fruit from Kent. The neighbouring Southwark Depot, reached from Ewer Street Locomotive Depot at

continued
and shut off momentarily. This brought all buffers violently together and the couplings loose. As this happened, the shunter hanging on to the train threw all his weight on to his end of his pole, the other end jerked up and threw the coupling off the hook, and he fell or jumped to the ground as the engine instantly opened up again wide and, with the first half of the rake only, raced ahead down the yard followed slightly more slowly by the rest.

If they had gauged it properly – they usually had – there would be just enough time for another shunter to throw the facing points the other way between the two rakes of wagons, so that the rear rake went on to a different line. 'Fly-shunting', was incredibly dangerous, but the GWR had to be beaten and so it happened every night except Saturdays and Sundays.

Much pleased were the guards when bogie goods brake vans – originally constructed from the shell of early LBSC overhead suburban motor coaches engines but later built specially – made their appearance on the 10.20. non stop Nine Elms to Salisbury, always an 'Arthur', and then with a Maunsell S15 non stop to Exeter. Non stop, but a slow climb, no more than 8–10mph, up Honiton Bank, a wonderful beginning to the day, the 5.15 dawn raising the echoes, past Ivygreen Farm with the smell of cows and earth and Devon, for the official who had slept on cushions under the canopy.

Cross-London Freight Links with Southern Railway

Route	End Points	Between Main Marshalling Yards		Remarks	Post War History
East London Railway	Liverpool St/ Spitalfields to New Cross and New Cross Gate	Temple Mills	Hither Green Norwood	Heavy gradients and very limited traffic capacity due to operating limitations at Liverpool St. Wagon hoist for two wagons at Spitalfields to depot Passenger service (LT) Shoreditch to New Cross/NC Gate	Freight traffic ceased 1966 and junction at Liverpool St removed soon after
Metropolitan Widened Lines	St Pancras/Kings Cross to Blackfriars	Brent Ferme Park	Hither Green Norwood	Very heavy gradient requiring banking engine Farringdon to Snow Hill and steam locos condensing fitted. Local passenger services south of Blackfriars	Freight traffic ceased 1969. Line re-opened for electric Thames link service May 1988
West London and West London Extension Railways	Willesden Junc to Clapham Junc and Longhedge Junc	Temple Mills Ferme Park Willesden Acton	Hither Green Norwood	Hither Green traffic via Nuneaton and Lewisham loops from 1929 Through express passenger services (eg 'Sunny South Express') also local service Clapham Junc – Addison Road (now Olympia). Electric service Willesden Junc – Earls Court withdrawn 3 Oct 1940	WW2 connections at Gospel Oak and Harringay made this a principal route for traffic to/ from Eastern and Central Sections. Additional through express services to South Coast from 1986. Ferme Park Yard closed 1969
North and South West Junction Railway	Brent Junc to Kew Old Junc	Temple Mills Ferme Park Brent Neasden Willesden	Feltham Hither Green Norwood	Primarily for Feltham traffic. Passenger service over almost entire route except Brent Junc to Acton Wells Junc	Ferme Park Yard closed 1969. Neasden Yard closed 1965
Staines Moor	Yeoveney to Staines	Acton	Feltham	WW2 single line connection from West Drayton – Staines GWR branch to give diversionary route. Opened 1940	Closed and lifted. Not used after war.

Other passenger/freight links with Southern Railway/Region:

Reading – Aldershot	Still in use
Reading – Basingstoke	Still in use
Didcot, Newbury & Southampton Rly (Didcot – Winchester)	Closed in 1964
Midland & South Western Junction Rly (Cheltenham – Andover)	Closed in 1961
Westbury – Salisbury	Still in use
Somerset & Dorset Joint Rly (Bath – Broadstone)	Closed in 1966

Metropolitan Junction, was the depot for Continental Goods traffic. Important suburban goods depots were at Surbiton, East Croydon, and Plumstead.

All the constituent companies sought access to wharves on the Thames where traffic could be exchanged with lighters working to and from the Docks. The Southern's Thames outlets were at Nine Elms (ex LSWR), Deptford Wharf (ex LBSC), Angerstein Wharf (Charlton) and North End Sidings (Erith) (both ex-SER). From Deptford Wharf an ex-LBSC D1 class 0-4-2T would make an occasional foray over one of the odder Southern backwaters, along Grove Road to the Admiralty Depot. Coal landed at Deptford went to the gas works and power station at Waddon and from North End to the gas works at Lower Sydenham.

As we have seen, the Southern was not without originating traffic. As far as the 'Withered Arm' was concerned, the Southern shared in china-clay traffic, though the GW dominated. This came from the Wenford Bridge goods branch, worked by the three Beattie 2-4-0Ts later to gain fame from their longevity, and the North Devon & Cornwall Junction Light Railway, opened between Halwill Junction and Torrington as late as 1925, the first six miles replacing a 3ft gauge mineral line. In the far west rebuilt LBSC tank locomotives were used. China clay was shipped at the Southern's own River Torridge port of Fremington (where locomotive coal was imported), at Fowey (for North American-bound ships), or rail-hauled to the Potteries. Southern rails were of course utilised where ever possible, so the clay for Fowey went via Launceston and Bodmin Road, involving four reversals, and that to the Potteries via Exeter, Templecombe and the Somerset & Dorset. China clay was also transferred from narrow gauge lines at Furzebrook on the Swanage branch.

Most of the output of the four Kent coal mines was distributed locally. Among the many short runs was the five miles from Shepherd's Well, where the trains from Tilmanstone were taken over from Colonel Stephens' East Kent Railway, to Dover Town gasworks. Block trains of Kent coal however were despatched to the paper mill at Overton

> **Elephants**
> 'Bogie Scenery Trucks . . . Note, No 4584 equipped for tethering elephants' (extract from *Appendix to Carriage Working Notice (Steam Trains) London East and London Central Districts.* And one day, sure enough, the van in the carriage dock at Ashford had its doors open so that passers by could see several tethered elephants.

Up South Western freight. The morning goods from Portsmouth to Nine Elms toils up the long 1 in 80 gradient between Rowlands Castle and the summit of the South Downs near Woodcroft Crossing on 20 November 1951. The engine, U class 2-6-0 No 31795 is ex River class 2-6-4 tank No A795 River Medway rebuilt following the Sevenoaks disaster of 1927.

No 595's Triumph

The down *Atlantic Coast Express* failed at Woking with a burst steam pipe. The station pilot was No 595, one of the notable Adams 'Highflyers'. Decrepit, leaking from several firebox stays, far from clean and with pressure, nominally 175 lurking nearer 140; the beautiful outside cylinder 4-4-0 with her great 7ft driving wheels was shunting vans.

When built in 1892, they had been the most powerful express passenger engines in the country; they were always game engines. So when the express ran in and stopped, with steam everywhere, everyone noticed two things. There was no other engine in the station. And No 595, was facing the South West.

A frenzied conference; the London crew wanted to stay with their damaged engine; our chap knew the road to Salisbury. It would take about 20 minutes to summon anything from Guildford and – well, it was decided that we should try.

The 'Nelson' limped off its train and we backed on – to be told we had THIRTEEN on! The fireman, wild with excitement, was working desperately. We had a nearly full tender, but 'We'll never even get the brakes off' said the driver. And indeed it took all of seven minutes to manage 18¼ in the vacuum at the rear end. But the guard said that was all it had been, and the seven minutes had been gainfully employed by the fireman. The pressure was about 167 and she was seething.

The inspector said that if we could get the train to Basingstoke, some 23 miles, they would have an H15 or S15 more or less available. The regulator was thrown open – they didn't slip, the X2s, and really the engine said 'Cor!' For an appreciable time nothing happened. Then, inch by inch the gap between engine and tender moved slowly forward over the sleepers and some time after that, it seemed, No 595 emitted

continued opposite

(Hants). Gypsum came from Mountfield on the Tonbridge–Hastings line to the North Kent cement works, sand and fuller's earth from Redhill, while flints from Newhaven and Dungeness went to the Potteries.

The port traffic was dominated by Southampton, for the South Western and afterwards the Southern cultivated this as much as they did the more prestigious ocean liner traffic. The traffic mainly went to Nine Elms and other London depots, though trains were also despatched to Birmingham via Basingstoke. General freight traffic came from the Continent in smaller quantities through Newhaven, Folkestone and Dover. Traffic through the latter was only a pale shadow of its present dimensions, though it increased with the inauguration of the train ferry in 1936. The line across the swing bridge to the West Quay at Newhaven was one reason for the long use of the 'Terrier' tanks, as the one along the sea front at Dover led to the retention of the equally diminutive P class 0-6-0Ts. The goods branch from Hamworthy Junction to the quays at Poole was kept busy.

The Forces were among the biggest of the Southern's customers, private sidings to the Dockyards at Chatham, Sheerness, Portsmouth and Devonport were provided, as well as to Woolwich Arsenal. The army camps on Salisbury Plain also received much traffic even in peacetime when manoeuvres were as much part of the season as harvest.

Along the North Kent line and from Strood to Maidstone was a concentration of private sidings and large goods depots unique on the Southern. They included sidings to cement plants, paper mills and engineering works. The goods depots were at Plumstead, Dartford, Gravesend (the depot was at West Street and served by the branch from Fawkham Junction), Strood and Chatham. Frequent trip workings concentrated the traffic on Hoo Junction and Hither Green. And there were interchange sidings at Liss on the Portsmouth main line and at Bordon with the army's own Longmoor Military Railway.

Apart from the large London depots and the medium sized provincial ones, there were some eight hundred small local depots, the vast majority combined with passenger stations, though there were a few sidings dealing with public traffic remote from passenger facilities, such as the 'wharves' on the Wenford Bridge (Cornwall) branch, Mislingford and Farringdon (on the Meon Valley) and Graveney (between Faversham and Whitstable). These were served once or twice a day by ambling short-distance pick-up freights, depositing and picking up a few wagons, and putting off some 'smalls' consignments from the 'roader' wagon at each. The Southern's policy was also to concentrate collection and delivery services at a more limited number of larger stations. This was carried out from Alton (Hants) among other centres.

As London spread outward, many rural depots became suburban. Agricultural traffic was replaced by increased coal traffic and by bricks and other building materials, while outwards traffic largely disappeared. At the rural wayside stations and at the market towns the traffic in many ways reflected the agricultural year. Inwards the universal coal traffic would tend to build up in the late summer as merchants laid in stocks for winter. Inwards fertilisers would be mainly a winter and early spring traffic, though feeding stuffs were less seasonally influenced.

The winter would see outwards agricultural traffic at its lowest level.

Cabbages and cauliflowers though would be despatched from East Kent stations, and as spring advanced market garden traffic would build up. Conditional (Q) semi-fitted 'Market' trains were run to pick up traffic from wayside stations in Kent for Blackfriars Goods Depot. The 1937 working time table shows the 19.15 from Deal via Ashford, the 18.10 from Ramsgate, the 16.50 from Adisham and the 17.20 from Sittingbourne, all via the Chatham Line.

The early summer would see the soft-fruit season. Trainloads of mainly passenger-rated strawberries and other fruit were despatched from Swanwick on the Southampton–Fareham line, from Paddock Wood and from the North Kent stations, and even from the Tamar Valley. A seasonal increase of tomatoes and cucumbers from the glasshouses of the Worthing & District Growers' Association would mean the daily train of vans from Angmering to London Bridge, picking up at stations to Hove, would be fuller than usual. Channel Islands early potatoes and tomatoes were shared with the GW but still important.

Later on the tree-fruit traffic would build up. Cherries from Newington would be succeeded by apples from Marden, Wateringbury and other stations in Mid-Kent. This was sufficiently important for a temporary control office to be set up at Paddock Wood. The hop season would see the despatch of 2 cwt 'pockets' from Yalding and the Hawkhurst branch to breweries in London, Alton and Burton-on-Trent.

Autumn lamb sales involved livestock specials from markets such as Ashford (Kent), Steyning (Sussex) and Salisbury. Cattle traffic was rather less seasonal and livestock would be despatched regularly from West Country stations such as Launceston, Halwill and Okehampton. The southern and western counties were not great grain-growing areas between the wars. But wheat and barley in sacks would be forwarded from stations in Hampshire. The last crop to be harvested was sugar beet. There were no factories in the south, so block trains were run to East Anglia from Chichester, where traffic from local railheads such as Lavant was concentrated. Agricultural products included beer from Alton and cyder from Whimple (Devon).

Milk was of course a passenger-rated traffic. It was conveyed in churns from a wide variety of stations, usually in vans attached to advertised passenger trains. As early as 1906 the LSWR was carrying five million gallons annually in this way from its Dorset stations. To take a random example of a typical train, in 1930 the 07.10 from Hastings to London Bridge via Tonbridge and Redhill was described as a milk train conveying passengers from Wadhurst. Progress was leisurely, Tonbridge being reached eventually at 09.24, a far cry from the burgeoning 'Southern Electric'. A milk special left Polegate via Lewes and East Grinstead and calling at all stations to Oxted, its destinations being East Croydon and Tulse Hill.

The early thirties saw the introduction of farm collections based on factories from which milk was sent to the bottling plants in glass-lined rail or road tanks. This led to the loss of short distance traffic. But trains now ran to London from the factories at Torrington, Lapford and Crediton, Seaton Junction, Chard Junction, Sherborne and Semley. The terminals in London included Clapham Junction, No 8 Platform at Vauxhall and Mottingham.

continued

her first tremendous beat. The road is very, very slightly uphill rather than down except the initial rise to milepost 31, which is definitely a hill, if not a bank. The old engine struggled, shook, pressure slipped, held, slipped.

We all took turns at the firing and the speed rose to a breathtaking 28mph. But once over the top things changed. The old engine did splendidly and her injectors *worked*. Speed rose to 46 and then 52. It was gorgeous. The driver said 'She'd get to Salisbury!' to which the reply had to be 'What? Up the bank to Grateley?' 'Well, if we was going fast enough at Andover and had plenty of water in the glass.' Damn it! I didn't properly catch what he said about Basingstoke – if they give us the road, I'll go through!

But as we approached Basingstoke the distant was on. Alas! Unable to bear it, an unauthorised reach for the whistle and she yelled. The driver looked very disapproving and shook his head – we were clearly meant to stop at the station – and then the distant cleared. The signalman must have thought we had a better engine than expected and could go on. Our passage of Basingstoke – at just under 50 – with the engine shaking all over with the effort, the loco foreman on the platform ready to supervise the engine change looking at us aghast with his mouth open, were unforgetable.

It was quite a fight to get over the rise to Oakley but, once we did, things were easier. But we had to ease the engine to get some pressure back and some more water in the boiler, so through Overton and Hurstbourne, usually fast places, the speed was still not over 50. But then – *then* with the splendid downhill to Andover Junction we really threw caution to the winds and with the motion clanking like a runaway traction engine we managed 74

continued overleaf

continued

through the station with everyone on the platform running gloriously for cover, or so it seemed.

We had to work very hard, in spite of our speed, to climb to Grateley; and there were smells and noises and speed at the top beyond Grateley had fallen below 20 and it was a question of whether we might become a failure. Pressure was very down and bearings were hot but the rest of the way was down hill and we crept on, nursing the engine and virtually allowing the steam to do little more than take the weight of the motion off the big ends. But, largely by not noticeably slowing at Salisbury Tunnel Junction (the noise in the ensuing tunnel was frightening) we managed a splendid *Atlantic Coast Express* sweep into the platform, even though the white metal had mostly run out of the bearings. Possibly No 595 never ran again under her own steam. If that is true, it was a splendid death for an Adams 7ft 'Highflyer'. – Patrick Stevenson.

There were a number of rather peculiar traffics. One train which had a particular aroma was the late evening departure from the City of Southwark's refuse depot at Walworth Road to Longfield Dust Siding between Fawkham and Meopham. The town refuse was conveyed in ordinary sheeted open wagons. There was even some goods traffic on the Isle of Wight, principally coal landed at Medina Wharf (near Cowes) and cement.

For a number of years after 1948 BR essentially maintained the freight system it had taken over. Southern Region freight in 1960 was virtually unchanged from Southern Railway freight in 1947.

The first general change was in motive power, steam being eliminated by 1967. The 1960s were generally unhappy for BR's freight, but prosperity's move to the south was now under way and industrialisation in the South East was reflected in an 11 per cent increase in tonnage carried in 1961 over the previous year. The main feature was the growth of originating traffic, previously less important. Between 1964 and 1973 this traffic grew from 5 million to 8.3 million tons.

But the new Beeching policies began to have an effect. After 1966 closure of freight depots accelerated, so that by 1980 only a handful of depots remained dealing with general wagon load traffic, Poole, Plumstead and Chatham among them, while the London depots mentioned have all disappeared. Freight is handled mainly in block trains to and from a limited number of terminals.

To list these would be tedious, but important sources included the train-ferry railhead at Dover, the oil refinery and chemical plants at Fawley; petroleum distribution depots at stations such as Micheldever (Hants), Earley, Horsham and Selsdon; the Transfesa perishables depot at Paddock Wood; railheads for steel at Brockley Lane and Farningham Road; car forwarding from Ramsgate; and fertiliser distribution depots at Gillingham (Dorset), and Andover. With the growing aggregate deficit in the South East, terminals have been established at Botley, Crawley,

The vintage LSWR X2 class 4-4-0, which was inherited by the Southern. No 586 was a sister of the locomotive described in the accompanying paragraph.

Ardingly, Chislehurst, Salisbury and elsewhere. Most of the traffic originates from outside the Region, but aggregates are railed from Lydd and sea-dredged material is landed for railing from Cliffe.

Now Betteshanger is the sole remaining Kent coal pit. Domestic coal is now handled at 11 concentration points, two on the Chessington branch. Cement traffic remains heavy. In 1970 APCM concentrated their Thames-side manufacture at a huge rail-served plant at Northfleet. Coal is brought from the East Midlands in merry-go-round trains. Cement is forwarded in block trains of bulk wagons.

In spite of the great surge in light industry in the South East, the Region lacks any freightliner depots other than the two at Southampton virtually specialising in shipping containers. On a normal weekday in 1987 about 17 trains were received and despatched daily from these two terminals and on the quadrupled section of the Southampton–Basingstoke route it is still common to see a freight overtaken by a passenger train. But no regular freight goes west from Basingstoke to Exeter and today's railway is even more a passenger one than in Southern Railway days.

Many surviving traffics are still short haul. One of the most interesting is the aggregate traffic from Lavant over the 5 miles to concrete works at Drayton. The County Council encouraged the use of rail to keep lorries out of Chichester. As an example of Speedlink working, Dover Town despatches at least 11 trains on a normal weekday. The scene may yet be totally changed, freight greatly increased, by the Channel Tunnel.

Bulleid utility. Bereft of all unessential items such as footplating, the unorthodox appearance of the Q1s raised a storm of popular protest. Even the enginemen, hardened to the realities of life on the footplate were disconcerted by the sight of coupling rods whirling round under their noses. Nevertheless the weight saved allowed a large boiler and the Q1s were successful engines. No C8 leaves Guildford with an up goods just into nationalisation, on 25 November 1948.

191

14
SOUTHERN RAILWAY TO SOUTHERN REGION

VE Day found the bomb-battered Southern Railway as busy as ever with continuing military traffic to and from the armies in Europe, and the ending of restrictions on travel to the South Coast unleashing a flood of holidaymakers. On the Saturday before the 1945 August Bank Holiday long queues waiting to enter Waterloo stretched along York Road, and the 72 main line departures carried an average of 812 passengers. The SR coaching stock was depleted by 10 per cent due to losses, delayed repairs and government requisitioning. Many of the 4,040 carriages which had been damaged were running with windows boarded up. The company did well to build 539 coaches between 1945 and 1947. (By 1950 the electric stock exceeded the 1939 total by nearly two hundred vehicles.)

Train services to Kent and Sussex were improved as early as June 1945; October saw two trains per hour on most suburban lines and the resumption of restaurant cars to the West of England, followed in January 1946 by those on other routes. Pullman trains recommenced on 15 April 1946 with the *Golden Arrow* reopening the short sea route to France, followed by the *Bournemouth Belle* in October 1946 and the

BR standard motive power comes to the Southern. Standard Class 5 4-6-0 No 73081 heads a mixed rake of new BR Mk 1 and SR stock forming a Ramsgate to Victoria morning express from Dumpton Park in June 1959. Even a decade and more into nationalisation well over 90% of the trains on this line were still hauled by ex Southern engines including King Arthurs, and 4-4-0s.

official return of the *Brighton Belle* a year later after repairs to a bomb-damaged unit. By October 1946 over 81 per cent of the pre-war timetable was being provided, but the bitter winter of 1947 and its fuel crisis reduced this to 78 per cent, though the SR relieved the coal shortage by the rapid improvisation of oil-burning for locomotives based at Eastleigh.

Under these circumstances the introduction on 20 June 1947 of the new *Devon Belle* Pullman service was a remarkable achievement. At a time when weekend travel from Paddington often involved queuing and standing in corridors, the *Devon Belle* offered Pullman comfort, reserved seats and an observation car: initially it was very successful but with the return of normal conditions its slow schedule became unattractive. The story of its decline and withdrawal and of the post-nationalisation Pullman has been told elsewhere. The point here is that the Southern was quickly on the ball. The short time between the end of the war and nationalisation was indeed an exhilarating one on the Southern, with Eustace Missenden in enthusiastic command as general manager, though anxious about the political future. 'First in the field', cried the posters displaying one of Bulleid's shining new 'Pacifics', while his prototype post-war corridor coach was exhibited in October 1945, the first of the production series going into service on the *Atlantic Coast Express* in December 1946. These were followed in late 1947 by some six-car restaurant sets for the Bournemouth line. Some Maunsell restaurant cars had been modified in 1947 to provide a buffet area for drinks and snacks. (These inspired Bulleid's 1949 Tavern Cars with their olde worlde imitation brickwork and wooden beams, and the accompanying restaurant cars without windows, to make diners concentrate on the business of eating and thus speed the meal service.)

But most long-distance services were not restored to pre-war frequencies and timings until after nationalisation, an almost hourly service to the South Coast and twenty-minute frequency suburban services coming in the 1948–9 winter timetable. The pre-war Atlantic Coast Express timing to Exeter was not restored until 1952; the following year brought the return of eighty-minute timings to Folkestone; but it

Through the Downs. The Oxted line remained steam worked well into BR days with BR standard and LMS 2-6-4Ts taking over from former LBSCR classes on Victoria and London Bridge services. Then it was dieselised, and was electrified in 1987. In the photograph BR Class 4 2-6-4T No 80153 heads a London Bridge – Tunbridge Wells West train in the late 1950s. In the bay behind is a push-pull service from Tonbridge.

Still Meeting

After nationalisation, only the Southern's chief officers continued to meet in an organisation under the original company's name, and the score of remaining ones still do, now supplemented by those who served on the Southern Region. Thus today's BR chairman, Sir Robert Reid, attends the annual Southern Railway Association lunch, of course at the Charing Cross Hotel.

The changing face of Victoria. By the early 1960s the variety of steam classes and the glamour of the Golden Arrow *had given way to the dull but efficient monotony of electric working, the last steam* Golden Arrow *leaving the terminus on 11 June 1961. Its replacement (with a smartly capped driver) waits for the 'right away' a year later.*

was not until 1957 that the Bournemouth two-hour trains were permanently restored. Punctuality at the end of 1945 had been abysmal, with steam trains averaging 8.06min late and electrics 4.97min; by the determined efforts of S. W. Smart, the Superintendent of Operation, these figures had been reduced by November 1948 to 1.55 and 2.09min respectively.

Bombing had badly affected the SR. Over one hundred of its eight hundred stations needed repairs. First priority was the restoration of Portsmouth Harbour station, where only one platform was useable. This was achieved by the summer of 1946. At Blackfriars the destruction of the signalbox in 1941 closed the terminal platforms to traffic until a new box was completed in August 1946. The 1935 buildings on the down side at Southampton Central had been destroyed and their reconstruction was urgent. Within the docks war damaged sheds alongside the Ocean Docks were replaced in July 1950 by the Ocean Terminal, designed to accommodate the two *Queens*, which has followed them into oblivion. Elsewhere, repairs had to wait; the stationmaster at Wimbledon was housed in a former LSWR restaurant car berthed in one of the terminal platforms for over a decade after the war. The Clasp system of prefabrication provided a cheap means of restoration at several stations during the 1960s. Even today some war damage repairs have still to be made, as travellers who emerge on a wet day from the subway at Clapham Junction on to platforms 9 and 10 will realise.

Restoration of the war-damaged buildings at the City termini was linked to office development. Holborn Viaduct was rebuilt in 1963 and Cannon Street in 1964–5 but the reconstruction of London Bridge was not completed until 1978. Schemes interrupted by the outbreak of war were slowly resumed; the rebuilt and resited Twickenham station opened in March 1954, but Chichester had to wait until 1960. Powers had been obtained in 1939 for an escalator at Bank station to spare Waterloo & City commuters the weary trudge to the surface. When the project was revived in 1955 a travelator was substituted for the escalator but completion was delayed until September 1960 by limitations on capital expenditure and interruptions to work during Mansion House functions. The new towns at Crawley and Bracknell required appropriate new station buildings. Increasingly the rebuilding of stations has been carried out in partnership with property companies, examples being Blackfriars and Dorking. The use of the air space over London terminal stations for office development, first suggested by the LBSCR in 1921 and again by the SR in 1946, has been achieved at Victoria in the 1980s.

In June 1939 the SR board had approved electrification from South Croydon to Horsted Keynes, but work had not commenced when war broke out and in July 1946 it was announced that it would be carried out when manpower and materials became available. Sir Herbert Walker proposed to his fellow directors in March 1942 that plans should be prepared for the post-war electrification of the whole of the Central and Eastern sections. The success of Raworth's electric locomotives (CC1 and CC2) would now enable freight traffic, boat trains and cross-country services to be electrically hauled and this could lead to the elimination of steam traction from Kent and Sussex.

The committee which reported in February 1946 offered two options; (a) the electrification of all lines east of Portsmouth and Sturt Lane Junction (Farnborough) and (b) to extend the electrified area to Salisbury and Bournemouth. Option (a) involved increasing the electrified route mileage from 714 to 1,337 at an estimated cost of £13 million. It was soon realised that it was unrealistic to electrify such lines as the Sheppey Light and the Elham Valley, and a party of SR officers visited the USA early in 1946 to study diesel traction.

The electrification plan announced in November 1946 was consequently limited to 284 miles of the principal routes, which it was hoped

A new image emerges. The Bournemouth electrification of 1967 changed the whole face of services out of Waterloo to the south west. 4REP unit No 3014 hauls two sets of 4TC trailers (414 and 413) round the curve at Pirbright on the 10.35 semi-fast Bournemouth to Waterloo service on 25 May 1978.

Light ACE

The Atlantic Coast Express stood in the platform, a shining green four coaches, with a rather grubby Bulleid Pacific No 34076 *41 Squadron* at the head. I had neither travelled over the line before, nor travelled on the footplate of a Bulleid Pacific, so my attention was fully occupied. The similarity with Doncaster practice was obvious on the footplate, and the driver spoke of his charge with an enthusiasm that one might expect, where the capacity of the engine is so overwhelmingly in excess of the demands of its rostered duty.

Promptly at 08.30, No 34076 moved off, rumbling over the bridge at Little Petherick Creek, and along the level run alongside the Camel Estuary. The tide was upriver just for once, and the light blue blended well with the mellowing colours of early autumn. The Pacific did not endear herself to me by exhausting a great deal of smokebox char everywhere, but her riding was superbly smooth. We exceeded 50 mph for some distance before coasting into Wadebridge.

We restarted at 0846, taking the single North Cornwall line, which ran alongside the single Bodmin and Wadebridge line as far as the site of the old Wadebridge Junction, where the North Cornwall swings north-eastwards on a sharp 20 chain curve. The old North Cornwall railway was built on a shoestring budget, but for all that it was well built. It crosses difficult terrain, but gradient and curvature although severe, are consistent. From mp 253 at Wadebridge Junction to mp 242 there are 11 miles rising at 1 in 73-75, with almost continuous curvature of about 30 chains, roughly equivalent to 1 in 60 on straight track. From mp 242 to the summit at mp 237¼ the gradients ease, but the curvature remains. Much of the route to Otterham is exposed to strong winds off the Atlantic, which can

continued opposite

to complete by 1955 at a cost of £15 million. There may have been a political motive behind its publication as the railway companies were trying to display their future policies before the nationalisation proposals reached Parliament. There was no public money for railway investment in the 1940s and though the Railway Executive approved the main part of the scheme in principle in 1952, its realisation had to await the 1955 Modernisation Plan.

The first stage in the scheme comprised the former Chatham lines from Gillingham to Ramsgate and Dover, where eventual electrification in 1959 also included the Sheerness branch on which diesel operation of the through trains to Victoria would have created problems – today there is only one through train daily anyway. The second stage comprised the routes from Sevenoaks and Maidstone via Ashford to Dover and Ramsgate, also the Medway Valley line, completed in sections during 1961. Both stages involved major widening works between Bickley and Swanley, Rainham and Newington and through Folkestone, including reconstruction of stations at St Mary Cray, Ashford and Folkestone.

The third and last stage covered the lines from Tonbridge to Hastings and Bexhill West, from South Croydon to Horsted Keynes and from Christ's Hospital to Shoreham. However, the urgent need for new rolling stock on the Hastings line brought diesel-electric multiple-unit trains in 1957–8 and electrification only took place in May 1986 after the restricted tunnels had been singled. October 1987 at last saw electric trains as far as East Grinstead, but the lines to Horsted Keynes and Bexhill West have long been closed. Christ's Hospital to Shoreham was intended as a diversionary route for the Brighton main line, though Hurst Green Junction–Uckfield–Lewes was considered as an alternative; the former has been lifted and the latter closed beyond Uckfield, so during emergencies or engineering work travellers to Brighton are loaded on to buses for a tour of the Sussex lanes or sent on a two hour detour via Littlehampton.

Regular passenger services on the electrification extensions were operated by the customary multiple-unit trains, but a fleet of twenty four electric locomotives was provided to work main line freight traffic and such prestige, but non-standard, trains as the *Golden Arrow* and *Night Ferry*. One of the recommendations of the 1947 report on diesel traction was the use of dual electro-diesel locomotives. Six prototypes appeared in 1962, followed by the production series in 1966–7 in time for the Bournemouth electrification. This route also sees the combined operation of diesel locomotives and electric multiple-unit stock controlled from one cab – another idea which had been envisaged in 1947.

Essential but less obvious was the renewal of the power supply system throughout the suburban area, where the manned rotary converter sub-stations transforming 25Hz ac to the traction current of 600 Volts dc were life-expired. Between 1950 and 1957 these were replaced by remotely-controlled rectifier sub-stations fed from the national grid at 50Hz ac. Consequently the former LSWR power station at Durnsford Road was closed and in 1976 its site was used for the East Wimbledon rolling stock maintenance depot.

With diesel traction now to be used on the secondary routes and branch lines it was decided in May 1947 to employ it also on the main lines for pick-up freights, for cross-country trains such as the Birkenhead–Margate and for relief trains and hop-pickers' specials. Shunting was an obvious task for diesel traction and orders were soon placed for twenty five 400hp locomotives which were built at Ashford in 1949–52. The general purpose diesel locomotive planned was a small machine of about 600hp, adequate for the three SECR coaches which comprised most branch trains or for local freights, and capable of being coupled in pairs for more onerous duties. Railcars were suggested for use on self-contained branches such as Westerham or Hayling Island. In fact it was diesel-electric multiple-units (the SR showing its preference for electric traction even away from the third rail) which replaced steam on the secondary routes in Sussex and Hampshire between 1957 and 1962. Sadly many of these lines soon became victims of the Beeching axe.

Having tried the small LMR 800hp diesel 10800 in 1952–3, the need in Kent and Sussex was now seen to be a line diesel able to hold its own on the electrified main lines. Pick-up goods trains were soon to give way to the bulk movement of oil, cement and aggregates. With the adoption of electric train heating for the few remaining locomotive-hauled services it was possible to adapt the Birmingham Carriage & Wagon Co Type 2 diesel into the very successful 1,550hp Class 33 design. Push and pull working which had been suggested in 1947 for diesel operation on local services was introduced on the South Western Division in 1967 with nineteen of the ninety eight locomotives being modified.

The third type of locomotive envisaged was a 2,500hp machine for the West of England services capable of 100mph and able to haul 500ton trains – a specification which was only met with the arrival of the Class 50s in 1980. Instead the SR placed orders in August 1947 for three 1,600hp diesel-electrics. Publicity showed two of these working in multiple providing 'Deltic' level power. Diesel traction was not accorded high priority by the Railway Executive and 10201 was not delivered until December 1950 and then the nearest it came to Waterloo was a stand on the South Bank within the Festival of Britain exhibition. Eventually all three locomotives were completed (10203 uprated to 2,000hp was the prototype for the BR Class 40) and were joined by the two LMS-designed main line diesels (10000 and 10001) during 1953–4 on four daily rosters from Nine Elms which involved eight return trips to Exeter, Weymouth and Bournemouth, covering up to 688 miles per day for each locomotive. As first published the 1955 Modernisation Plan included the early dieselisation of these routes, but in the event Waterloo was to become the last stronghold of steam in London.

As for steam traction, 890 of the SR's 1,819 locomotives were over forty years old in 1945. Electrification and dieselisation would have eventually eliminated most of these, and the remaining steam main line duties on the Western section could have been covered by the 140 Bulleid 'Pacifics' built between 1941 and 1951. However, there would remain a need there to replace the veteran LSWR M7 tanks on branch line work and for this task Bulleid devised his complex Leader locomotive. Of thirty five contemplated, only one was ever completed and made some unsuccessful trial runs before its inventor took his fertile mind to Ireland. BR then provided tank engines of simple LMS or standard design for this work.

continued make the run yet more difficult for the smaller engines. There is only one tunnel on the whole line, Trelill tunnel just west of Port Isaac Road, and apart from three multiple span river bridges and some rock cuttings, this is the only major engineering feature as far as Meldon Junction.

The driver worked his engine on about ¾ regulator, giving about 210-220lbs. in the steam chests, and what appeared to be about 20-25 per cent. cut-off on the uphill section. I say about, since the steam reverser was faulty, and the engine persistently notched herself down until the driver reset the reverser, so that the cut-off was in a continual state of flux! He set the cut-off as well as he was able, and drove on the regulator: with a light train, the difference between 1 in 75 up and down is so great of course as to make the cut-off somewhat irrelevant. The driver was a master of the brake, running quickly into the platform and stopping smartly, and it was this work which I found the most impressive of the day's travel.

The coal consisted of wet dust and cobbles, rather more of the former than the latter, but of generally passable quality. The fireman ran with a very thick fire, well built up in the back corners, and fed the engine right under the firehole door. The engine steamed perfectly around 250lbs sq in although her appetite seemed to me to be somewhat excessive. So many Southern men seemed to have trouble in firing Gresley Pacifics when they visited the Southern in the last years of steam, possibly due to poor fuel, but on the occasions I have witnessed, due to their failure to keep the back corners filled. Yet here was a young fireman making easy work of it, using the technique that took A4s to Edinburgh and back. – P. J. Carter in *Stephenson Locomotive Society Journal*

SOUTHERN RAILWAY TO SOUTHERN REGION

In 1939 the Southern planned to lengthen its suburban electric units from three to four cars by incorporating coaches from the two-car trailer sets and by new construction, which would also replace vehicles with vintage pre-grouping bodies. Further prototype series appeared in 1946–7 until the 4-SUB design settled on the arrangement of three saloon and one compartment coach in each unit, produced under BR in large numbers during 1948–51. The use of trailer sets ceased in 1948 and the last pre-war wooden bodied units were withdrawn in 1962.

New suburban electric stock was usually allocated to the Dartford group of lines, where post-war overcrowding was so acute that whenever the Minister of Transport appeared at House of Commons question time he was invariably assailed by complaints from South East London MPs. Bulleid's double-decker experiment has been described elsewhere: there was no alternative to the difficult course of running longer trains. Not only did sixty six two-car units have to be built to make up the new ten-car trains, but platforms had to be lengthened and track and signalling altered to accommodate them throughout the South Eastern suburban area. At Cannon Street this involved a major £1¼ million reconstruction and it was not until the summer of 1957 that the ten-car trains came into general use out of Charing Cross and Cannon Street.

From 1952 onwards suburban electric construction was to the EPB design, a close successor to the 4-SUB, and these units were concentrated on the South Eastern Division. While prototype sliding door stock appeared on the South Western in 1979 and later generally, and on the Central Division in 1985, EPBs will remain the norm on the South

Really the end. The final departure of the Night Ferry *from London Victoria on 31 October 1980, the BR brake second next to the engine leads the original Wagons-Lits coaches which ran through to Paris via Dunkerque. The locomotive is No 33 043, a Bo-Bo diesel-electric built by the Birmingham Railway Carriage and Wagon Co, Smethwick, entering service on 8 July 1961, allocated to Hither Green depot. A sad occasion.*

Eastern until the 'Networker' stock appears in the 1990s. Many units have been refurbished, but those in their original condition often offer grime, graffiti and the chance of being mugged in their compartment coaches.

The peak hour suburban overcrowding of the 1950s has been succeeded by increased traffic from dormitory towns and villages throughout the South East. The decline in the inner suburban traffic is most marked in the evenings and at weekends, when many stations and lines in South London are now closed. No longer do the suburban units carry crowds of excursionists to the seaside on Sundays and Bank Holidays.

At nationalisation the Southern Railway had 148 route miles of line controlled by colour light signalling. Its board had approved in November 1946 a £1.2 million scheme to convert the Central Section main lines from Battersea Park and Bricklayers Arms Junction to Coulsdon North. The start of work was delayed until 1949 and in the meantime there occurred the disastrous collision in fog at South Croydon on 24 October 1947. The scheme was eventually completed in stages between October 1950 and May 1955 and the area of operation was later extended to cover the Tulse Hill and Crystal Palace areas. All these boxes had a short life, being replaced between 1975 and 1984 by the signalling centres at London Bridge, Clapham Junction and Three Bridges.

In contrast, ex-LSWR structures still control the colour light signalling out of Waterloo until the resignalling scheme there is completed. A modest extension from Wandsworth to Barnes was made in 1959, following the collision at Barnes on 2 December 1955. The Kent

Try taking this lot over – all the 8.15s to town, and the 8.16s and 8.17s. The lead into a booklet Want to Run a Railway *produced by the Southern Region in 1962 firing back at the barrage of criticisms it was then receiving about train service reliability, at a time when it had just completed the final stage of the Kent Coast electrification but was still trying to soldier on with outdated equipment on many other lines.*

Which 8.15 to Town?

There are *forty* eight-fifteens to Town every weekday on the Southern. There's an 8.15 through the ABC from Ashford, Bookham and Carshalton down to Upper Warlingham, Virginia Water and West Wickham. You've got to take the forty. After all, *we* have to.

Every one of the forty stations marked here has an "Eight-fifteen to Town" on weekday mornings.

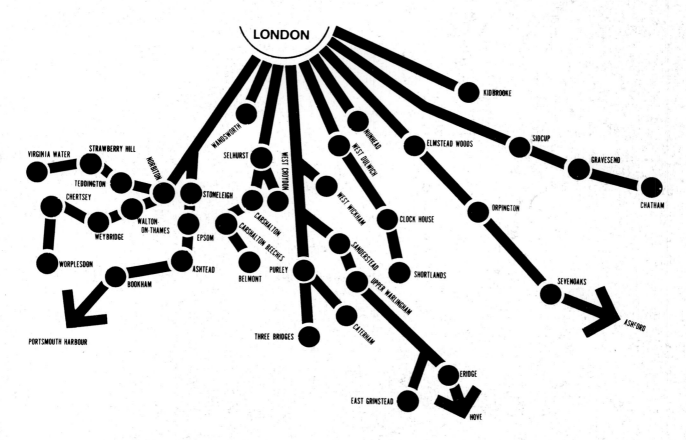

Well Performed

The summer of 1948 saw a tournament which, in a Britain starved of pageantry during the war years, struck a receptive chord among the participants and a limited but keen number of supporters. But these were no caparisoned horses ridden by hard men in armour with lances, bent on the destruction of their adversaries. They were iron horses, manned by men in bib-and-brace overalls, armed only with tea can, sponge cloth and shovel, being put through their paces in the interests of future engineering excellence. The Interchange Trials were under way.

The Southern Region, as it had now become, participated directly in jousts in the express passenger and general purpose stakes, fielding three 'Merchant Navy' Pacifics in the first and three 'West Country' light Pacifics in the second for trials over a variety of longish routes in England and Scotland. The Southern engines, used to shorter gallops and no water troughs from which to refresh themselves en route, found themselves harnessed to LMS coal-and-water carts for their 'foreign' excursions.

It was a difficult time at which to undertake meaningful comparisons, for there was still traffic congestion, temporary speed restrictions abounded on the war-worn track, and the whole ethic of hard driving and punctual arrival had taken a beating during the last eight years and could not be swiftly recreated. Though there were occasional cases of serious slipping, the Bulleid engines acquitted themselves well. Indeed, spurred on by keen jockeys, they often outperformed their rivals.

Southern watchers will long remember with pride the outstanding running of the light Pacifics on the Marylebone–Manchester route and above all in Scotland. No 34006 *Bude* covered the Great Central line in a fashion

continued opposite

Coast electrification of 1959–61 was accompanied by colour light signalling of the main lines to Ramsgate and Dover (the secondary route via Maidstone East had to wait until the 1980s). The new signalling centres have replaced most of the early SR colour light installations of the 1920s and 1930s and have extended power signalling throughout the suburban area. On the South Western Division colour lights continue all the way to Bournemouth and Salisbury and at passing loops as part of the tokenless block system from there to the outskirts of Exeter and as the coastal and cross-country routes are gradually converted, the semaphore signal will soon be an extinct species on the SR. The region has always preferred to spend money on colour light signalling, with its positive advantages to traffic, rather than on automatic warning systems.

The 1945 Labour government's nationalisation of air transport ended the Southern Railway's hopes of participation in the new European air line. As the Victoria – Poole flying boat specials ceased with the opening of Heathrow airport in 1946 so began a succession of schemes for its rail connection with Central London in which the SR has continued to be involved without result. However, the rail link to Gatwick airport (first served by the SR in 1935) has been a success story bringing ever increasing traffic since it became the second London airport in 1958, which has required major railway investment in rolling stock and in the stations at Victoria and Gatwick.

From all this it can be seen that nationalisation made little immediate practical difference. Even before it came into effect, Sir Eustace Missenden had left to become first chairman of the Railway Executive, but John Elliot, schooled by Walker, had long been playing a vital role as number two and happily moved up. That the two men knew each other well, and Missenden had problems enough north of the Thames, resulted in the Southern being left to handle its own affairs to a greater extent then any other part of the new BR. It succeeded in retaining the famous green for electric trains, as well as many of its individual practices. But there can be little doubt that electrification would have been persued more vigorously had it controlled its own investment programme. The Transport Commission and Railway Executive not unnaturally gave priority to the modernising of the nation's long-distance freight traffic, though it has to be added that much of what was spent on that was wasted and Southern electrification always proved a sound investment.

The omens were not good. The combination of the practical ex-Southern man at the Executive and the Civil Service mandarin, Sir Cyril Hurcomb, at the British Transport Commission over it, was not happy. Elliot may have acted as though he was general manager, but from 1 January 1948 his bureaucratic title was that of Chief Regional Officer. And in the game of musical chairs that was to become all too-familiar in following years, in 1950 he was moved to Euston, succeeded by an ex-LNER man, C. P. Hopkins.

The Secretary (Brigadier L. F. S. Dawes) and the Solicitor (H. L. Smedley) were important officers of the Southern Railway; nationalisation transferred their functions to BTC headquarters. Once the Southern Railway preferred to leave its catering in the hands of outside contractors, but it showed signs of more active participation in the post-

war years by appointing a special assistant to the general manager, by extending its parliamentary powers to cover such enterprises as holiday camps, and in 1947 by purchasing the Knowle Hotel at Sidmouth. Under the BTC, this activity passed to the Hotels Executive.

The Southern Railway in 1930 brought its operating and commercial departments under the authority of a traffic manager (R. M. T. Richards since 1940). Under the Railway Executive organisation these activities were separated into regional Operating, Commercial and Continental departments, R. M. T. Richards became Deputy Chief Regional Officer until the post was abolished on his retirement.

Within the engineering field, signalling and telecommunications and civil engineering became separate departments in succession to the SR's Way & Works organisation, whose head, V. A. M. Robertson remained as chief civil engineer until 1950. On the other hand the departments of mechanical engineer under O. V. S. Bulleid and electrical engineer under S. B. Warder were merged following the retirement of Bulleid in September 1949 and Warder's transfer to RE headquarters. The formation of the combined department acknowledged that the SR was now primarily an electric railway. The SR board had allowed Bulleid considerable latitude during the years of government financial control and it is difficult to imagine 140 Pacifics and such projects as the Leader being sanctioned in the days when Sir Herbert Walker guarded the purse strings. The motive power department had long been independent of the chief mechanical engineer and its superintendent, T. E. Chrimes, was

continued

that made the efforts of her 4-6-0 rivals look positively puny, and at one stage turned out the second highest horsepower recorded in the whole series, 2010 equivalent at the drawbar. On the Highland line to Inverness No 34005 *Yeovil* made utter hay of the timetable over the great climbs to the summits at Druimuachdar and Slochd, recording over 1900 equivalent horsepower on occasions. On both routes the combination of two Londoners, Driver Swain and Fireman Bert Hooker from Nine Elms shed, brought a strong dose of 'joie-de-vivre' to an otherwise prosaic series.

But such brilliant running had to be paid for. The Bulleid Pacifics were never frugal with coal and water. Hooker was having to shovel almost two tons more coal on each round trip than his rivals. To paraphrase the French, 'It was magnificent, but it was not what running railways was all about'.

Holding their own

Today Exeter Central is little more than a glorified halt, often in the charge of a single member of staff. But for many years after nationalisation it remained one of the West Country's most important trading posts. It was the place one went to for the first express to London and the last one back, as well as for frequent trains on the West Country's busiest and best-run branch to Exmouth. It was headquarters of an actively-run Division whose manager's *continued opposite*

Today's trains. Waterloo station in April 1983 with the new BR electric units, of Classes 455 and 508. The class 508s took many Southern Region suburban services particularly on the South Western Division, and sliding doors with push button controls ousted the seventy year reign of compartment stock inaugurated by the LSWR. The Class 508 units were then transferred to Merseyside, and were succeeded by the Class 455 units, each of which incorporated one trailer from the 508s before they left.

the last Southern officer to remain in the post; after his retirement in May 1958 it was absorbed by the operating department.

The Transport Act 1953 abolishing the Railway Executive created regional area boards, restored the general manager and brought the name Southern back on to publicity material. Steam-hauled stock could now also again be painted malachite green – though a surprising number of coaches had only 'required' revarnishing of their green paint during the years of the official 'blood and custard' livery. There remained a solid core of middle-management brought up on the Southern and loyal to its ideas, but musical chairs continued at the top, the region perhaps being at an all-time low when David McKenna, elevated to the BR Board, was replaced as general manager by another LNER graduate, Lance Ibbotson. Not merely was the region taking a great critical onslaught from the media, partly because of the very overcrowding and lack of reliability that investment in the first BR years along former Southern Railway lines would largely have avoided, but increasingly the appointment of top men from outside was seen as a means of 'teaching' Waterloo how to behave. Though an able railwayman in himself, Ibbotson was disliked during his term of office and (as he had been previously as general manager at Paddington) even more after his retirement when he supported a campaign to convert railways (including main lines into stations such as Waterloo) into roads. Investment was however belatedly stepped up.

Within the traffic department, the Southern Region was controlled by five divisions (later called districts) corresponding broadly to the former SE&C and LBSC systems and three divisions of the more extensive LSWR territory. From 2 April 1950 the SR lines west of Exeter were transferred to the WR and in exchange the ex-GWR routes south of their

West of England main line went to the SR. Under the system of penetrating lines operating arrangements did not change, but chocolate and cream signs appeared on Southern stations beyond Exeter, while upper quadrant signals were erected at Weymouth.

A further rationalisation of regional boundaries from 1 January 1963 transferred to the Western Region all the former Southern lines west of Wilton. Pannier tanks appeared briefly on some of the branches, but closure soon followed (Exmouth only surviving), together with most of the Withered Arm beyond Exeter. The Atlantic Coast and the other West of England expresses were replaced in September 1964 by a diesel-hauled semi-fast service between Waterloo and Exeter. Many intermediate stations between Salisbury and Exeter were closed in 1966 and the line was reduced in 1967 to single track with minimal crossing facilities. Some improvement in these has followed the SR's recent regain of control as far west as Sherborne.

These changes (in summary form for there were further small transfers) resulted in a considerable reduction in the size of the Southern Region and the whole of the remaining ex-LSWR system now comprised a single South Western division. When the divisional organisation was abolished in 1984, the emphasis was transferred to sector titles. The end of the war found the SR headquarters scattered between the surviving offices at Waterloo, Victoria and London Bridge, the wartime retreat at Deepdene (Dorking) and Brighton Locomotive works. The divisions were accommodated in temporary hutments at Orpington, Redhill and Woking. More recently the Region's administration became concentrated within modern office blocks at Croydon and elsewhere.

Many of the operating methods of Herbert Walker's Southern Railway became institutionalised under the Southern Region. Thus the absence of sliding door stock until 1979 and the continued ritual of the guard's green flag until the 4SUBs disappeared. The pre-war suburban trains had carried destination boards but these had been removed to confuse the enemy and post-war attempts to restore them never succeeded. Regular travellers relied on the headcodes on the front of the train, which within the complex SR suburban area often provided more precise indication than the roller blinds on today's sliding door stock. Formerly many Southern services divided en route (only a few remain) and in the absence of destination boards the staff at junction stations such as Woking or Swanley were bombarded with anxious queries. Even the regulars would be baffled when the portions were unequal.

The Western Region was often accused of being different and trying to follow GWR tradition, but the Southern Region has been just as tenacious in keeping to its own way of doing things, even though in outward appearance its identity is steadily being concealed within the red, white and blue colours of Network SouthEast and with all the changes forced on it the general view would be that however efficient it is not as friendly as the pre-war Southern. And it could be argued that the very creation of Network SouthEast – the case for a separate organisation handling commuter areas had been suggested by MPs from the 1960s – was a vote of no confidence. The mixture of success and failure, continuity and change, common sense and dogma, has been subtle and will undoubtedly be argued over for decades to come.

continued

chauffeur vied with his opposite number at St David's to turn out the smarter car for rounds of inspection increasingly undertaken by road.

Central men had their own esprit de corps, and were naturally adept at putting the St David's ones down. Independence meant everything. A journalist's suggestion that Southern trains for North Cornwall might more economically be routed via Lydford, enabling Halwill Junction–Launceston to be closed, had the manager driven to the two intermediate stations the very next day to assure the staff that no such nonsense would happen.

The Western of course pretended it was superior, and nothing as minor as nationalisation broke the rule that everything coming down the hill from Central should be halted well and truly at St David's. Only a Surbiton–Okehampton weekend car-and-passenger train (complete with restaurant) once or twice passed through non-stop, more by accident than design. True, for operational purposes it was agreed that a summer Saturday train for Manchester would start at Exmouth; but the Western forbade the Southern to advertise it as such lest Exeter passengers bought their tickets at Central.

With minor exceptions there never was proper co-operation leave alone integration. Oddities such as a Saturday through train from Tavistock North to Tavistock South, and the Plymouth and Kingswear portions of a Swansea express changing positions during the evening both running via Okehampton, were quickly terminated by the Beeching closures.

As someone put it: 'Time stood still until it ended.' The fossilisation was great for enthusiasts, extraordinarily expensive for the nation. Yet how many of the services controlled from Exeter Central are still missed?

Southern Chronology

1923 1 Jan. Railways Act 1921 came into force.

Sir Herbert Walker (LSWR), P. C. Tempest (SE&C) and Sir William Forbes (LBSC) appointed joint general managers. Tempest knighted in the King's birthday honours. Forbes retired on 30 June and Tempest on 31 December.

1924 1 Jan. Sir Herbert Walker appointed overall general manager.

Jan. First hole made in wall between the SE&C and LBSC stations at Victoria. Later in the year the Chatham platforms realigned, concourse enlarged and second connecting way to Brighton side opened.

A charming matter came up in July. It had been decided after consultation with Lord Stamfordham on behalf of the King that the Royal waiting room on Windsor SR station should be dismantled; it had not been used since Queen Victoria's day, presumably because neither King Edward VII nor King George V wished to journey from Windsor to Osborne. Lord Stamfordham wrote to ask whether the directors would accept a casket and New Testament which had been kept in the waiting room, as a memento of HM Queen Victoria, and this was gratefully accepted.

1925 20 Jul. Totton Hythe & Fawley Light Railway opened.

27 Jul. North Devon & Cornwall Junction Light Railway opened.

The Southern carried 7,000,000 passengers between 12 July and 21 September and ran 7,031,000 steam and 1,784,000 electric train-miles. Said Walker in the *Southern Railway Magazine*: 'The staff's efforts brought increased facilities to the public we serve and credit to our railway. Keep it up!'

21 Sep. Victoria's platforms numbered 1–17 from East to West in a single sequence.

1926 2 Jul. New lines Margate to Ramsgate opened (Thanet Loop) and closure of SE and LCD lines to Margate Sands and Ramsgate Harbour.

Aug. 'Lord Nelson' class 4 cylinder 4-6-0 introduced.

19 Jul. *Atlantic Coast Express* introduced, 11,00am Waterloo to various destinations in Devon and Cornwall.

1927 1 Jul. George Ellson appointed chief engineer.

1928 Classes K and K1 2-6-4Ts converted to 2-6-0 tender locomotives classes U and U1 following Sevenoaks accident of 24 August 1927.

1929 15 May *Golden Arrow* 1st class Pullman service Victoria–Dover and Calais–Paris introduced.

7 Jul. Wimbledon to South Merton opened (electric).

Sep. Class Z 3-cylinder 0-8-0T introduced.

Pleas that the Continental-style 24-hour clock should be adopted were rejected pending its use nationally.

1930 5 Jan. South Merton to Sutton opened (electric).

Mar. 'Schools' class 3-cylinder 4-4-0 introduced.

7 Jul Lewisham loops opened.

1931 1 Jan. Canterbury & Whitstable and Lee on the Solent branches closed to passengers.

1 Apr. Hythe–Sandgate closed to all traffic.

5 Jul. Hurstbourne–Fullerton Junction closed to passengers.

5 Jul. *Bournemouth Belle* all Pullman service introduced.

1932 14 May Stoke Junction (Port Victoria branch) to Allhallows on Sea opened.

10 Sep. Basingstoke–Alton closed to passengers.

Public address system first introduced at some stations.

1933 2 Jan. Botley–Bishop's Waltham and Kemp Town branch closed to passengers; Devil's Dyke branch closed to goods.

1 May. Sentinel rail bus introduced on Dyke branch.

2 Jul. King George V graving dock at Southampton opened by His Majesty King George V.

Aug. Bank Holiday created a record number of bookings at Waterloo; 78,052 tickets issued.

1934 1 Jan. Ruthern Bridge mineral branch closed – last train 29 Nov 1933.

News theatres built at Waterloo and Victoria.

1935 6 Jul. Chichester–Midhurst closed to passengers.

30 Sep. Lynton & Barnstaple and Ringwood–Christchurch closed all traffic.

1936 1 Jun. Basingstoke–Alton closed to freight.

14 Oct. *Night Ferry* through sleeping car service London–Paris inaugurated.

Sep–Oct. First 350hp diesel electric shunting locomotives introduced.

1937 4 Jul. New line through Lydd opened and part of New Romney branch abandoned.

Ash Junction–Farnham via Tongham closed to passengers.

14 Oct. Sir Herbert Walker retired.

15 Oct. Gilbert Szlumper appointed general manager.

15 Oct. J. B. Elliot appointed assistant general manager.

1 Nov. R. E. L. Maunsell, chief mechanical engineer, retired; O. V. S. Bulleid appointed.

1938 Last gas lit coach withdrawn.

Jan. Class Q 0-6-0 introduced.

29 May Motspur Park–Tolworth open (electric).

1939 Jan. Charles Sheath, probably the oldest serving railway director retired aged 90; he joined the SER in 1863 aged 14 when that company's secretary was Samuel Smiles (of *Self Help* fame). Sheath became secretary in 1899, retiring from office on Grouping and joining the Southern board.

1 Jan. Devil's Dyke branch passenger service withdrawn.

28 May Tolworth–Chessington South opened (electric).

25 Sep. G. S. Szlumper moved to War Office as director general of transportation and movements.

E. J. Missenden appointed acting general manager with J. B. Elliot as deputy.

1940 27 May–4 Jun. British Expeditionary force evacuated from Dunkirk. 319,000 troops conveyed in 620 trains from SR ports to destinations throughout country.

1941 Jun. 'Merchant Navy' class 3-cylinder 4-6-2 introduced.

Dec. CC1 main-line electric locomotive introduced.

1942 Mar. Class Q1 0-6-0 introduced.

1 Apr. G. S. Szlumper released from government service and resigned as general manager; E. J. Missenden appointed.

1943 LMS Class 8F 2-8-0s constructed at SR works for LMS and LNER (130 built between 1942 and 1944).

1944 26 Jan. Robert Holland-Martin, chairman, died.

1 Feb. George Ellson, chief engineer, retired. V. A. M. Robertson, ex London Passenger Transport Board appointed.

Feb. Col Eric Gore-Browne appointed chairman. Eustace Missenden knighted, King's birthday honours list.

1945 May 'West Country' class 3-cylinder 'light' 4-6-2 introduced.

1946 May and (Apr to Nov 1947) 14 ex-US Army 0-6-0Ts purchased for shunting at Southampton Docks.

1947 20 Jun. *Devon Belle*, Pullman train with observation car, introduced.

Aug. Sir Eustace Missenden appointed Chairman of Railway Executive.

1 Oct. J. B. Elliot appointed acting general manager.

Southern preserved. Former LSWR T9 4-4-0 No 120 seen here preserved in LSWR livery at Wadebridge on 27 April 1963 after working an enthusiasts special on the North Cornwall line. Although No 120 is part of the national collection it is currently used on the Mid Hants Railway which has preserved part of the former Alton – Winchester line.

ACKNOWLEDGEMENTS

As with companion volumes to this work we have sought out railwaymen who not only worked on the Southern but lived for it too, as well as putting together an advisory team who have kept an eagle eye on the work from its inception to final proof reading. This team comprised R.A. Savill who began his railway life as a Southern Cadet and ended it (after meritorious war service) at British Railways Board, John Powell who was a Derby apprentice rising through the ranks to Traction and Train Crew Manager at the Board and John Edgington who worked in LMS control and the PR department at Euston prior to joining the National Railway Museum in 1975. The newcomer to the team, Raymond Savill, and his leavening coupled with the experience of the other two deserves uninhibited thanks. To be able to rely on this corporate fountain of knowledge has been worth a very great deal indeed. Not only this — we were also able to unearth a further ex Southern Cadet in Patrick Stevenson, hotelier extraordinary, whose memory and human touch has not only guided us but is particularly apparent in the snippets which he has been able to provide and which do so much to make the book a living thing. Mention must also be made of the courteous and kindly help given by Sir John Elliot, the Southern's very last General Manager — an erudite man of tremendous charm who has not only written the Foreword but also made very positive suggestions to ensure accuracy and depth of research. Thus it has been a first class team.

Others too have searched their memories and note-books. Basil Cooper, perhaps stands out here and our thanks go to him and those other friends who have stood on the edge with welcome comments. We have been able to use material from many sources which has been able to add character and a balance of historical matter. Particularly we would like to thank Richard Hope, editor of *Railway Gazette International*, for permission to use extracts from special supplements issued by the *Railway Gazette* and John Slater, editor of *Railway Magazine* for similar permissions: both these long standing publications have been, as always, of tremendous value in any research. Another fascinating and worthwhile series of dips have been made into the inter war volumes of the *Meccano Magazine* which along with issues of the *Southern Railway Magazine* has produced not only some human gems but also pieces of month to month information not necessarily available in technical publications. Last there must be made mention of the preservationists who have seen to it that whole sections of railway as well as locomotives and rolling stock have been lovingly restored and once more put to work. To do this they too have had to seek out information which has willingly been passed on.

A special work of thanks also goes out to the photographers — as has been said before no matter how large his collection or how prolific his photography no author can fill a book of this kind with his own pictures and hope to get the best. C.R.L. Coles, S.C. Nash, H.C. Casserley, and the National Railway Museum have been able to work wonders adding to the comprehensive collection available from the Millbrook House picture library. Geoffrey Kichenside too, who comes from a family who served on the Southern has delved into his negatives and other material to provide illustrations and text matter. Wherever the photographer is known then full credit is given below, when we have been unable to discover the photographer then the credit is given to the author's collection but our thanks to the unknown photographers is given here too. George Heiron has again put brush to canvas in producing the jacket painting of a notable Southern junction with a scene representative of SR operation all over the system.

We would like to pay tribute to *all* those who have made this book possible, section authors, the providers of fillers and snippets and the photographers — and those who have unwittingly helped, the railwaymen of past years who have run the trains, made the black smoke when asked, provided unauthorised youngsters with footplate or signalbox access and who have made the railway hobby a joy.

The authors who have contributed to the feature chapters are recorded below and to them and all those listed above our grateful thanks. This book would not be here without them. The contributors to the main feature chapters were:

1. Introduction, **David St John Thomas**
2. Personalities and Characters, a composite chapter from several contributors
3. Electrification, **Basil Cooper** and **A.J. Powell**
4. The Ultimate in Steam, **A.J. Powell**
5. Boat Trains, and Pullmans, **D.W. Winkworth**
6. Stations Great and Small, **Alan A. Jackson**
7. Coaches: Old, Rebuilt and New, **Geoffrey Kichenside**
8. From Kent Coast to ACE: The Holiday Expresses, **D.W. Winkworth**
9. Ships and Docks, **John F. Hendy**
10. The Southern at War, **R.C. Riley**
11. Running Sheds and Workshops, **A.J. Powell**
12. The Southern in the West, **David St John Thomas**
13. Southern Freight, **H.P. White**
14. Southern Railway to Southern Region, **J.N. Faulkner**

The between chapter fillers were by Geoffrey Kichenside with the exception of The London & Southampton by H.P. White, and the SR Locomotive stock lists which are reproduced by kind permission of the Railway Correspondence and Travel Society. The Tree of Growth was compiled by John Edgington, who also produced the Southern Chronology.

We would also like to make acknowledgement to the following photographers or collections for the use of their illustrations: J.H.L. Adams 11 upper, 86 upper; P.M. Alexander 9 lower, 14 upper, 40 lower, 56 lower, 58 upper and middle, 72 middle and lower, 76, 86 middle, 99 bottom left, 123, 128 lower, 129 upper, 158, 171, 178, 184, 187, 191; D.S.M. Barrie 55, 119 bottom; BR SR 95, 97, 105 (lower); W.A. Camwell 160, 190; H.C. Casserley 9 upper, 14, 15, 75, 157; C.R.L. Coles 4, 59, 60, 70, 83, 85, 92, 94, 118, 119 (two) 159, 183, 194, 195; Colour Rail 45 top left and left, 80 top left, left, 113 top right, right, 149 top right, right; Basil Cooper 87 lower, 160; Derek Cross 17; J.G. Glover 202; P.W. Gray 167, 168/9, 171, 172, 174, 176, 179; G.F. Heiron 60, 175, 180; John F. Hendy 132, 133, 137, 139, 147; P.J. Howard 195; Geoffrey Kichenside 36, 39, 40 upper, 99 bottom right, 101 (three), 102, 103 (two), 105 (three), 127, 129 (bottom), 155, 193; L&GRP/David & Charles Frontispiece, 93, 121, 126; LPC/Ian Allan 128 upper; Millbrook House Collection 13, 56 upper, 57, 68, 70, 117 (two), 122, 144, 150 top left, left, 199, 201; National Railway Museum, York 7, 11 lower, 24, 28, 29, 33, 34, 43 (three), 50 (two), 51 (two), 52, 53 (four), 55 (two), 61, 62, 67, 72 upper, 74, 88, 91, 95, 106, 110, 111 (two), 135, 140, 141, 142, 153, 163 lower, 164, 180, 181; J. Scrace 99 bottom centre; SR 101 (top), 103 (two), 109; Eric Treacy/Millbrook House Collection 84, 163 (upper); P.B. Whitehouse 192.

INDEX

INDEX